WHen
anImaLs
speaK

ADVANCED

INTERSPECIES

COMMUNICATION

when
animals
speak

PENELOPE SMITH

BEYOND
WORDS
Publishing

Beyond Words Publishing, Inc.
20827 N.W. Cornell Road, Suite 500
Hillsboro, Oregon 97124-9808
503-531-8700
1-800-284-9673

Originally published by Pegasus Publications, copyright © 1993 by Penelope A. Smith as *Animals: Our Return to Wholeness*

Proofreader: Joseph Siegel
Design: Principia Graphica
Cover photography: Randy Wells and Jill Rickabaugh
Composition: William H. Brunson Typography Services
Managing editor: Kathy Matthews

Printed in Malaysia
Distributed to the book trade by Publishers Group West

Library of Congress Cataloging-in-Publication Data
Smith, Penelope.
When animals speak : lessons, healings, and teachings for humanity / Penelope Smith.
     p.   cm.
     "Originally published by Pegasus Publications . . . as Animals: our return to wholeness"—T.p. verso.
     ISBN 1-58270-009-5 (trade paper)
     1. Extrasensory perception in animals.   2. Pets—Psychic aspects.
     3. Telepathy.   4. Human-animal communication.   I. Smith, Penelope.
Animals—our return to wholeness.   II. Title
QL785.3.S583   1999
133.8'2—dc21   99-10101
                                                                        CIP

The corporate mission of Beyond Words Publishing, Inc.:
   Inspire to Integrity

IN MEMORY OF PASHA

Photo by Jim Craven. Photo © 1991 by *The Mail Tribune*

"With great warmth and precision Penelope expands the field of interspecies communication to a spiritual awareness of the interrelatedness of all beings. With refreshing clarity she teaches the reader how to listen to and communicate with our animal friends and all of the nature kingdoms. This revolutionary book will shapeshift the reader to a new level of connection, understanding, and appreciation of the magical world in which we live."

—Linda Tellington-Jones

Founder of TTEAM, the Tellington-Jones Equine Awareness Method and "the Tellington Touch," which promotes healing, training, and communicating with animals

contents

Foreword

ONE OF THE THINGS I most admire about Penelope Smith is that she is very clearly a participant in the overall dance of Nature. This is rare. Most people are onlookers, watching Nature as something that is outside of themselves.

We are rather inclined to "look at" Nature, but never quite see it. Penelope's new book, *When Animals Speak*, compels us to look beyond the purely physical realm, into the metaphysical aspects of Nature. Just as it is accepted that humanity is spirit clothed in flesh, so also Nature is spirit that is expressed through form. While we can admire the beauty of form, it is the spirit of Nature with which we may communicate.

People in modern society have inadvertently isolated themselves from Nature. We look through our eyes at Nature in the same way that we stand in a room looking out through the windows. We have a longing to connect with the Nature "out there," but we are unable to find the door that will allow us to get out of the room.

In many ways this book will provide that door. If you apply what you read and learn in your everyday relationship with Nature, be it through your animal pets or the garden plants, you may well open the door, step through it, and experience a greater wholeness in your life.

—Michael J. Roads

Author of *Talking with Nature*
Journey into Nature
Simple Is Powerful
Journey into Oneness

Introduction

ANCIENT AND MODERN tribal people have recognized the need for humans to remember their deep connection to all of Nature. They ritually acknowledged all other species as part of themselves, necessary for their physical, mental, and spiritual wholeness. They communicated with all forms of life as their sisters, brothers, guides, and teachers.

We, in our culture who are inculcated with the separation of existence through an emphasis on logical analysis and scientific rationality, need the reconnection to the rest of Nature more than ever. Of all species, humans appear to require the most education to remember who they really are and master their existence. The animals and other nonhuman beings can teach us about our own true nature, since most of them always know and never disconnect from awareness of themselves as eternal Spirit functioning within the whole web of life. Humans need the animals and other life forms on many levels, from biological to spiritual. All the other beings on this Earth— by their presence, their honest communication, their wholeness, and their love—can, if we are receptive to their help, lead us back home.

Interspecies telepathic communication is a direct link to the spirit present in all species. It is based on the recognition that all beings are intelligent in their own way and that they can understand, interrelate, and communicate. It is the experience of receiving direct thought transmission, images, feelings, impressions, and concepts from individuals of other species. It is confirmed by positive changes in behavior and enhancement of cooperation, peacefulness, and closeness among the beings communicating. When deep mutual understanding occurs, harmony, dignity, and mutual respect usually replace fear, aggression, and dominance.

When people divorce themselves from Nature, from the spiritual essence that flows through all of life, their relationships with their fellow creatures of different forms often assume the shallow character of owner and possession. When we connect as spirits and share each other's worlds or unique expressions of life, there is no need for categories and hierarchies that divide us.

Opening up and listening to anyone, of whatever species, requires a quiet attentiveness and calmness. Our overstimulating modern lives often cause us to shut down our sensitivity to the world around us. We learn to deny the subtle realities, the communication of thought and feeling. We build psychic walls and cease to see, hear, feel, and smell most of what's around us. We ignore even our own inner selves and feelings. Our minds race frantically to keep up with all the expectations of the culture around us so that we rarely or never have a quiet mind, a peaceful outlook, or a calm receptivity.

As babies and small children, we were open to the world, eager and curious about the sights, sounds, feelings, and thoughts of all the beings around us. We, like all other species, are naturally telepathic, but most humans in our culture are conditioned to accept only verbal language as valid. However, if we don't understand the thoughts and feelings behind the words—the true meaning of what people communicate—then we don't really understand the words anyway. Dictionary definitions are not enough. So even human language requires reception of thoughts to be complete.

When we do slow down and tune in, we become much more aware of the nature of life around us: the behavior, habits, feelings, energies, and spirit or essence of other species in our environment. As we continue to spend time in a quiet, receptive mode with other species, we may get images, impressions, thoughts, messages, feelings, and energies in different forms, which we can learn to interpret or understand.

Sigh like the wind, open your arms and your heart, and all creatures will hum to you, answering your questions about themselves and the nature of the universe. You'll learn that all of us have our deepest natures, the universal truths, and the essence of spirit in common. We can learn from the smallest microbe to the largest whale. While we each may be very different in form and function in the whole ecosystem, we all are intelligent, perceptive, uniquely vital and part of the same Divine Spirit.

Growing numbers of people are reexperiencing the spiritual awareness of our innate unity with the rest of creation. Increasingly, this awakening is being manifested as an urgent desire to understand our fellow beings by learning from other species and living in harmony on the Earth

This book has been written for those who want to rekindle their essential awareness of their fellow beings; to deepen their connection with other species; to live in harmony, peace, and joy with all beings; to recognize the spirit in all things; and to understand how we are all intimately part of each other. It's an exciting time, for it is now possible to affiliate all species through the universal language of telepathic communication.

Since about 1987, it's as if a moratorium on recognizing animals as intelligent beings has been lifted. This is evident in major newsmagazines, nature publications, television programs, and animal-related conferences, as well as in the general public view regarding animals. Before that time, accepted thinking in Western society dictated that animals were lower on the evolutionary scale, had less complex brains, and were therefore incapable of the thoughts, feelings, purposes, and accomplishments of humankind.

Any suggestion, perception, or awareness of "higher" thought processes or communication abilities in "subhuman" animals was belittled. Mental and emotional blinders were to be kept on during "scientific" experiments, eliminating any possible awareness of responses that might have led to the investigation of animal intelligence beyond the accepted notions

Even many religions, philosophies, and doctrines of "ageless wisdom" regarded animals as second class, not involved in spiritual consciousness, and irrelevant in planetary evolution. Now, animal researchers credit animals with having complex languages of their own, emotions, and potential for thought processes similar to humans. The human potential and spiritual growth movements have also moved from a solely human-centered focus to recognizing the unity of all of life and the importance of all of Nature in our evolution.

These rediscoveries and acceptance of animals as fellow beings can be discussed without an immediate accusation of "anthropomorphism," a term that means "mistakenly ascribing human thoughts and emotions to animals." This expression has long been used in a negative way to discourage the idea that other species can have feelings and thoughts similar to our own. But the word is out! Animals are intelligent beings with their own special awareness and wisdom, and many humans can learn to communicate with them directly.

Most investigations into interspecies communication are still mainly concerned with communicating with animals indirectly, getting them to learn our symbols and communicate in human language or respond to our cues. However, there is a growing realization, an awakening cultural awareness, that we all are linked—physically, mentally, and spiritually

Our disrespect and ignorance have veiled the telepathic link. It is possible that our damage to the planet's ecosystem and our unbalanced relationship with the rest of Nature may be largely resolved through interspecies respect and understanding.

All my life I have been communicating telepathically with animals. Since 1971, I have done counseling and healing work with animals and their people and have offered books, tapes, and courses. I rejoice in the burgeoning awareness that has encouraged many people to rediscover, develop, and use their interspecies telepathic abilities. May what you read here increase your joy and connection with all of life.

WHO animals really are

IN THE BEGINNING of all things, wisdom and knowledge were with the animals, for Tirawa, the One Above, did not speak directly to man. He sent certain animals to tell men that he showed himself through the beasts, and that from them, and from the stars and the sun and the moon, man should learn.

—Pawnee chief Letakota-Lesa

THE ESSENTIAL CONNECTION

The cornerstone of my work and the positive results I have experienced with animals over the years has been my connection with them as total beings. The acknowledgment of their essential spiritual nature has formed the core of our ability to understand each other. Nonhuman animals are not some lower forms of life, living with only automatic reactions or stimulus-response programming.

Yes, animals are different from humans. Various species have unique bodies, genetic backgrounds, and senses, and therefore they experience the world in their own particular ways. They are also individuals, who combine their physical species nature with their own unique mental and spiritual qualities and awareness to express themselves and fulfill their purposes in this universe.

Approaching animals as objects or biological forms does not promote the deep understanding and equitable relationship that become possible when we are able to overcome our culturally ordained perceptions and allow ourselves to become fully aware of their physical, mental, and spiritual natures. While it's good to study the biology and behavior books to learn about animals' general and species-specific needs and patterns, this will not tell you all about an individual's particular personality, ideas, hopes, purposes, and dreams. You can't separate the physical from the spiritual aspect of a living being. We need to recognize the whole being when we approach an animal of any species.

When you make the spiritual connection, it's almost as if bodies disappear. They can be seen as vehicles of life in the physical and individual expressions of divine creation. When the essential, spiritual contact is made—being to being—recognition of likeness, even oneness, occurs. It is magical to feel this deep affinity and respect. It engenders open communication, trust, and understanding.

This type of relationship is not based on sentimentality, nor can it come about if we treat animals as babies or dependent underlings. It is a blend of compassion and kinship. If you have experienced this kind of soulful communion with another creature of any kind (including human), you are, by your approach or attitude, acknowledging your union or commonality as spiritual beings. Even if you don't think about it or phrase it in these terms, the animals know.

This doesn't mean that every animal is going to fall at your feet, be calm in your presence, or even want to communicate with you. They make their own choices, and they have their conditioned fears from centuries of experience of their kind plus their own personal experiences. Their first response may be to flee or attack according to their biological chemistry and their function in nature's pattern.

Some animals will be more aware of you as a spiritual being and have more ability to connect with you. Others don't particularly want or see the need to relate to humans or any other species. However, I have found that if you remain quiet, attentive but unobtrusive, respectful, and willing to make a connection, most animals will be interested or at least will accept you as a part of their environment.

Domesticated animals who have experienced humans positively all their lives don't view humans as predators, and so they can often communicate more easily. You may find it easier to connect with companion animals than with wild creatures you have never met. Experiencing both can be a pleasure and a privilege. To have a wild animal accept your human presence and connect with you as a kindred spirit is a deep honor.

I don't regard other animals as humans in furred or feathered clothing. They are themselves: individuals with different senses, forms of thinking, means of expressing themselves, and ways of seeing life. The joy comes when you connect spiritually and share each other's worlds. Then there is no need for categories and hierarchies that separate and lead to condescension or alienation. You celebrate the experience of differences and rejoice in the oneness of your essential nature. This opens the door for learning from one another, sharing wisdom, and growing together in harmony.

ANIMAL INTELLIGENCE AND AWARENESS

All over the globe, there is a vast body of experience and learning that is not yet widely known. In particular, the scientific knowledge that man currently possesses cannot begin to encompass the wisdom held by plants and animals. The utilization of this wisdom is greatly to man's benefit, and we can expect that sooner or later its fruits will merge with the mainstream of science.

—*The Christian Science Monitor* (January 2, 1992, p. 6)

What do animals think about—only food? Are they intelligent? Do they remember the past? Can they reason? These are some of the questions people ask me in curious or disbelieving tones with regard to my experience with animals. In human history, these kinds of questions have been posed about other cultures, races, or any other groups that are considered different, inferior, or simply incomprehensible.

How do the people who ask these questions judge animal intelligence? They usually expect animals to prove their intelligence by using the same language, symbols, or expressions as we do. Experimenters test animal IQ according to human standards and laboratory models. But animals don't act or see or think in the human mode. Animal intelligence or ability must be perceived and understood in its own context and on its own terms.

DIFFERENT PERCEPTIONS

There is a vacuum in human understanding: the absence of direct and unre-
stricted observation, communication, and understanding of other species.
Having communicated with thousands of animals as fellow intelligent
beings, I am sometimes astounded that many people do not see animals as
intelligent and aware individuals.

Yes, other animals think and perceive differently than humans. They fulfill different functions in the world. When humans transplant animals out of
their natural environments, the animals can be inhibited in expressing their
native intelligence. Human modes of thinking can seem very chaotic and
confusing to a more direct and less analytical way of being. Humans often ask
animals to do things that are alien to their nature, which can be difficult for
them to understand. Animals may also panic at human-made machines,
activities, and manners that offend their finely tuned senses.

Living with humans can cause a kind of culture shock to an inexperienced
domestic animal. For example, some people consider horses stupid or crazy
if they bolt or get anxious when they see flapping plastic, hear rain on metal
roofs, or jump at things that they've seen before. Horses were not designed
for the confinement of human-made structures and spaces, and their vision
is very different from human sight. Nature has adapted them to open spaces.
Perception of strange movement is a signal to flee. If we see things from their
viewpoint, their behavior seems logical. It is a credit to their willingness to
help us that they usually adapt to and do well in the alien situations to which
humans expose them.

One visitor remarked, while I was showing her my chicken friends and
extolling their beauty, alertness, and sharp perception, "But chickens are
stupid, they'll run in front of a car." So will children or people unfamiliar with
cars. Automobile noise, speed, and headlights can be very confusing for the
keen senses of nonhuman animals. We are accustomed and have even dulled
our senses to live with the sights, sounds, and smells of our fast paced,
industrialized world. The chickens, deer, rabbits, mice, and others that are
not accustomed to the sudden onslaught of cars or other machines may
become sufficiently confused and terrified at their approach to freeze or run
in front of them. Try lying down on the road at night, with your senses tuned

in to everything around you, and on that level experience the overwhelming rush of noise and lights and the danger of an approaching car.

We can demonstrate *our* intelligence by stretching out of what we are conditioned to see. Rather than looking at animals as dumb cows or birdbrains, we can stop and see what is actually there in front of our eyes, our ears, our minds, and our open hearts. It takes clear observation and receptivity to appreciate the intelligence and expressions of another culture, group, or species, without trying to measure it by our own standards. An experience will illustrate:

I have enjoyed creating an extensive garden of native and climate-compatible plants, as well as a vegetable and herb garden. Our most frequent uninvited samplers of garden delicacies are banana slugs and snails. They have inhabited this area far longer than humans, and they certainly have an important place in the ecosystem. I don't mind their consuming a small percentage of my tender vegetables, but continued foggy weather is so conducive to their propagation that they sometimes gain an unfair (from my point of view) advantage. So, I pack them off in a bucket to a part of the forest down the road and ask them not to return.

One summer, in the process of transporting as many as a hundred slugs each week, I became very close to their ways of being. I have found them to be gentle, sensitive creatures with flowing and aesthetically acute perceptions of the world. Stepping into their viewpoint, I have seen a world pulsating with waves of energy. They don't seem to see with the same kind of visual receptors as we do. They sense waves of energy, auras, so that other creatures are "shaped" according to their body form, including the energy that is emanating from their bodies. We appear to slugs as more amorphous than solid—bands of heat and colored patterns with sharp or smooth energy projections that our movements and intentions create.

Slugs "hear" or feel sound vibrations throughout their whole bodies. Every pore in their flexible forms is sensitized to give a feeling-picture of the world. They are supremely sensuous gourmands of the animal world and ultimate teachers of experiencing eating and sexual activity as fully as possible. They totally become one with their food and envelop it gracefully and lovingly into their being, whether it be tender leaves or dog excrement.

I was digging in the garden and uncovered two slugs mating in a pile of leaves. Slugs are hermaphroditic, so they easily find a mate! Contradicting the common human conception that sex is a strictly mechanical affair to animals, the slugs were intertwined in what I could feel as ecstatic communion. I respectfully covered them again. Several days later I ruffled the mulch to see if they were there, and they were still engaged in mating—obviously a pleasurable affair not to be rushed. Again, I felt their intimacy, their joy in communion, their orgasmic oneness.

Slugs and other creatures that are very unlike humans physically and mentally may be hard for people to think of as intelligent and aware. To see the beauty in their expression of life requires getting past stereotypes and prejudices, communicating, and becoming one with them in feeling and understanding. We expand when we embrace other creatures' ways of sensing and thinking.

Certain animals, considered as pests by humans, have managed to outwit human attempts to eradicate their kind and instead live and thrive along with humans. Their survival demands that they be alert to human thoughts and intentions. Examples are rats, raccoons, coyotes, and cockroaches. Being omnivorous also helps them to live on human throwaways. These survivors are amazingly intelligent, quick, and perceptive, and they often enjoy their relationship with humans. Unfortunately, other wild animals who are not attuned to human thinking and activities often do not survive human encroachment on their territory.

The same behavior that people evaluate in humans as rational and conscious is often regarded in animals as instinctive or unconscious. Dogs lift their legs and urinate and bark to mark their territory and announce their presence to other canines. People may view these behaviors as automatic stimulus-response mechanisms, over which dogs have no control. When humans build fences, mark boundaries, or fight over territory, it is considered laudable or at least acceptable as a right to private property or expressive of individual or group identity. Dogs and other animals are assumed by many people to have no conscious reasoning behind their actions, while humans are considered to understand, or at least be capable of understanding, their own behavior.

We limit our communication with animals to our own awareness and ability to understand. Animals watch and learn to communicate on a level that's real or acceptable to us, whether by body language—such as barks, nudges, scratches, tugs—or by transmitting emotions or intentions, or through deep spiritual communion. Many behavior books show not what the animals are capable of, but what is the bottom line for humans in communicating with animals. When your animal companions resort to peeing on the bed or barking incessantly to communicate, you have probably missed the subtler levels of thought and emotion that convey their concerns and needs. Animals have to communicate on the level that you can perceive.

Accepted thinking in our culture tells people to expect little from animals in the way of rational understanding and conscious decision-making. There is no concept that animals possess awareness of the deepest truths and laws of the universe. Those people who deeply tune in to other species, without the intermediary of words and cultural limitations, experience animals' understanding that is beyond concern for survival needs. Whole vistas of sharing and learning with animals become available when people are open to mind-to-mind and heart-to-heart contact with other species.

THE LANGUAGE BARRIER

Verbal communication can be a wonderful human ability, enabling complex ideas to be represented, viewed, and manipulated. It is also a major contribution to misunderstanding and removal from full communion with other humans. In interpreting human language, we can weave webs or layers of misunderstanding because they are abstracted from direct experience. We become entwined in things we *think* happened or what we *think* people meant or thought about our actions and us. Words can cause us to judge others, not by experience of who they are and what they really intend, but by what they say or how we interpret what they say.

Language can be a barrier in resolution of problems in human interaction and in counseling. With nonhuman animals, counseling is direct. Questions and concepts can be conveyed rapidly back and forth telepathically. We can usually clear problems by getting directly to the feelings or issues involved. Animals generally do not wrap their experiences or memories in veils of abstraction or considerations of underlying meanings of the experience or the beings involved. They, too, may misinterpret, but they usually don't go through mental gymnastics over what their experience means to them or anyone else, as humans often do.

Recent or deep-seated emotional or spiritual problems and traumas are usually simpler and faster to resolve in nonhumans than in humans. Obvious and permanent behavioral and emotional changes can be seen in minutes—as opposed to many hours, as in the counseling of humans. Often animals quickly realize why problems developed and what past decisions are affecting them now, and then can release old patterns and change dramatically.

Humans take longer to figure things out. To get to the power of simple, direct experience and understanding of profound truths, humans often spend many hours or years through counseling or other means of education. Most animals live the truths of life directly, understanding them without having to expound verbally or write volumes about them. That's why they can be our best teachers.

The human mind can entrap itself in complexities that cripple action, eliminate much joy in living, and cause endless suffering to self and others. The accomplishments of using the mind as a tool to interpret and symbolize can be interesting and exciting, but language, at its best, expresses thoughts in ways that lead us back to experience the fullness of life *beyond* words.

Animal companions are capable of understanding our verbal abstractions by getting what's behind them to what humans *really* mean. Their normal mode of communication is direct transmission of intention and feeling. Most animals do not make living and interacting as difficult or complex as humans do. They generally convey directly what they feel to each other and to humans, unless through close contact they have been influenced by the more indirect modes of human communication. Human thwarting of animal companions' needs and goals can also cause them to develop psychological complexities and difficulties that mirror their humans.

Some people think it would be boring to live life so directly, with such innate understanding or intuitive expression. They think it would be too simple or limited. They want complex mental games. That's part of the experience of being human. But getting lost in mental complexity can make people miserably alienated from the world, from self, and from others. They may then seek—through counseling, meditation, prayer, or other spiritual practices—to be free of mental patterns which inhibit the experience of pure joy in living.

When we meet animals on their own ground and drop our acculturated human ways of judging and analyzing and get beyond the limitations of human language, we see animal individuals of beauty, uniqueness, perceptiveness, intelligence, warmth, humor, and wisdom. These qualities appear as if by magic, where before the animals were perceived only as labeled objects, separated into neat categories that removed any possibility of relating to them as fellow beings. When we are able to "become" another of a different kind, we expand and become more whole. Another part of the universe is experienced. Another part of us is recovered. We are closer to the true divine nature, present in us all.

This free-form soliloquy came through me in June 1992:

Thinking does not make a being wise
But knowing
A process native to spirit in all form
From bees to rocks to elephants
Thinking can be fun
It can lead to realization
It can lead to confusion
And its own blind alleys
Spinning around on itself.

Knowing
Feeling deep from the core of the soul
Brings truth and light
Consciousness equals knowing
It does not evolve from logic
Or sequential thinking or rationalism
Although a leap from thinking
Can be made into pure knowing
But the leap can be made by being
Totally being who you are
Spirit whole and eternal.

Thinking is not the be-all
And the end-all of consciousness

It often must be transcended
To reach pure beauty
Wisdom
Truth.

Thinking is found in many species
None consider it an end point
Or something that places them
Above all things
Except modern humans
Who miss the point
That deep peace, tranquillity
Are found in spirit
Not in mind or mental cogitation
Or logical argument
Mind above matter
Is spirit conscious in all things.

We reach our ultimate knowledge
Our source
When we reach ourselves
As knowers
Without words it comes
And dwells in the heart.

Who is most conscious among all species?
Is it those lost in thought?
No, it is those who know
Who feel, who see
Whose extent reaches beyond boundaries
Of skin and brain and form.

I have found knowers in all forms
From trees to butterflies to humans
We can learn from them to let our intellect
Be our game board
Our means to juggle ideas

That is our right and inheritance
But not to let it rule us
And make us separate and alone
With the notion of higher and lower.

Recognize the knowers
And you may find your Self.

SEPARATION OF SPECIES

How do we separate ourselves from each other? By race, sex, size, species, belief systems... let us count the ways! Differentiation and separation are analytical functions that, when used in certain ways, can cause discord. When we emphasize differences instead of unifying qualities, such as our common essence and feelings, we can end up with varying degrees of domination, exclusion, harshness, and even cruelty to those perceived as different.

You've probably heard and been subtly conditioned by statements about the separation between humans and other animals. Until recent years, ideas about other species' inferiority were widely accepted. Now, however, many scientific researchers are recognizing and shedding fixed ideas that had prevented open observation, and they are coming up with different conclusions.

One of these ingrained ideas was that animals were not intelligent or were greatly limited in brainpower compared to humans. They could not really think or make conscious decisions, as their lesser brain mass and complexity prevented that. Recent studies have revealed complex decision-making and problem-solving abilities in many species, even in those with relatively small brains.

Then there was "tool using." Only humans were considered evolved enough to create and use tools to survive. Now this ability has been noticed in species as varied as chimpanzees, birds, and ants. Another idea was that only humans could be altruistic—that is, do things for others without any self-serving reward in sight. Countless tales of animals of various species helping and saving humans and each other, despite danger to themselves, have refuted that notion.

For centuries it was accepted that only humans used language and symbols. In recent years, much to the amazement of scientists, complex languages and use of symbols have been noted in a variety of species, from elephants to birds to bees. There is still a widespread belief that animals really don't understand as much as we do about the world, and are unable to express what we can through understandable language, but those ideas are gradually undergoing transformation, as people connect with animals in deeper ways.

Many people think animals lack self-awareness and a sense of right or wrong, as in our systems of ethics and justice. However, modern researchers are seeing self-awareness and ethical concepts expressed in animal behavior and communication. In addition, through direct telepathic communication, it becomes clear that many animals have a deep sense of who they are and their purposes in life. They also have their own systems of right and wrong, and they deal out justice according to their group customs. While their ethical constructs may be quite different from what we're accustomed to, compare this with the vast differences in these concepts and systems among human cultures on the Earth.

Animals usually do not belabor and question their awareness as much as humans do in modern societies. The awareness and acceptance of their own consciousness is present nevertheless—different in degree or quality in each individual, but present in all species.

I have read the opinion that human beings are distinguished from all other animals by their ability to reach beyond the present and perceive the reality of other places and other times—to see things from a great height, above the usual scale of everyday life. My experience with countless animals refutes this opinion. They have revealed their awareness of other places and times in this life, in other lives, on Earth, in other places, in other dimensions, and out of body. They have insights as deep and astounding as any human I have ever communicated with. They usually feel and describe these states in less complex ways than intellectually oriented humans, but the deep understanding is there.

It makes much more sense to me to look at differences as expressions of the universe that make life wondrous, rather than trying to create barriers that segregate beings. The more you communicate directly and have a rapport with others of a variety of species, the more the wisdom and unity of all are apparent and can be sources of mutual expansion. We can learn from our nonhuman friends to accept what is around us *as it is now* and feel the unity underlying all creation and the divinity that we all share.

Animal intelligence, awareness, and connection with the rest of life was profoundly demonstrated in an encounter I had with a tree frog. It occurred on a cool February night in 1991. We had just come home from our community center after a slide show by a local naturalist. I was intrigued by his thoughts regarding the possible underlying causes of drought conditions: that we are not asking the Thunderbird for rain, as native peoples have done for eons, and that we need to listen to what the animals have to tell us. I took to heart the familiar and true words, which become more urgent as human ways disrupt the natural environment for many creatures on the Earth.

On our doorstep, facing the door as if waiting to go in, was a tree frog, resplendently green. Picking him up gently, I intended to place him among the plants in the garden. He had other plans. Instead of jumping away, as I expected, he refused to leave my hand, crawling back on as I tried to coax him off. I brought him close to my face, to find out why he wanted to stay. He calmly and clearly conveyed his warmth and appreciation of me. I felt an ancient kinship. He said that I should let people know: "We need clean water; we need pure air." I knew he was speaking for all the Earth's amphibians—frogs, salamanders, newts—whose vast numbers are noted to be shrinking at alarming rates worldwide. He wanted to spend a moment with me, feeling it was important that we connect, that the message be carried forward.

When he finished, he gently pirouetted in my hand, and as I lowered him to the ground, he hopped away. Later, I heard his voice, along with those of his companions, calling for the much needed rain to come.

EVOLUTION AND INTERRELATIONSHIPS

Humans in our culture have been inculcated with the idea that *Homo sapiens* is superior to and almost separate from the rest of the animal kingdom. While humans are more biologically complex than most species in brain development and manipulative ability, we are not separate from the rest. We have our place in the functioning whole, as do all the other animals.

The idea that there is a difference in evolution of spirit, or that different kinds of spirit inhabit different forms, also creates a chasm separating animals from humans. I have found that we are all the same spiritual essence, and we are free to evolve as individuals through any form.

Bodies of different types evolve according to their needs to adapt to changing environments and to stretch their capacities. We, as spiritual beings, have a variety of choices in how we can express our creativity during life on Earth. We inhabit bodies of different species according to our purposes and express ourselves within the limits of biological forms. Each species, groups within species, and individuals have their purposes and their evolution in the physical universe and as spirits moving through form after form, dimension to dimension. It is an interwoven pattern.

I have looked at the relationship of humans to the rest of the animal kingdom for a long time. We have unequaled power to create and destroy environments. No other species categorizes, separates, and synthesizes the meanings of life as humans do. Humans may get lost in the process and never arrive at integration, complete understanding, and knowing. Nonhuman animals can abstract, but the fundamental knowing of their place in the universe and the purpose of life is intact and does not need to be rationalized, taken apart, and put back together for them.

We play with language, study, write, and record stories about the world and ourselves. Other animals pass down their observations and memories through custom and group consciousness, cellular memory, and direct knowing. I have often felt that humans are the students of all of life around them. Our function is to study and communicate with each other about what we see and experience. Humans are the mental expressionists of life realities, finding numerous imaginative ways to bring forth meaning. We increase our empathy and communion with others as we express our discoveries with music, dance, writing, and other creative forms.

An American woman, researching Australian aboriginal life, asked an aboriginal woman about how humans differ from animals. The aborigine explained, with disbelief at the other's ignorance, that *we are the ones who can tell all the others' stories.*

FORM AND SPIRIT

About twenty years ago, while living in Edinburgh, Scotland, I had a cat friend named Ipsis. He chose his name, which means "himself" in Latin. He was a striking black cat, who would look deeply into people's eyes and cause them to make remarks like "That is not just a cat!"

Ipsis was a special friend and helper and would accompany me in my spiritual counseling sessions with people, usually greeting the client, then quietly curling up in the background. He would often know when we were nearing the resolution of an issue and the person was about to have an important insight and release of emotional energy. He'd jump up on the desk and gaze at the person, encouraging, and listening for the realization. People would laugh, saying they knew the session was nearing its conclusion, as Ipsis jumped up to help them recognize and voice their incipient insight.

I remember, in particular, another way Ipsis assisted me. We lived in a high-ceilinged, drafty apartment, whose only source of heat in the damp and chilly climate was a small electric heater that you had to feed precious coins to operate. It was often difficult to rise from a warm bed in the morning darkness before the sun came up, but Ipsis helped to make it easier. He often slept under the covers at my feet. Just before the alarm would sound, he'd come up to my face and gently pat it with his paw to wake me. I'd smile and pet him and sometimes drift back to sleep. If the alarm sounded, and I still didn't get up, Ipsis became more insistent, licking my face with his scratchy tongue or biting my chin. He'd say to me, "You have to get up and do your work. It's very important." With his help, I'd manage to face the cold room, and together, we would go to the counseling center where we worked.

I would laud Ipsis's virtues to my boyfriend, and, while he loved Ipsis, he would become impatient with my perceptions. He said to me, "All I see is a cat. Ipsis is *just a cat.*" I replied, "But, if I look at you in the same way as you're looking at Ipsis, all I see is a human. You are *just a human.*"

You see what you can perceive, what you allow to enter into your aware-ness. Being in the physical world, we are masters of limitation, working with apparently finite boundaries, senses, mortality, and change. For me, life would lack meaning and richness without also having the consciousness of the pulsing of spirit infinite throughout everything and the understanding of thought and feeling that reveals the depth of beings.

So, I saw both the deep and wise spirit that was Ipsis and the beauty and grace that he manifested through his cat form. It was all wonderful—the spiritual communication and wisdom, cat instincts, senses, and habits—all to be enjoyed, all part of the whole, all good.

Separating the physical from the spiritual is a risky proposition. Even what we call *physical* is spiritual in essence. As modern physicists have discovered, when you look at what the universe is composed of, down to the energy forms in each atom, it all disappears and reappears, like magic. It is neither here nor there, although the illusion is that these energies form solid particles and fairly permanent objects. The energies that form the basis of matter are so influenced by our perception, we appear to be a part of them and share in their creation, their continuance, and their form. We are not separate from them in essence. How fascinating!

We, as individual spirits who are animating forms, are also elusive, taking on identity, personality characteristics, and ways of being that we may think are our real selves. These are all changeable as we shift from state to state within physical reality, beyond physical reality into spiritual dimensions, and returning to the physical. We can have identities in infinite variations. We can be one with individuals, with groups of beings, or with all or No-thing/God. Who can pin a name on us and say that's all there is?

To be practical, in the physical realm, we (of any species) are capable of expressing ourselves as spirit within the limits of the physical form and agreements of the other players in this dimension. We can be wise and wonderful, balanced, aware beings, or full of fears and strongly influenced by what has been done to our bodies, or both, at different times and circumstances. We can rise above negative influences or environments and determine our own futures, or we can consider ourselves totally formed by them. We can also come through our restrictions to express ourselves in the fullest possible way, manifesting the potential of our species and our purpose as individual spirits.

Each of us, as individuals, has a unique body-mind-spirit combination and approach to the universe. Our bodies influence us as we communicate through our physical senses. We can identify with others of our own species in our common physical, emotional, and social needs and natural behaviors. We can identify with all species in our sharing of life on Earth, symbiotic relationships, physical and emotional similarities, and in our essence as spirit.

Beings generally choose to incarnate as certain body forms and in certain situations that help them fulfill their chosen destiny or next step on the winding road of adventure through life. They can be very conscious about what they are doing or very unaware, hiding their own decisions about life choices from themselves to enhance the intensity of limitation and element of surprise or adventure, or because they've become too mired in unknowing and the physical game. The game of life can be played in many ways, and eventually beings come back to full knowing of self as spirit. To not know self as a spiritual being for very long is to become very miserable indeed.

As human beings, apparently at the top of the biological totem pole and most involved in analytical mind functions, we need the other species to help us use our forms without losing our way and our connection to ourselves as spirit. Animals can teach us the joy of being, enjoying the senses and potentials of the body and universe each moment, maintaining that high connection to self as infinite spirit that most animals never lose.

Not all animals are more spiritually evolved than all humans are, as some people suppose. Animals have their spiritual paths and make "mistakes," as we all do, which they suffer or learn from. Some animals become deranged by living under the influence of human cruelty or imbalance and mimic or create human-type neuroses. Natural forces normally eliminate unbalanced animals, as they usually cannot survive well. If humans intervene, breeding animals and saving deformed or deranged ones, we can get the same weakening of the genetic pool and disease we find in humans. Humans mirror their own state in the animals whose breeding they control. Animals attracted to these humans perpetuate their humans' states. Of course, an animal's development and well-being may be enhanced by positive human contact. That's really why different species are together—to help each other survive, grow, and enjoy life to the fullest.

We are individuals, making our way through infinity, taking different paths and crisscrossing along the way. All paths and all forms are valid. Depending on the viewpoint of the individual spirit at any given time, some are more fun or purposeful than others are. While it is wonderful to recognize the abilities of any species, whether human, dolphin, dog, cat, llama, or bird, it is essential to understand each individual uniquely. Not everyone is an embodiment of the spiritual fullness or purpose of that species. Each can express that species' purpose as they choose.

Some animals appear wise beyond their form, beyond any form. People look at them and say they are like humans. What they usually mean is that they are exceptionally conscious and aware or intelligently responsive. Some individuals will be shining examples of their species and of themselves as infinite beings and are exceptional as individuals of any form. Generally noted for their joy in living and their confidence in self and love of others as fellow spirits, they are conscious of their choices in incarnating from life to life. I call them *master beings*.

It can be fun to characterize species according to traits or purposes. We humans love to categorize. However, we gain the most insight into individuals by looking at them in their wholeness, noting who they are in their travels as spirit throughout this and other planes. What an adventure it is to discover each other in and through and beyond form!

HIGHER SELF/LOWER SELF

Many people love to divide themselves and other species into parts—soul, spirit, mind, body, higher self, lower self, emotional body, astral body, etc. There are many systems that people have promulgated to explain conflicting impulses or different functions. While you can learn from analysis into parts, to understand beings fully, you have to put them back together again.

Some people have told me that they talked to an animal's Higher Self, as if the rest of the animal was inferior. This presumes a Lower Self that is not as pleasant to experience or wouldn't know what the Higher Self was talking about. I recommend that you communicate with living beings, including yourself, as they are, body/mind/spirit united, with all their experience and knowledge. This approach acknowledges them respectfully and with full appreciation, and they have an opportunity to respond to you as whole beings and to grow accordingly.

Animals can tell you about anything from the highest values and purposes to what they want for dinner. You don't need to split them up into parts of consciousness and correspondingly negate or prioritize communications.

On March 15, 1986, just before a workshop, this discourse on the subject of elements influencing the level of our exchange of communication with animals came through me:

There are the manifestations of the animal in its physical form—its function, operation, and purpose on Earth as that type of animal.

There are our judgments, our ingrained conceptions, societal attitudes, and personal interpretations of experience that color our perception of the animal.

There is the individual spirit who animates the animal form, with all its purposes, drives, desires, needs, lessons, energies, loves, choices of ways to be, life.

There is the spirit of energy (God, life force, divinity, great spirit, essence) uniting us all and calling forth the unique contribution each has to the other to walk in balance on the Earth. In physical form we complement each other and make each other whole. In spirit we recognize each other as equal, parts of the whole, aspects of divinity, and one in essence.

To recognize the beauty and transcendence of each form is to recognize the essence and commune with spirit, and is the highest purpose.

On all levels we can commune (become one with or know without words or analysis) and communicate (exchange energies and understanding) and know each other as we manifest. Beauty and truth come out and speak for themselves as we allow them.

Don't be fooled by an emphasis on one topic, level, or state of communication. Spirit in any form has infinite potential and innate wisdom. It is your job (and your joy!) to *see*. See deeply. See the whole being. See behind the disguise of the physical. See, feel, and know the spirit, and be willing to receive communication on any level.

GROUP SOUL

Some people have posited that animals, especially those who live in herds or large groups, do not possess individual consciousness but have a group mind or group soul. I have found that all species and groups that operate in harmony for a common task have leaders who coordinate activity and keep a link, telepathic or otherwise, with the rest of the group. They may have a physically present leader and/or a discarnate, spiritual leader—sometimes referred to as an *oversoul*. You can address any animals, from elephants to snakes to termites, as individuals and experience communication with them. You may also address the oversoul or group or species leader, through communicating with an individual of the group or with the oversoul directly.

A workshop I led in Cambridge, Massachusetts, in April 1993 was heightened by the presence and messages from a barred owl and gopher snake brought by Suzanne Ballard, a representative of "Animals as Intermediaries." These animals were some of those who could not be returned to the wild due to injury or human habituation and were willing teachers in human education and therapy programs.

Owl, whose right wing had been amputated, was presented to us seated on Suzanne's arm. I asked our group to tune in quietly to Owl, but I could not restrain myself from excitedly relaying her thoughts. First she surveyed the entire room and thought, as she looked at a floor lamp about fifteen feet away, "Oh, that's a tree; no, it's not, but I could fly to it anyway if I need to. There's the window. What's that noise? Oh, traffic outside." She proceeded to analyze the lighting from the windows and all around the room, and I could see all the various shades of light in the room, highly differentiated through her eyes.

Owl broadly surveyed us and found us to be safe and compatible with her. She then looked directly at people, focusing her big, dark eyes briefly from person to person, taking those who dared to follow into her sanctified realm of deepest mystery, a vast pool of floating darkness and peace. She gave us this message:

> You may think that I am broken and cannot fly, but I can. Even now I
> look for a place to land. I am wild and free. You can fly with me in your

dreams. I will take you to realms where you can fly and be free to expand as spirits. I am glad to be here as your teacher.

I represent all owls, all keepers of the realm of mystery from which spirits come and to which all return. You will not forget me, and I will not forget you. Come fly with me. Be free. In your dreams, I will take you flying. We are One.

As Owl delivered this message, Suzanne softly commented, with surprise, that Owl was presenting her vulnerable right side without the wing to the audience, showing how safe she felt and that she was comfortable with staying out longer than ever before. In group presentations, she generally stayed with her winged side exposed only. Owl conveyed to me that she felt that we all understood she was whole and free, even without her wing, and we were at one with her. What a breathtaking experience to communicate with her and receive her blessing!

Then Snake was presented. Beautiful in lithe form and multicoloration, light and humorous in spirit, Snake contrasted the somber wellspring of dark beauty and wisdom given by Owl. Snake first looked up at Suzanne, winding toward her face and thought, "Oh, it's you my friend, how beautiful you are." Then she turned her face to the group of spellbound people and noted how their energy surged toward her in interest. As she relayed her feelings through me, the group of workshop participants relaxed and their energies receded. Through Snake's perception, I could see the many colors of the energies all around the people.

Your light is beautiful, like rainbows. You are all very aware of me and sensitive to my feelings. I like that. I feel a kinship with you. My world is one of beauty and peace. I came to share that with people, and I delight in your awareness. I feel the heat and light all around you, intermingling, questioning, and changing. I am happy in my life. I do not think of living in the wild as my path, yet I bring the joy and knowledge of all snakes. We are an old and ancient people on the Earth and have much to share. I am a young and free spirit, enjoying bringing warmth and joy to people. Come talk with me.

Both Owl and Snake shared much with individual people later as the human students went to the animals to learn how to telepathically communicate with them.

I experience the oversoul of a species or group as the unifying energy, the One Voice, the consciousness or total wisdom of that group or species. The oversoul is a guiding presence within each individual of a species, yet greater than the individuals as separate entities. I have read that those souls who are bears, for example, return to a group soul and reincarnate in the same form. This has often been confirmed by animals who have revealed their paths to me. Yet my experience also suggests that beings can go wherever their purposes and choices take them, to any form of life, kingdom or dimension, according to their path.

Many spirits may choose to reincarnate in one form repeatedly and remain part of that consciousness or group energy or soul. Others shift to different species, including human. We can be a part of one tribe, race, species, or any form, from life to life, if we desire. We can also share in the experience of many forms, energies, and purposes as our awareness of connection with all life expands, while we still have one particular body as our identity.

When individual spirits adopt forms of whatever species, they adopt the overall programming, function, purpose, and way of being of that species. They can immerse themselves into that pattern totally or alter it to some extent in that life experience, determined by their desires, purposes, and spiritual abilities or mastery of form.

A history of a species can be presented, but, as with human history, you many find in communicating with individuals that you get other viewpoints or pieces of the puzzle. This planet is a place where souls can incarnate in whatever form of body they choose and have opportunities to learn from their adventures, to bring out the very best in themselves, physically, mentally, emotionally, and spiritually.

LIVING WITH animals

NAMING

PEOPLE NAME THEIR ANIMAL companions in different ways. Some
name them by their physical characteristics, like Shorty, Chocolate, or Fluffy.
Others give them names according to their own whims or according to certain
systems or traditions. Others perceive mental or spiritual qualities that the
animal embodies and name them Valor, Libre, Magnifico, Hawk, or Shaman.
Some names seem to pop right out of the animals; they seem to fit, and the
animals seem to give them to you. Some names people give to animals can be
self-fulfilling, as they convey the meaning and emotion of the name when
they use it. Names like Killer, Rambo, Wild Thing, Demon, Dodo, Stupid,
Poof, or Bonzo may need to be changed, according to what the people
and animals think about them and how they influence emotions and behavior.

So, what's in a name? What do animals think of the names that we give
them? Some animals don't really care what they are named. The name
becomes familiar and is associated with you and your affection for them.
They don't react, even if it were a name we would consider negative. Other
animals do not like their names at all. The names do not fit their qualities or
way of being, and they respond negatively or won't respond to them at all.

Many animals prefer to choose their own names. Like us, they have personalities and traits they embody. They may like names that symbolize these
qualities. To get these names, you need to listen to the animals. Where do
they get their names? As spiritual beings, before they reincarnate, animals
usually have an idea of their purpose for the coming life, and they may give
names that remind them of this. Or they may give themselves names that

they have had in previous lives that they feel exemplify their characteristics in this life. When a name comes from them, it feels right to them and to you, if you are attuned to them as whole beings. Sometimes they cannot find a word that represents the concept of their name, and you have to do your best to approximate it in human language. They normally will let you know if they approve of your choice.

For some animals, naming them incorrectly can cause resentment. Regina Heynneman talked with a woman who named her cat Francis and had a hostile relationship with the cat for seventeen years! Regina discovered that Francis hated her name and wanted the name *Holly*. After she was called Holly, the cat, who had been staying outside and away from her person, became friendly and came into the house.

When I picked up my male Afghan hound, Pasha, from the animal shelter, I asked him about himself and a name he would like. He told me he had been a Russian man in his last life, and his nickname was Sasha, which he liked. Since my name was Penelope, my other Afghan at the time was Popiya, and my van was called Pegasus, I asked if he could be called Pasha. It sounded good to him, so Pasha he was. I later found out that *pasha* signified a leader or lord in Arabic, which suited our Pasha just fine. Being a Leo astrologically, and a leader naturally, it all fit.

Rana, my female Afghan's name, came to me with the meaning "queen." She showed me images of herself as royalty in India long ago with a red jewel in the center of her forehead.

I asked our fluffy Angora calico cat what her name was when I picked her up as a kitten in June 1982. She gave the name *Chico San*, which she said meant "wise boy." Although she turned out to be a female, she liked the name. It suited her gentle, wise nature, so Chico San it was.

A deaf white kitten who appeared at our front door in July 1982 gave me an unpronounceable name that he pictured having on another planet. I told him we couldn't manage that name here on Earth. The *Star Wars* movie was playing at the time, so I checked out a few names from that movie. When I mentioned *Obi Wan-Kanobi*, he glared at me disdainfully. I tried *Yoda*, and he nodded his head and squinted his eyes approvingly.

My first cockatiel friend was given to me, fancy wrought iron cage and all, in October 1982 by a client who was tired of battling with him in angry screaming matches at three in the morning. The woman's life was full of stress, and she didn't want to try to handle the problem with him. She asked if I would take him. I agreed, and home he came. He disliked the name *Pishta*, which she had given him, so I asked him what name he wanted. He gave me an image of a moving carousel with colorful, wooden horses going up and down. I thought, "Carousel?" He said no, and gave me the image again. I got the concept of turning, with the name *Pirouette*. That was it! In a few weeks, he was saying his name, after never talking aloud before, as well as "You're terrific," which I had said to him to shift the formerly contentious relationship with humans to a positive note. He never screamed angrily again at three in the morning or at any other time.

My first guinea pig gave himself his name before he was born in December 1982. His mother was black and white and was pregnant when a friend got her from the pet store. He pictured that he would be orange and white, and said his name was Cinnamon. Later, he sired two males with Lara, who was black. The babies were brown with black ticking. They did not give me any names for themselves. Because of their appearance and their father's name, they became Nutmeg and Gingerbread, which suited them just fine.

When my yellow-green and gray parakeet came home with me from the pet store in March 1983, I was thinking of names like Misty, because of his muted coloring. Then he made me aware that he was the same being who had been my parakeet, Winky, when I was a child, and he would be quite happy with that name again. Others of my animal family have given themselves different names when they reincarnate and come back to our family, but in this case, Winky wanted the same name again.

Our tortoise-shell cat, Yohinta, came to us because our black cat, Heyoka, summoned her. In about January 1988, Heyoka told me that an old friend of his would arrive as a kitten in June. She would be born in early April, as he had been, and she would be his playmate. When I contacted her spiritually, she said she should be called Punk or Punky. After she arrived, and we called her that for a few days, she appeared to me in a dream at 3 A.M. and told me that her true name was Yohinta and that she should now be called that. I woke myself up and wrote it down. When I called her Yohinta, her eyes twinkled, and Heyoka felt much better also. It emphasized the ancient Native American connection for all of us and suited her perfectly.

I was driving home with an orange tabby kitten the same year Yohinta arrived. I asked him what his name was or what name he would like. He clearly said to me, "Sherman." Since my then husband's family name was Sherman, I queried the kitten to see if I was really getting it right from him. He said clearly and somewhat impatiently, "Sherman, Sherman, like General Sherman, do you get it?" I got it.

When Sherman arrived home, I told my husband the kitten's proposed name. Michel didn't like it. He didn't want to constantly hear his last name. So, I tried to change it. I called the kitten Samson, hoping he'd accept something close. No go. For days, he ignored me when I used that name. I tried other names, like Peter Pumpernickel or Periwinkle, since he was such a magical, fairy-like character, but he was not amused. I told Michel that the kitten was not happy with any other name. So Michel asked me to ask him why he wanted that name.

Sherman explained to us, as he had revealed to me when he first arrived, that he was from the angelic realm. In order to be stable in his cat body and fulfill his mission on Earth, he needed to have a solid name, a name that helped him plant his feet on the ground. That name was Sherman. Michel then understood and accepted the name. As soon as I began to call Sherman by his chosen name, he regarded me warmly and came when he was called.

In June 1991, Rosana and Kelly Hart and I were visiting Elk Hill Farm in Eagle Point, Oregon, where they kept their llamas. They particularly wanted me to meet a new male llama, then about five weeks old. I had long been in love with llamas and considered having a few someday as part of our family of teachers and friends. Michel was concerned that we had enough animals to care for. At the time there were more than eighty animals of various kinds, including fifty chickens. This could be a burden for us, particularly when I was away doing workshops and he had to take care of them. There was also the consideration of space for them, which would involve fencing a large, mostly forested area of our property.

The young llama and I connected with each other, and he particularly connected with Pasha, who was traveling with me. I felt strongly that he was meant to be with us, but because of Michel's objections, I tried to maintain some detachment. Since it would be about six months before he'd be weaned and ready to go anywhere else, we had time to consider it all prac-tically and carefully.

In the meantime, Rosana and Kelly hadn't come up with a name for him. They asked me if I got a name, but I didn't want to look or ask. I felt he might go with someone else, and I was trying to keep an emotional distance. As I was returning home, thinking about this wonderful llama, the name *Regalo* came to me. I thought it was something to do with "regal," which certainly fit. I didn't mention the name to anyone.

Months later, Rosana wrote to me, saying that they'd named the young llama *Regalo*, meaning "gift" in Spanish. Reading that sent chills over my body. This confirmed that the name indeed came from him, since they had received this independently. With research into llama care and meeting other llamas, Michel came to see that they wouldn't be that hard to inte-grate into our family. We began to prepare the land for Regalo and another llama's arrival.

Another llama-naming encounter occurred in August 1992, when we went to visit Elk Hill Farm again to see baby llamas born in April and May. Regalo's full brother did not yet have a name, and Rosana was interested in learning it from him. When I communicated with him, he gave me various descriptions of himself: Joker, Jack of Hearts, Jack of Diamonds, and finally the name he wished, Heyoka. In the Lakota Indian tradition, *Heyoka* is the Sacred Clown, or Fool, the one responsible for making people laugh at them-selves and their folly.

Another young, unnamed llama told me he was in the same spiritual brotherhood as Heyoka, Regalo, other friends, and myself. He had known Heyoka as a Native American centuries before, and they were warriors together, doing many brave deeds and honoring the Earth. They had come back to help enlighten people toward further connection with themselves and the Earth. He showed me a picture of them both with arms outstretched to the sky looking at the clouds. He told me we could call him White Cloud or White Thunder. He was a white llama with black on his rump. Rosana pointed out how appropriate this was since his sire was called Thundercloud! He is now called White Thunder.

When Elfie, our Netherland dwarf rabbit, left her body in September 1991, within a day I was contacted by two dwarf rabbits named Chester and

Molly. Their names came with the thought of them. After calling various breeders, I was told that a nearby feed and pet store had some dwarf mixed-breed baby rabbits for sale. I felt strongly that Chester and Molly were there. When I went, transporting cage in hand, Chester and Molly came forward to greet me in a cage with two other rabbits.

Below their cage I saw a creature I had never seen before—a chinchilla. He came forward to greet me, played "peek-a-boo" in his box, which he busily shred, and looked me right in the eye. I felt a deep connection with him and sensed that he was very special. I knew nothing about chinchillas, and the store attendant did not have a book on hand with information about them. I talked to the chinchilla a bit and decided, although I had a strong pull to take him with me, that I'd have to find out more about chinchillas to ensure I could take proper care of his needs before I considered bringing him home.

Another pet store had a book on chinchillas, which I devoured. Although the chinchilla couldn't be mixed with the rabbits and guinea pigs, as his nature was more aggressive, it looked as though I could manage with our current habitats. I had picked up the rabbits on Friday, read the chinchilla book on Saturday, and now it was Sunday, with the feed store closed. I thought, "If he's still there on Monday, then he is meant to be with us." As I took a nap on Sunday, I got the name *Peter Quince* and saw images of an explorer in the sixteenth century. He told me that he knew me and was meant to work with me now as a chinchilla, and I could call him Quince.

Many of my chickens have given themselves names, such as Chiminy, Iglet, Guido, Jeffrey, Celeste, ChaCha, Pepper, Peter, Aureo, Orion, Antoinette, Dominique, and Andromeda. Others have given no names in particular, so I have given them names that strike me as suiting their characteristics, such as Sugar Pops, Plum, Buttercup, Spinky, Plato, Rosie. If a name I give them or they give themselves does not sit well with any of us, we discuss and modify it as needed for all of us to be happy.

For fun and affection, we also have variations of the animals' names. My Afghan, Popiya, was known as my "Popiya Pizzeria." Pasha also was known as Pasha Pazoo, Pazoo, or Prince Pasha Pazoo. Rana was Rana J. Banana (ba-*nah*-na, to rhyme with *Rah*-na) or Bananas; we didn't know what the "J." stood for. Sherman is also Shermanoni Marconi Cat, Oni, or Shermes. Heyoka is playfully called Heyoka Moka Toka or Toka or The Kid. Yohinta is

Yoyo or YoYo Ma, Yoyo Buttons, Buttons, or Bebe Chat (French for "baby cat"). Pirouette is Pirouetta Katwetta Katwoo. Winky was Winky Doodle or Winky Doodle Boy or Doodly Boy. Chico San has the most variations: Chico Bunny San, Chico Pico, Chico Pico Little Mico, Chico Cuddle San, Chico Fussy San, Chico Baby San, Chico Lovey San, and more. The llamas, Regalo and Raindance, are known as the Doobie Brothers or the Doobers. The animals enjoy or at least tolerate the name variations and the kisses and hugs that go with them in the warm, playful spirit we all share with one another.

ARRIVALS

People have asked me what our animal companions and I communicate about, assuming we must talk a lot with each other. We actually don't chat a lot unless we are getting to know each other or there is some difficulty or teaching that the animal wishes to relate. Our understanding is like a running current among us, so we don't need to question each other or chitchat very much.

I do talk aloud and sing to our animal companions as a natural part of living and my expression of joy and harmony being with them. They let me know their needs. Problems don't usually have a chance to develop, because we listen and supply what we can. If anyone is unhappy, we find out why and remedy it in cooperation with all concerned. New arrivals are a time of joy and intense communication, as we learn about each other and the animals explore their new environment.

Pasha came into my life on February 24, 1979. At the time, my animal family consisted of an Afghan hound, Popiya, and a pert black and white cat named Peaches. We lived in an apartment in Los Angeles, and I was the manager of the twenty-unit building, where no animals were allowed!

I've always managed to convince landlords to allow me to have animal friends even when their policy dictated otherwise. I've assured them that my animals and I will be quiet and responsible and that upon our departure we'd leave the apartment or house in equal to or better than original condition. By the end of the interview, all my past landlords have agreed to have us as valued tenants.

After Popiya was with me a few years, I felt it was the right time to adopt another Afghan. I put my request out to the universe and visualized having the male Afghan puppy who was meant to be part of our family. The message floated around the planetary airwaves, and then Pasha contacted me telepathically. He pictured himself as a puppy in a kennel with other Afghans in a desert area. He was not considered to be "show quality," so the people were considering selling him as a pet, though with a price tag that was well beyond what my 1979 income could tolerate. I asked him—if he was meant to be with me as he indicated—to somehow get himself out of the kennel and into an animal shelter where I could pick him up.

Two days later he contacted me and said he was in the shelter. He had managed to get over a six-foot fence and run about twenty miles to be picked up and taken to an animal shelter some thirty miles away from where he had lived. I called all seven shelters in the greater Los Angeles area on that Monday, and only one, about thirty miles from where I lived, had an Afghan puppy. I was told that I had to wait five days, until Saturday, before he would be up for adoption.

When I arrived at the shelter Saturday morning, I looked around at all the anxious, upset, barking dogs and at first couldn't find the Afghan. I had missed him because he was lying upside down with one foreleg stretched straight up (a pose that would become very familiar to me and that I named the butterfly position), relaxed, and napping. He was in the same cage as a frightened, whimpering black dog. The keeper pointed him out, and when I found him, Pasha sprang up enthusiastically and looked at me with bright and deep eyes. As the man was taking him out for me, a woman who was looking at an Irish setter down the row spoke up, "Oh, they're taking the Afghan!" Even though I knew Pasha was meant to be with me, her words created a "nick of time" feeling.

As we drove home, the six-month-old Pasha told me the story of how he had jumped and scrambled over the high kennel fence to get out. In the process, he had caught and hurt a rear foot (that nail remained crooked all his life), which the person at the shelter had pointed out to me. Pasha wanted to make sure he got to the shelter, so he ran from his kennel in the desert about twenty-five miles before he "arranged" for someone from the shelter to pick him up. It amazed me that the people did not call the shelters to find him. I got that they figured cars or coyotes had killed him. We knew we were meant to be with each other, and no obstacles could get in the way.

I had consulted several times, long distance, with a very wise and wonderful Appaloosa horse named Nishumi. In June 1983, I got to see him in person. When I approached Nishumi, he had a personal reproach for me. He said that I had not acknowledged the help he had given me spiritually in my work with people. He had contributed his energy and wisdom several times, and he wanted me to know that. I apologized for not being aware of his contribution, since I have many animal helpers who send their healing energies and guidance to animals and their people during consultations and workshops, and I didn't single him out.

He accepted my apology and said that he would give me something so that I would never forget him. He didn't tell me what it was, but I thanked him in advance. His people and I headed toward the barn, and on the way I found a large feather from a raptor in the path. I picked it up and said, "Oh, this must be Nishumi's gift." The woman felt that there was something else. I walked into the barn and saw a litter of kittens with the most beautiful, shiny black mother cat I had ever seen.

A black male kitten stopped his play with his brothers, came up and made known his connection with me. I knew then that this was Nishumi's gift. I asked the mother cat if it would be okay to take him home, and she approved. I checked telepathically with our cat at home, Chico San, then one-year-old, to see if it would be okay for her to have a kitten. She tuned into him and approved. Our younger cat, Yoda, also approved. Nishumi was right. With this gift I would never forget him.

When I asked the kitten's name, Nishumi's person got *Heyoka*. When Heyoka and I arrived home, Chico San was very upset at his arrival. I reminded her that she had okayed his admission to the family. "I approved of him spiritually, not physically," she disclaimed. Now he was here. He was obviously meant to be with us, so we'd do our best to help Chico accept him as part of the family.

Chico San had been chief lap and cuddle cat. Heyoka also liked to sit in my lap. While I gave Chico San priority, she was miffed about Heyoka and refused to sit in my lap for months after he arrived. Yoda had a great time playing with Heyoka, but Chico never became a playmate to him, although she soon tolerated his presence.

An important point about bringing in new members to your animal family is that those who were there first should be consulted about who comes to live with them. People bring in new cats, dogs, birds, or horses without discussing or even informing the other animals. They often figure that the animals should just adjust to human decisions. This can be a source of disharmony, extreme emotional distress, illness, and even death in your animal family. Animals can feel rejected, confused, resentful, and disoriented by an unexpected arrival. Jealousy and competition among family animals is often caused or exacerbated by human actions and intentions. You can make all the difference in maintaining or restoring harmony.

A couple complained to me about the behavior of their senior cat toward their new kitten. The older cat was hissing and swatting at the new arrival, and they were shouting angrily at her behavior. They protected, played with, and were delighted with the new kitten. They had not asked their older cat if she wanted a kitten or prepared her in any way for his arrival. She considered the new cat a usurper, and the people were proving how right that was by behaving negatively toward her since the kitten arrived. I acknowledged the older cat's feelings and explained the situation to her people.

I asked the people to pay little attention to the new kitten for now, and to explain to their senior cat why they got the new cat—for her and their companionship—and that she was still "number one." I told them to ask her to teach the new kitten her wisdom and the ways of the family. They were to give the older cat priority attention and thank her for being there as a wonderful cat and respected senior member of the cat group. They were to let her interact with the new kitten and establish her own relationship before they lavished the kitten with attention. At first the people thought this was unfair and that the older cat should be punished for her behavior, while the new kitten should be welcomed with lots of attention. I advised them that if they continued to do so, they would have a very unhappy, if not ill, older cat, and a disharmonious family.

They reported that following my advice made a difference immediately. After the consultation, the senior cat relaxed toward the kitten and loved the return of affection from the people instead of their anger. She then enjoyed the idea of having a younger cat to teach, look after, and play with, and the two felines then got along great.

The results may not be so immediate in every case, and there are variations in handling, depending on the individuals involved. I generally find that including the established animals in the decision about a new animal in the family, by asking them for their permission, makes all the difference. If your heart is set on adding to the family anyway, explain to them in advance what is happening, and make it comfortable for them by not letting their space and habits be altered stressfully by the new arrival. Instead of feeling displaced by the new animal, they know about it and are more prepared. Then they may feel part of the new one's life, and usually end up taking care of the newcomer.

Some people adopt stray cats or dogs after having only one animal companion for a while, or several who are close friends. They may be surprised or shocked that new ones are not accepted. They ask me, "Why won't they accept a poor homeless cat or dog and share their home, when they were strays or abused also when I rescued them?" I ask these people how they would react if their husband, wife, or other family member brought a stranger home to stay with them, eating their food and sleeping in their bedroom, without asking first. How many homeless people have they invited to stay with them recently?

Why should animal companions accept someone into their space automatically? Even if they would happily live with some animals, that doesn't mean they could live and share with just anyone. Aren't we the same? I find that letting the animals at home help pick out a new family member—whether in person or telepathically connecting at a distance—can help to create happiness all around, instead of possessive jealousy and aggressive behavior.

In 1984, we moved from Los Angeles to the forested edge of Point Reyes National Seashore northwest of San Francisco. The cats went from being mainly indoor dwellers to being at ease both indoors and outside and enjoying their freedom in a healthy, natural environment. Yoda spent less time playing with Heyoka and became more interested in a neighbor cat. Heyoka had a good time, because there was so much to do in the new environment.

Through difficulties with the landlord and Yoda, Yoda departed for a new home after a few years, and Heyoka missed having a cat buddy. Chico San refused to play with him. She found him too boisterous, and she wanted to play by her rules. I would play with Heyoka or send him to play with the nature spirits outside, when he was restless for companionship. While he enjoyed playing with the fairies, he still wanted a cat playmate. I talked it over with Chico. She didn't want another cat in the family and had long refused my desire for the envisioned orange cat. I had honored her wishes, but now reasoned that if she didn't want to play with Heyoka, then he had a right to have his own cat playmate. She had no argument.

Early in 1988, Heyoka told me that he had called an old friend of his to join him in cat form. She would be born in April and arrive in June. I got an image of her as having orange on her body. I thought she might be my orange-tabby-cat dream come true. Heyoka and I looked forward to her arrival.

In early June 1988, I had to fly to Chicago to help care for my sister, who had undergone spinal surgery. I kept wondering how the new kitten would arrive. If she appeared in Chicago, I'd have a problem, since my sister is allergic to cats and we were a long way from home.

Michel phoned me to announce that he thought he had found Heyoka's companion but wanted to check to be certain before he brought her home. He was at the annual Western Weekend Fair in town, and there were a few litters of kittens for adoption. One kitten had called to him and said to take her home, that she was the one. I asked if she had any orange on her. Yes, some orange spots and stripes mixed into her black coat. As I tuned in further, I knew she was Heyoka's friend. I instructed Michel to take her home and put her in the bathroom with the door open a crack, so the other cats could get used to her smell and discover her themselves.

Michel brought her home and kept her in the bathroom briefly, but because she didn't like it, he let her out. Heyoka came in through the cat door and found Michel and the new kitten together in the living room. Heyoka was startled and went back out the door. Michel called to tell me that Heyoka had gone and not reappeared for two days, which was totally out of character for him.

I checked with Heyoka telepathically, long-distance. He told me that besides being shocked at a new cat in the house, he saw Michel and the kitten together, felt their closeness, and thought that the female kitten was a replacement for me, since I had gone out of town! I explained to him that Michel hadn't meant to frighten him and that I wanted him to come back and meet his new kitten companion; I would be home in a few days.

This shows how differently an animal can respond to the spiritual connection versus the actual physical presence. Although Heyoka had called his friend to come, his emotional surprise when she arrived did not permit him to recognize her spiritually as his old-time friend. Her strange smell and his misinterpretation of her presence made him feel alienated and confused.

Heyoka listened to me and came home, but he stayed away from the new kitten, whom we were calling Punky at the time. Even after I returned, he was wary of her. When I got her permanent name a few days later and began calling her Yohinta, Heyoka became much more comfortable around her and began to accept that she was his companion. After six weeks, he dropped his cat reservations, and they became best friends. They have since lovingly groomed, slept, played, and communed with each other.

When I walked in the door after returning from Chicago, Michel had Yohinta in his arms, and we laughed when she made the introduction to me, "This is my friend, Michel."

In January 1986, Paisley and Sharmay, two female domestic rats, became members of our family. When I brought them home, they assessed me with their keen intelligence. Connecting mentally within or across species, when mental patterns or ways of thinking are very different, may be difficult. Since rats, as a species, have survived alongside humans for millennia, they have developed a keen awareness of human thought and intention. Rats have a lot in common with humans. They are very social animals, living in groups, engaging in frequent communication with each other, and enjoying mutual grooming, play, and contact.

Many animals are not interested in what humans are thinking, and may consider human thought as chaotic, scattered, too complicated, scary, or so different from theirs as to be incomprehensible or repulsive. This is somewhat species-specific, but there are vast variations among individuals as to how much they are attuned to or alienated by human thinking. A lot depends on their previous (including past life) experience with humans or *as* humans. The ones who have been with humans before or have been human themselves, as is the case with many animal companions, are usually comfortable and can comprehend human thinking more easily. Those with only wild animal experience, especially as prey animals, may find their first domesticated contact with humans a terrifying and mind-boggling experience.

When Paisley and Sharmay arrived, I felt my "mental innards" being examined. In a few hours of assessing my thoughts and ways of moving and being, they decided that I was okay. They relaxed their wariness, and we became very good friends.

One of our first conversations was about cleanliness—not theirs, but mine. The one thing that they found disgusting about me as a human was how dirty I was! They washed themselves vigorously after I touched them. They asked me if I could do something about my filthy hands. My hands were clean by human standards. I realized that the feel and smell of the oils from my pores offended them. I explained that I could do nothing about that, no matter how much I washed; they would have to get used to it as part of me. I discovered that rats are meticulous about keeping their bodies clean, grooming themselves even more than cats do. After a few weeks, they calmed their cleansing frenzies after I handled them, having become accustomed to my hand secretions and appreciative of my warm and loving touch.

Paisley and Sharmay died in September 1988. I was missing their physical presence, though I felt them in spirit all around me as I entered our local feed store on the way to an appointment in the late afternoon. In the store was a lovely, orange male tabby kitten that a number of people were playing with and admiring. I had long wanted an orange cat. Gold and golden orange are very special colors for me. I was in a hurry, and only briefly connected with the kitten, figuring one of the other people would adopt him.

As I was driving away, I got the message from Paisley and Sharmay that the kitten was their parting gift to me. It was too late to return to the feed store after my appointment, so I called about the kitten the next day. He was no longer there, having been taken home unadopted. I contacted his person at work. She told me where her home was in Bolinas, a twenty-five-minute drive, and that I could go there and pick up the kitten myself!

When I went to see the eight-week-old orange tabby, he was playing vigorously with his litter mates and very uninterested in me. His mother was very warm and friendly to me and looked strikingly like our tortoise-shell cat, Yohinta. I asked my angelic guides if this kitten was really meant to be with me, as he was giving no sign confirming our connection. The answer was affirmative, so I picked him up to take him home.

Aside from giving me his name, Sherman, he was rather distant. Even when we got home, he played with objects and was interested in playing with Yohinta, who was five months old then, but he displayed a cool disregard for me. I was surprised, as my animal friends generally make a strong connection from the start.

I thought this would pass, and accepted it as just his way, but it was unsettling. I even considered finding a new home for him! After a few days of being treated like an object by him, I asked Sherman what was going on, why he ignored me. He looked at me in surprise. He said he thought that's how humans wanted to be treated, because that's how they had treated him and how they treated the other cats. I explained that I recognized him as a fellow spirit, and I did not appreciate being treated otherwise. Now he understood! From then on he was affectionate and playful with me, and became a close buddy.

Chester and Molly, dwarf rabbits, were born and raised in cages. One of my greatest joys is to take animals from limited environments, such as small cages, and give them roomy and interesting habitats. For our rabbits, guinea pig, finches, cockatiel, and parakeet, we built "The Beatrix Potter Bunny Cottage." It was a storybook dream of mine that was fulfilled after we moved into our own home in September 1988. The cottage had about fifty square feet of indoor floor space, woodframe walls and floor, and a wood and wire floor covered partially with straw. Two and a half sides were covered with windows and one and a half with aviary wire. There was also a large bay window wire extension for the birds to fly into, to sun or shower in the open air under a tree. The rabbit had a lower twenty-five-square-foot extension along the entire back of the cottage that rested on the ground and connected with the main floor by a wooden ramp.

Elfie's departure saddened her companion guinea pig, Gingerbread, although he understood and accepted her transition to the spiritual realm. He withdrew into his box shelter and hardly came out for his vegetable and fruit treats, for which he usually whistled joyfully. He felt that he was getting ready to join her. However, I was getting messages from two young rabbits who were ready to join our family. I told Gingie to hang in there, that soon he would have bunny company.

The new bunnies arrived about ten days after Elfie's death. Gingerbread welcomed them. I gave them a chance to sniff each other to get familiar while the bunnies were in their traveling cage. Gingie checked them out and found them very peaceful and liked them. Chester and Molly immediately accepted

Gingerbread, and showered him with love that he had never received from a rabbit before—snuggles, licks, and eager sharing of vegetable treats. What a pleasure it was to experience their warmth and happy thoughts with each other! Gingerbread no longer thought of dying. Instead, he spent a lot of time seeing what his two bunny friends were up to and felt rejuvenated in his new role as Uncle Gingerbread.

Young Chester and Molly—five and seven weeks old, respectively—were astounded by the amount of space they now had and enjoyed exploring. In a short time Molly was looking through the wire at the rest of the garden, asking when she could go out there. I had to explain that "out there" was off limits and that she wouldn't survive for long with the owls, hawks, weasels, foxes, and other predators. Our dogs would also have a hard time resisting chasing rabbits who hopped freely around the yard.

While they initially passed up the carrot and apple offerings as foreign and went to the commercial rabbit pellets that were familiar, it didn't take them long to savor the new delights of fresh vegetables. They accepted the birds as natural elements of their environment. The rabbits and birds that have lived in our family over the years have enjoyed each other's company. My cockatiel, Pirouette, often had nose to nose conversations with Elfie.

I brought in handfuls of wild plants and watched as Gingerbread, Chester, and Molly huddled in a happy munching group together. I laughed at their conversations. Molly said to Gingerbread, "We sure get a lot of interesting things to eat here." Gingie replied, "Oh, yes, she brings in all kinds of things for us. We always come running when Penelope arrives, to see what's next." Their communication then revolved around what plants they liked in the mound of greens, who was eating what, and could they have a nibble. I delighted in seeing Molly and Chester nuzzle and kiss Gingie.

I planned to have Chester neutered at the proper age, so we would not have a population explosion, but I was evidently a day or so late. On January 17, 1992, Gingerbread, guinea pig, was the proud "grandfather" of six baby bunnies. He stayed with them and kept them warm, and Molly never minded his care of her babies, despite the difference in species and protective mother rabbit instincts. She groomed Gingerbread in appreciation whenever he was off duty, and he got accustomed to having his eyes very well-washed, rabbit style.

We found wonderful people and new homes for four of the babies. Gingerbread had plenty of bunny-love for his senior years, since we kept two of the babies, Periwinkle and Velvet. I felt that Gingerbread had a part in the "mistake" of this pregnancy. He was so happy with his bunny friends.

In late September 1992, a tragedy struck that took all of our rabbit family from this Earth. After Gingerbread lost his bunny friends, he was nurtured by their sending him lots of loving energy from the spirit realm. I had no call to find a new rabbit companion, and I felt it was too late in the year to acclimatize a baby rabbit to outdoor living. I saw rabbits in pet stores but had no attraction to them. I was thinking it would be nice to have an adult rabbit, when Regina Heynneman, who attended a workshop at our home in October, mentioned that a friend of hers knew someone nearby who had an eight-month-old, spayed female lop-eared rabbit who needed to find a new home. I preferred rabbits with upright ears like their wild cousins, but I thought I would check her out. I could let go of that prejudice or preference if she were the right being for our family.

The lady who had the rabbit had just moved from a ranch to a town house, due to divorce, and had to keep the rabbit caged most of the time. She didn't feel that was a good life for her rabbit. She would put Etta, the rabbit, on her patio when she came home, but Etta hated to be returned to her cage and had managed to escape once for a few days. The woman was afraid predators would attack Etta. Etta was already acclimatized to outdoors, as she spent most of her time there or in the cage in the garage. The fact that she was already spayed was a big plus; according to the House Rabbit Society, 80 percent of female rabbits who are not spayed develop reproductive system tumors.

I arranged to see her, but first I went to the feed store where I had found Chester and Molly. They had two baby bunnies. One looked just like Molly. I held them and loved their sweetness, but I had to see Etta as planned. As I left the baby bunnies, I got the message that they were inbred and would not live a long life, and I was not to get them.

Etta was over twice the size of our former dwarf bunnies—about six pounds. Her fur was a lovely agouti coloring (a gold, brown, and gray blend) and was very thick and luxurious, perfect for outdoors. She had beautiful brown eyes and those long lop ears. Etta showed strong character, yet was gentle and loving and personable, a lot like Elfie and Molly were. Another important and interesting point about Etta was that she was born on February 25, Michel's birthday! Conditions seemed right, and I liked her, but keeping her was contingent on her being gentle with Gingerbread and on their liking each other.

Her name came to me as Elea or Ellie, so combining with her original name, we called her Ellyetta. She loved her new home and was fine with Gingerbread. Although she was far larger than our previous dwarf rabbits, she did not intimidate Gingie. At first, she tried to nudge him around and play, but she listened to me when I told her to be very gentle and let her know that he could not run around with her. It brought back a sparkle to his eyes to have bunny company again.

Ellyetta was very active—jumping on her big wooden box and stump and down the ramp to the outside, lower level. At first she ran from me when I came into the cottage, thinking I was going to take her away, but I reassured her that this was her home and that she wouldn't be put in a cage. After that she came up to me for strokes and nose to nose conversations. Perky Pete (cockatiel) crashed around when Ellyetta first ran around, unable to figure out what she was. She looked like a dog to him. It took the birds a day to adjust to her presence and movements.

She expanded emotionally and spiritually in a very short time in her new home. Her former person had warned me that sometimes she was grumpy and would lunge and bite. Instead, she quickly became affectionate, bright, and filled with purpose.

Less than three weeks after she arrived, we had an advanced workshop at our home. Ellyetta made us all laugh when the eleven participants gathered around the Bunny Cottage to meet all the animal inhabitants, and she stretched out toward everyone and said, "Have all these people come to see *me*?" She shone as a teacher that weekend, relishing her newfound purpose. She raced around to show people how much she loved her home. She conferred with Gingerbread to answer people's questions at first, as he is an experienced teacher. Then she came up to give people encouragement and answered them wisely.

Ellyetta was elated when she saw how she could use and stretch her abilities to help people understand. She kicked up her heels and laughed and asked when these new friends would be back and when more people would come. Her love for people expanded as she saw how she could help them. We were delighted with Ellyetta's presence and joy in participating in our family purpose to enhance interspecies understanding.

GROWING TOGETHER

Sometimes, when people learn to respect and communicate with animals as fellow beings, they are puzzled that their dog or cat friends still display their dog or cat nature. Animal companions will not proceed to do everything your way or behave like human adults (thank goodness!) or fulfill your personal concept of enlightenment. Their actions and ways of thinking will still be influenced by their particular sensory equipment and genetic inclinations, just as yours are filtered through your human senses and programming.

When we domesticate animals, we alter their genetic programming to some extent, so they learn to live with us and sometimes become more human-like. We usually like them more when they harmonize with our life patterns and obey human rules. It can be a challenge for animals to change their physical nature to conform to human needs. As with humans, their ability to adapt is influenced by their body type and other aspects of genetic inheritance, such as hormonal cycles and temperament.

Among those animals who like and want to serve humans, many choose to *act* more like humans. Some *want* to do so, but have such strong opposing genetic tendencies that are almost impossible for them to override that they run into conflicts with people and themselves. Understanding and accepting individual nature and needs is the beginning of working things out for mutual benefit.

Humans sometimes misinterpret animals' actions as ungrateful, if the animals don't express appreciation according to human expectations. People can also blame their horse, dog, or cow for their own shortcomings and resentments. Animals can have their own emotional problems, too, and they can get into manipulative games, as people do, often to cope with people's inability to understand them. It's hazardous and very courageous to volunteer to live with and try to help some people.

Many humans of our time think of themselves as superior to other life forms. Nonhuman animals do not view humans in that position. They look at humans as simply another life form—for some a predator, for others a friend and symbiotic partner. Many animals don't give us much notice at all. Some individuals of different species consider their species to be the best or most enjoyable and wouldn't consider being human.

A cat named Paisley philosophized to me, "I prefer to be a cat, which is vastly superior to being human. Cats use their intelligence much more wisely than people do. People are much more emotional, and when you're human, your emotions get the best of you. I feel agile, quick, and astute. I like to associate with humans, but I recognize my superiority to them."

Individuals of whatever species will have their own viewpoints about any subject. A common thread that I find in most nonhuman animals is enjoyment of who they are and life in general. Except for abused animals and those who have adopted human ailments and neuroses from close contact with unbalanced humans and misguided breeding, as well as a few wild animals who are misfits and don't survive long to pass on their aberrations, most animals have high self-esteem, confidence, and joy in living. They don't need psychiatrists or mental hospitals. Many animals will tell you very naturally, with no boasting or assertiveness, that they are great. They have a healthy appreciation for who they are.

Animals are not just extensions of humans. They have their own choices and their own paths. In my experience, it is erroneous to assume a direct link in all cases between animal problems and their human's ailments. However, we do attract each other to work things out and help each other and often mirror each other's weak and strong points. Those things that we deny, resist, or suppress can become our teachers or tormentors, depending on how we react to them. We may find these submerged qualities manifesting in our associates—those of either human or animal form. We who live together on the Earth can set each other's tone like tuning forks vibrating off each other.

Living with animals while being aware of their sensitivity and depth of communication provides wonderful opportunities for growth and expansion for all concerned. As humans, we usually identify with those species that are most like us in ways of sensing, behaving, and thinking. Understanding the viewpoints of many animals and appreciating their senses, knowledge, intelligence, and ways of being is like immersing oneself in other human cultures. You come back with expanded, freshened outlooks, not limited to one particular social upbringing or locale.

Yohinta, our small, dark tortoise-shell cat, is an excellent huntress. She has patiently waited at the edges of gopher holes, and has often been successful in her catch. One day, she came into the house through the cat door lamenting, "Rana took my gopher." I was skeptical that Rana, our female Afghan, would do that, but Yohinta complained again that Rana had done so. I went outside, and sure enough, Rana was busy crunching down a gopher. I told Yohinta that since she was such a patient and effective hunter of gophers and Rana was not, that I'm sure she could catch another one. Somewhat mollified, she went about her business.

When we were preparing for our llamas to arrive, building their fence and shed and clearing the dead brush from their run, I also tried to prepare all the other animals for their arrival. I described what the llamas would be like as best I could. When the llamas finally appeared, the dogs, chickens, rabbits, and birds accepted their presence easily. My mental pictures of the llamas' size did not prepare the cats, and they acted at first as though King Kong had arrived.

Yohinta had the most to say about them. The llamas were in their run for a few days, and we were getting them familiar with the rest of our property by leading them around on halters with lead ropes. Yohinta gave me this commentary: "Did you see the big animals? I saw them. I was surprised to see you right next to them. Weren't you afraid? What are they like? I'm afraid they could hurt you. Did they hurt you? I'm going to keep watching them. They are scary but interesting." I interjected my feelings and thoughts during her questioning, and she listened very thoughtfully.

A few weeks later, Yohinta went up to the llamas' gate, sniffed Raindance's nose through the wire, looked him in the eye and asked, "What are you?" He looked at her puzzled, with no ready answer to the question! Months went by before Yohinta no longer questioned them but rather accepted their presence.

Since his introduction to our family as a baby llama, Regalo loved Pasha. When Regalo arrived at our home in December 1991, he got very excited, waggling his neck and prancing, when he saw Pasha. When the young llamas, Regalo (then seven months old) and Raindance (fourteen months old), first arrived, Pasha went into the llama run with me, and the llama "boys" and he played in the woods. Pasha dodged under bushes and had a good time sniffing around with the llamas right behind him. He ran out his dog opening in the fence when he had enough.

A few days later, Pasha again went in the run through the gate with me. The llamas were behind the shed, and Pasha puttered around. When Regalo and Raindance saw him, they charged off running after him, and Regalo caught him in the open and jumped on him. Pasha screamed as he was knocked over. As I was yelling and running toward them, Regalo jumped on him again. I chased the llamas away, and poor Pasha, a senior dog of over thirteen years at the time, was shaking. He was not injured but definitely unsettled, so I gave him a massage and comforting.

I talked to Regalo about what he did to Pasha. Regalo was puzzled that Pasha was hurt and scared, as Regalo was just excited and playing with him. I explained the situation, that Regalo and Raindance had to approach other animals slowly, or they could hurt them. Both llamas listened, still perplexed that their playfulness could have hurt Pasha.

Pasha decided not to get near those llamas again. I reminded him how he, as a puppy, had knocked a child over in enthusiasm and was puzzled when the boy cried and how he had to learn to control his playful impulses. Regalo was just a "puppy" and wanted to play in his llama way. However, that didn't make Pasha feel he could trust them, and he wouldn't go with us on our next walk with the llamas.

The next morning Sherman (cat) went into the run, and I cautioned him to use the exit hole in the fence if necessary. Regalo and Raindance approached him very quietly, instead of rushing over. He still headed out when they approached, but they were trying to be gentle.

We had various adventures on our walks on the dirt roads and wooded trails outside our home when the llamas were very young and inexperienced. We made the mistake of taking them for a walk just before sunset. They were jumpy and easily spooked, so we thought we'd make it short and turned around after a quarter mile. It was a fiasco. Both llamas refused to move. Regalo said he'd never seen this road before, though we had walked it several times. Through their eyes, the sides of the road looked like they dropped off, and trees loomed at them like shadowy, scary shapes. It took us a long time to get the short distance home, cajoling, ordering, calming, getting impatient. . . . Cars passed with lights on, and Regalo pranced all over. Even when we got to the yard, the llamas felt everything looked weird in the twilight and balked.

We all were exhausted and upset by the time we got them in their run. I fed the llamas some pellet treats for calming, but we all felt somewhat "violated." We were forced to pull and push them, which didn't feel respectful or harmonious, but was necessary at the time. Regalo, normally so brave and such a good walker, felt we were betraying him by forcing him to go where it was scary. Raindance withdrew more. The next day, Regalo wouldn't let me near him. We all needed to regroup. It was hard to experience the temporary rift. It showed, by contrast, how close we had been before.

The following day, everyone was relaxed and felt good about each other again. Now the llamas are experienced troopers, after many hikes at different times of day, but that early experience emphasized how important it is to see things through the other animals' senses.

Raindance had an interesting reaction when he first arrived. Our chickens checked out their llama neighbors through their wire enclosure, which was surrounded by the llama run. Aureo, our chief bantam rooster, loudly crowed to greet the llamas when he first saw them. Raindance stood back and stared and asked me in alarm, "Why is he screaming? Is he in pain?" After a few crows, he accepted my explanation and the rooster's intention that he was greeting and welcoming the two llamas.

A month after arrival, Raindance was standing looking out of his shed, humming in quiet distress. When I asked him what was the matter, he said he was lonely for his former group. He missed the herd of llamas and the feeling of security and anonymity it gave him. He could get lost in the interaction among the other llamas and not have to think about who he was or his purpose in life.

He wondered if he could fulfill his purpose of enlightening others and bringing peace, joy, and understanding, especially to humans—or if he really wanted to. He felt afraid. Raindance felt closer to Regalo daily, but Regalo was very different from him. Regalo was confident about his role, faced life bravely and with a sense of adventure, and was intensely interested in people, easily giving them his warmth. Raindance searched people deeply and pondered how he could relate to them. He felt he had a lot of responsibility here. He liked me and felt that we could learn to know and love each other more. He was not so sure about other people.

I felt his longing, his loneliness, his depth and beauty. Regalo and he were a good match: Regalo could pass along his mastership of dealing with people and helping them on the Earth, and Raindance could contribute his sense of the mystery of life and ethereal beauty. Raindance was a thinker, cautiously questioning why and how things were the way they were, while Regalo accepted everything in stride. After I told Raindance how I appreciated his sensitivity and that he had already reached people and helped them, he felt reassured and ceased his humming.

On her first llama walk with us, our friend and fellow animal communicator, Jeri Ryan, felt Regalo was adventuresome, curious, and playful. Raindance felt light, sensitive, ethereal, and wise to her. It heightened my enjoyment to walk with another person who noticed and appreciated the llamas' special qualities. She remarked that walking with them was an uplifting spiritual experience. We all floated together along the trail.

Raindance is the self-appointed guardian of the other animals. Soon after he arrived, he gave the unique llama alarm call several times when he thought another animal was in danger—once when Rana was approaching Molly (rabbit), who was temporarily in a cage outside the bunny cottage, and once when it looked like Sherman (cat) was in the chicken run.

The llamas also worked some magic with Michel. He realized that during the month or so since their arrival, he had experienced an enormous upsurge of energy—so much that he hadn't quite known how to handle it. He had been working like a dynamo since they came, almost unable to stop and rest. His body temporarily short-circuited, and he got ill with a flu. He was learning how to handle this energy that the llamas have given him.

Before the llamas' arrival, Michel felt that doing the animal caretaking while I was out of town took a lot of time and energy. After they came, he looked forward to tending the llamas and everyone else. During one trip, Michel had a wonderful heart-and-soul connection with Regalo and Raindance and with Quince, the chinchilla. (Interestingly, both llamas and chinchillas are originally from the Andes Mountain region and emanate the high mountain etheric energy.) Regalo and Raindance were very interested that

Michel was doing the things I usually do; it was a special time for him to get close to them.

A person who had done the advanced workshop was visiting this area, and I invited her to come on a walk with our young llamas. She brought a friend who was, unfortunately, not very appreciative of animals. I coughed and gagged from the woman's overwhelming synthetic perfume. The cats ran from her. The llamas wanted nothing to do with her, not only because of the strong perfume, but also because her energies were harsh and disrespectful to them. They balked and were jumpy on starting a walk with her. So, I explained to her about the perfume and asked her if she could walk another way. She assented, and we carried on with the advanced workshop student.

The student seemed somewhat scattered from being with her friend, so our young llamas were not enamored with her, either. Raindance thoroughly checked her out; he looked deep into her eyes with his intense focus, and asked, "Who are you?"

People had to become themselves, totally in the moment, with Raindance. He would not settle for anything less. It made him unsettled to be with anyone who was unfocused or unsure of themselves. Regalo, more self-confident and steady, was not so demanding of people. He let more of their scattered state roll off his back.

As Raindance sought to fully be comfortable with his identity and role in life, he desired others to be the same way if they were going to be connected with him by a lead rope. If he weren't on the lead, he would just move away, but on the lead he studied people very thoughtfully, questioning them until they responded from the depths of their being. He was jumpy until the person made a good spiritual connection and was present in a focused way with him. Everyone who walked with him felt their soul searched to the depths.

When we came back and were approaching the gate to the llama run, both Regalo and Raindance were very balky about reentering. We led them to another entrance. Raindance froze, stared at the run as though he had seen a ghost, and refused to move, standing about fifteen feet away from the gate. I got Regalo in and took off his halter, but Raindance refused to budge. Through his eyes, I saw a strange apparition in the tree branches. I acknowledged his viewpoint, but he wouldn't move—so I massaged his neck, then his head and ears, particularly the forehead, where mental stress is held and can be released with touch. We did that for a few minutes, and he snapped out of his fear and came with me.

Afterwards, he realized how much he valued handling and connection with him. The walk with a stranger had affected his perceptions of light and energies. When I helped him, he valued my presence. "You're like us," he thought. I was very honored. He is such a sensitive, beautiful soul.

I consider both llamas to be master teachers. Regalo was conscious of his mission from before his birth and Raindance was discovering his role in life more consciously by the day. What a joy to be with them and feel one with them! I can honestly say that I appreciate and delight in all the members of my animal family. The llamas have brought an added dimension to the experience, and I feel more complete and at home with them around.

FAMILY CHALLENGES

Not all our family relationships have been easygoing and filled with wonderment at each moment! I have learned a tremendous amount from those that were often a struggle.

I met my first Afghan hound in 1976 while renting a room in a large house where all the tenants shared a common kitchen. A young man who lived there had adopted an Afghan from the animal shelter. When I saw Mandy lying in the hallway, I fell in love. I had always been a cat lover, but when I saw her I thought, "Afghans are like cats, graceful and independent, only better—you can take walks and travel with them." I got to take care of Mandy when her person left town for months, and I very much missed her Afghan presence when I had to return her.

Through an ad in the paper, I found a woman who rescued Afghans from the pound and looked for homes for them. It was there that I met Popiya. She had apricot coloring and was very similar in appearance to Mandy. She did not like the other dogs that lived with her and growled at them, but she was calm with me. In her eagerness to have me adopt the dog, the young woman told me Popiya was about two years old. I didn't find out till much later that she was much older, almost eight at the time, although that wouldn't have swayed my decision. I felt close to her from the start.

The name *Popiya* came to me along with an image of a small, white, four-lobed flower, which represented her deep, gentle nature. In contrast, when I got her home, she bit me when I tried to groom her legs and paws. She growled if I approached her when she was lying down. I loved her and knew we could resolve anything—so, undaunted, the adventure began.

Popiya was in rough shape, physically and mentally. I learned through counseling her that she had been with a musician who had strange habits of being nice to her sometimes and then beating her paws when he was under the influence of drugs. He had also given her some mind-altering drugs. She started to have seizures soon after arriving, in which she would appear para-lyzed in the chest and front limbs; she would twist in an arc and shake her head and scream.

I had never experienced anything like that before, and it was unnerving. I realized that these seizures were caused by the aftereffects of the drugs she'd been given, as well as by past traumas and malnutrition. The vet had nothing to offer but drugs to calm her, which I didn't think would really solve the problem. Instead, we handled the seizures with good food, calcium/magnesium supplements, B-vitamins, counseling, bodywork, and loving care. The attacks decreased in frequency and severity, and after a few months did not recur.

Popiya wasn't accustomed to direct and honest communication but rather had learned to manipulate people out of fear of being hurt. After many months without seizures, she would start to turn them on when she didn't want to do something, instead of telling me directly. I'd notice her eyes beginning to glaze and the particular twist her body took, and I'd catch her before she'd created a full-blown seizure. I'd say firmly, "That's enough; you're not going to pull that on me. If you want my attention or don't like something, you just tell me. You know I'm not going to punish you, so don't try turning on a fit to get sympathy." Catching her in the act like that cut off the progression of symptoms, and she'd return to normal.

As I counseled her more, she cleared away her past traumas. Our rela-tionship deepened, and she stopped trying to use self-destructive means of communication. In the interim, I'd listen to her thoughts and watch her like a hawk for any attempt to get her own way by such dramatic and unhealthy means. I knew that basically Popiya was a very sensitive and beautiful being who needed help, and as she relaxed, her fine qualities showed more and more. She always was quite stubborn about doing things when and as she liked, but she learned to be very straightforward in communicating her desires to me, and we loved each other very much.

Popiya liked to test me. I would take her on walks to a very quiet neighborhood, with little traffic, where I could let her off the leash for exercise. She would run happily, but when I would catch up to her as she sniffed around, she would race off. When I wanted to return and had to put her on the leash, she would stay just out of reach for a long time, until finally she stood and waited for me and calmly went home.

One morning, unexpectedly, she raced off in a direction she had never gone before, away from the quiet neighborhood and into an area of heavier traffic. In typical Popiya (and Afghan) fashion, she wouldn't listen to my calls to come back. There was no way I could catch up to her, so I raced back to the house, got my car keys and drove off to find her.

When I found her, many blocks distant, she looked lost and confused. When she saw me, she gratefully jumped in through the open car door. Her rebellious feelings of breaking away to fun and freedom had changed to a fear that she wouldn't find me again. She never again ran off without knowing where I was and how to get to me easily.

Popiya growled at people, including me, if they approached her when she was sitting quietly or lying down. She never intended to bite but wanted to protect herself. I decided to lighten up the situation, so I would growl back at her and kiss her. Then she'd growl again, and I'd growl back and kiss her again. We would do this over and over, with Popiya's growls getting feebler and my laughter increasing. Just when I thought I got in the last growl and the game was over, I'd move away and Popiya would slip in a final growl. She'd look at me to make sure I noticed, and then flop her head back on her pillow, saying in her funny, stubborn way, "There, I got the final say."

Popiya would sometimes stop in the middle of the street on the way home and refuse to budge. Reasoning, pleading, or cajoling did not move her until she decided it was okay to move. Once, while trying to get her to move from the street, my patience wore thin and I began to yank at her leash and hit her rear end. Concentrating on her, I didn't see a drunken man careening toward me until he struck me in the neck. He would have struck me again except that

Popiya now saw the necessity to move, and we scurried away. I thought he muttered something about dog abuse, and the whole incident was shockingly embarrassing. I resolved never to hit Popiya again, and she apologized for getting me into trouble.

When we visited New York City for two weeks in 1979, Popiya was disgusted that I stopped to scoop her poop. She was accustomed to hurrying away from the site after doing her business. We stayed in an upper floor apartment of a tall building, and one day she went on strike. I couldn't get her to move from the couch for over thirty-six hours, and when she finally did, her bladder opened a floodgate right by the elevator.

She hated Manhattan noise, crowds, and traffic. On our way through the busy streets to Central Park, she registered her dissent by stopping in the middle of a street to poop. The light changed, and the impatient horns and angry voices of taxi and other drivers barraged us. Popiya blithely continued doing her business, with me standing tensely at her side. She was very pleased that this time she had engineered the situation so I did not hang around to scoop up the evidence.

On Popiya's birthday in April 1978, I held a party. I had a special leather collar made for her, carved with symbols that represented her name and some of her previous lives. Over thirty people attended, and as I gave a special dance performance for her, she lay regally on the floor near my feet, basking in the aura of appreciation from everyone. A poem inspired by the event, written by a person attending, gives a taste of the magic of that day:

A being's boundless energy, revealed
In bone and sinew, vibrant, bursting through
The source of life that cannot be concealed
Flares forth, leaps out, is new, is new, is new.

What is this world that beings bring it life?
What is this life that, growing, greens a world?
Life lives for love of living and of strife
And through its striving sees life's dreams unfurled.

These many beings, bursting on the Earth
Bring life to forms too manifold to count

And by their bounty bring to life its worth
From ever-new creation's flowing fount.

Stream forth the endless intersecting games
In myriad living shapes, with many names.

When Chester rabbit returned from being neutered and I let him out of his cage after the recommended twenty-four hour recovery period, his mate Molly rejected him totally. She chased and attacked him. Scent is much more important than vision to rabbits and many other animals; obviously, he smelled strange to her. I put him back in the cage and scented them both with herbal oil, but the next day she did it again. It was more than just his smell. Molly became very territorial while Chester was gone for the day. She even felt very contented without him! He became afraid of Molly after she attacked him, so I alternated each of them in the cage inside the cottage, hoping and pleading with them to reaccept each other. He tried to kiss Molly through the cage bars, but she continued to be overbearing toward him.

I had to make use of the cage for nine days, because Molly continued to aggressively chase Chester when I put him with her, and he continued to be so afraid of her. I encouraged him to stand up for himself, as I didn't want to keep them separate or find a new home for either. Finally, when I let Molly out of the cage, Chester stood up to her and fought. This was a difficult choice for Chester, since male rabbits are normally submissive to females and will not fight them.

I winced as I stood by and watched, but I knew we had to get through this for them to live peaceably together. Their guardian angels assured me that they would get through this now if I did not interfere. I held myself back and prayed. They bit and scratched and squealed for up to twenty seconds at a time. The fur flew. After about five encounters, Molly backed off. Chester had a few scratches around his eyes, but he healed quickly. They began again to groom each other, and Chester lightly chased Molly every now and then for a few days to show her he wouldn't take any bullying. She didn't try to chase him anymore. The appearance of six baby rabbits on January 17 further illuminated Molly's reaction to Chester as having been influenced by the hormonal changes associated with pregnancy. We were greatly relieved to get through that episode and see Molly and Chester become even closer.

DEEPENING UNDERSTANDING

Consultations with people and their animals are a source of growth and discovery for all involved, as they deepen their understanding of each other.

When Christine was about to move from California to Colorado, she called me to check with her Siamese cat, Tofu, on preparing for the change. Tofu made me laugh with her plain, direct, and adamant appraisal of the situation. She insisted that she wasn't moving, that she planned to stay in the house, and, of course, her people wouldn't leave without her. She reasoned that because they loved her, they would stay. Tofu was very satisfied with her "master plan."

Christine was flabbergasted, and hoped that Tofu would change her mind. Tofu and I talked further about the move, and I conveyed her people's viewpoint clearly and their plans to travel in a camper. Tofu was very reasonable about it and saw their purpose. We worked out, with the cat's agreement, how to help her adjust to the trip and pictured where they would live. Tofu changed from being insistent on staying to being willing to go with her family.

This is typical of how one may proceed when getting an animal's viewpoint: acknowledge it fully and then explain your reasoning, making the latter as positive as possible for them; they clear up their disagreement and then are with you all the way. After carefully listening to the animal, fully describe the situation as you see it and how it affects them, and work it out together. Not all animals will be as gracious as Tofu about changing their minds. You may have to work it out with them a bit each day, but communication goes a long way to resolving these matters.

Kathleen Bradley reported that her cat, Sharmin, was much happier after a consultation, and she too felt more relaxed and relieved. She wrote:

I had tried to call you many times and was unable to get through. Sharmy waited around, aware that I was up to something involving him. My cat opened this small cabinet where I keep my maps. He has never gotten into that cabinet before, so I watched him. He pawed out one map and let it drop to the floor, looked at it, then pawed out a second map, looked at it, and looked at me. I thought, "Maps, distance . . . okay, I'll give it another try." That is when I got through to you.

After we spoke, I wondered what maps were out; the second map he had pawed out was of Marin County (where Penelope lives). I am properly astounded and appreciative, whether this incident was a coincidence or not!

A horse called Chaca suffered so severely from a foot disease that she could not be ridden. When she became very depressed, she stood in one place in her pasture and did not want to eat. Her person, Elaine, phoned me for a consultation.

Chaca was depressed because her person could no longer ride her. Life was not the same without fulfilling the job she loved so well. Her foot condition was getting worse through lack of movement. When I suggested Elaine get Chaca a horse companion to keep her company and have someone to exercise with, Chaca brightened up. However, Elaine could not afford another horse. I suggested she find a goat or any four-footed companion to keep up Chaca's spirits.

Months later, I heard from Elaine again. She had followed my suggestion and borrowed a companion for Chaca from a neighbor. He was a seven-year-old, lonely donkey stallion named Charley, who had been kept by himself in a pasture, virtually unhandled by people. The donkey was not trained to a halter and lead rope, which made taking him home potentially difficult. Elaine told him that she needed him to be a companion to her mare, and if he liked that idea, he should follow her home. She held out a carrot to lead the way, and off they went, home to Chaca. In a short time Chaca and Charley became good friends and played around together. This companionship and exercise added a new dimension to Chaca's life, and her sore feet improved dramatically.

This might have been the happy ending, except for Charley's wild behavior, which prompted Elaine to call me another time. Charley was destroying Elaine's fruit trees, fences, barn siding, and anything else he could chew or trample. The last straw came when he damaged the fender on a friend's car.

Charley was untrained and powerful, and a stallion—a difficult combination. When I contacted Charley at a distance, he acted like a rebellious teenager, asserting himself and telling me what a wonderful time he was having and that he wasn't going to stop his behavior for anyone. He explained that he loved when Elaine came out screaming after he destroyed something. It was more attention than any person had ever given him.

In the course of the conversation with Charley, Elaine explained that she would have to return him to his lonely pasture at the neighbor's if he didn't change his antics. Charley wouldn't budge and defiantly said he didn't care what she did. Even though I carefully listened to Charley's feelings and acknowledged him, he was very stubborn. The situation looked grim.

Then Elaine said that she really loved Charley and would be sorry to have him go. I immediately felt his resistance soften. Since he was now open to listening to her side of the situation, I further expounded to Charley that Elaine really loved him and wanted him to be happy, and that he needed to cooperate with her to stay in his current situation, which he enjoyed so much. I asked Elaine to go out to see Charley after we finished on the phone; she was to tell him again how much she loved him, and detail to him the exact behavior she needed from him. He would need to have a halter on and be willing to be led around, even though he was not trained to do this. He would have to stay in a corral for a while to settle down and show good behavior before regaining his freedom to romp with Chaca.

Elaine called me the next day to tell me the results. After our consultation, Charley grew very quiet when she talked to him. He then let her put a halter on him and lead him to the corral, where he did not try to open the gate or monkey around as usual. He had previously demonstrated his ability to open any gate.

The crowning test came the next morning when she had to move boxes from the house to the garage for storage. Charley usually would be in the middle of any activity such as this, finding it irresistible to escape his enclosure and tear into the boxes. This time, when he saw from his corral what she was doing, he turned his back to avoid temptation. She was amazed!

Charley lived many happy months with good behavior, until earthquake disruption to the area he lived in created some havoc; he ended up going back to his former pasture home of his own accord.

Mary Lou Williams related another successful outcome:

Acting on your information, I decided the whippet girl had no home looking for her, and the Whippet Rescue people had homes waiting.

When the people came to look at her, she was again terrified of being "thrown out" and wouldn't have anything to do with them.

I kept sending her pictures of them loving her and having a permanent home for her. By the time we walked out and talked in the driveway for a few minutes, she'd brightened up a bit. Then she went by herself to their car door, waited for it to be opened, and climbed right in and settled down! She'd been going everywhere in my truck with me before, and walked right by the truck to their car! I felt so much better, then, as I had been feeling strongly that she thought I was throwing her out also, and I couldn't stand it!

Sue Goodrich describes a consultation she did:

Sherry called me, close to hysterics. When she arrived home she found her newly adopted female dog's week-old puppies in the swimming pool. They were very cold and made gurgling sounds. She thought the man she had rescued the dog from had done it. I told her to plug in her electric blanket, turn it on high, fill the sink with warm water, hold the pups upside down to allow any fluid to run out, wipe them off, and hold them in the water to raise their temperature, dry them with a rough towel, put them in the blanket, and call me back.

When I contacted the mother dog, she flashed me a picture of her putting the pups in the pool right before Sherry drove in. Thinking Sherry wouldn't keep her with the puppies, as they were a surprise to Sherry, she was desperate. Sherry and her roommate had recently discussed how they would ever find homes for mongrel puppies. They didn't know she was pregnant when they got her a month earlier.

The mother had not come near the puppies yet. There were three puppies that felt in shock and were getting ready to leave. I had her place her left hand on one puppy at a time, to help me find them at a distance. One after the other, the three were placed wrapped on a hot water bottle, and I had her work the ears to get them out of shock, then around and in their mouths to stimulate them, and tell them they were loved and would find wonderful homes. They warmed up and felt like they were solidly in their bodies. After they were placed back in the blanket, the mother came over and licked and licked Sherry and her roommates' hands. They told her she was wonderful and loved and this was her permanent home. The puppies were now crying for food, and the mother dog went to them.

After they shared the story with co-workers and friends, all the puppies were spoken for before they were six weeks old, and went to good homes. The mother was spayed and became a staunch friend and protector of Sherry's horses and home.

From Bobra Goldsmith:

After talking with you, I went right out to the barn to sit with Pequeño (llama), "tell" him things, and visualize as best I could the pleasant life he could possibly have with us, being a companion to the weanlings or whatever he liked. Although I'm very new at trying to do this kind of thing, I did "let him go" while I was trying to communicate with him.

The interesting thing is that his attitude seemed to change quite noticeably. It wasn't long before he got up from where he was sitting in his stall. I opened the door into the aisle, where feeders are for the females when they are inside, and just let him wander about as he pleased. Pretty soon he started eating and finally settled down by a partial bale of hay. When the weanlings came in, I let them all roam in the barn, and eventually Pequeño went into the same stall and corral as they did. His attitude toward me also seemed to change. He had been generally oblivious of people or not interested in them. However, in the next few days whenever I came and said his name, he would turn his gaze directly to me. I would talk to him in my normal way as I took care of him, laying a child's sleeping bag over him as he sat when he was chilly. He seemed to welcome my visits and seemed to "listen." I continued to try to visualize to him several times a day, too.

In the long run, it was evidently my mission to have him back in order to preside over his death, although I would have preferred to have him enjoy many more years of greater freedom and a more interesting life than he had for ten years. I was happy that we had him for a month and that he had a bountiful amount of love and care in his last days. I think he may have understood or felt that love, finally.

One of my most moving and memorable consultations was in Alaska with Joanie Doss and her parrots, the Amazing Amazons, who work with her to entertain, educate, and enlighten people by performing, especially for groups of children. The wise elder of the group was Pepper, who explained that he was about fourteen years old and very mature. He told his story of being captured from his wild habitat, how his parents were clubbed and killed, and how he and other parrots were treated very cruelly.

Unlike many animals who let go of memories of abuse and forgive people, he said that he hated people for a long time and wanted to kill those who captured him and the other parrots. He was grateful that now, after Joanie's nurturing, he considered himself a free bird and loved people and they loved him.

He described how angry he was when he met Joanie, when he expected people to club him if he expressed his feelings. How happy he was now to let the world know what happened to him and other parrots. Joanie confirmed how filled with hatred he had been when she got him. He bit chunks of flesh from her arm, lip, and scalp—every day for eighteen months. She felt he bit out of hate, not fear. It was a test of her patience, compassion, and determination that she helped Pepper to get through all this.

Joanie asked him why he stopped talking in human words, and he explained that people have to learn to listen to the mind, not just the words. Joanie felt that, through his actions, she did understand him almost as well as before. Pepper complimented her on how well she listened. After Joanie did my basic workshop, she understood how much she already understood telepathically from him and her other animal companions. Pepper explained further, "It is boring! You think that is all a parrot is about, learning new words and phrases? I know all these things. Just listen to me directly. I spell all things out."

Throughout the interview, where newspaper reporters were on hand and taking photographs, Pepper and I laughed aloud together when he repeatedly asked for the TV camera and said that he wanted this on television. The other parrots emphasized how much they admired him and considered him a wise grandfather and how much he taught them. What a character, what a wise and beautiful soul to live and grow with!

When she was sixteen years old, a cat named Lucretia talked to me about who she was and about her relationship with her person:

> When I was young I was a most beautiful cat, but unappreciated. My person didn't know my true self, and I didn't either. I lived much of my life repressed, hiding myself, encased in fear. In my thoughts I was not friendly.
>
> When you saw me today I realized who I am. You said I was beautiful and you meant not just the outward looks but my spirit, my self. I feel like a flower unfolding. Now, I realize I am wise and am blooming like a flower. I feel young again. I will live a long time.
>
> I feel the vibrations of the Earth. I feel the gophers moving under the ground. I call them and play with them. The small creatures are my friends, and I love them. They feel my footsteps and my presence. The Earth is alive and warm.
>
> I love to watch the sky—it is so beautiful. The clouds pass by. The birds pass by. I have never seen so many beautiful birds as in this place. There is so much to watch. I love the walks to the ravine. I hear the water underground, and it makes me happy. The small animals go there for water. I love it here. And I am loved.
>
> I am not the same. I am a new cat, a princess, like when I was born. I had shut off my true feelings. Now I can watch all day and feel the Earth.
>
> I like the colors around you, shifting like a rainbow—red, purple, and green. I wish you could stay. You see me as a spiritual being, and I am beautiful. Come back again. I am happy to have told my story.

In 1990 Dawn Hayman received this communication addressed to me from a very special horse companion:

> My name is Deeteza. I am a twenty-three-year-old Arab mare of incredible breeding. I met you back in July of 1987 when my friends

Bonnie Reynolds and Dawn Hayman called you about me. I was being very difficult at the time and you helped us. You told them that it was important to realize that I love to be listened to and to talk. The problem at the time was that I wouldn't get into their trailer, and, in fact, I had had a traumatic accident where I flipped over backwards in the trailer. You told them that it was important for them to explain what was going to happen in the trailer, and you were very right. I never knew how the trailer attached to the truck. I gladly went back home with them. The thing that really impressed me was that now I was able to communicate with them.

Bonnie and Dawn have created here at Spring Farm a place for all to learn to communicate. It is something that animals and humans have lost with each other through the years. It is not only important for people to learn to communicate with animals but also for animals to learn to communicate to people. Just as important is for the animals and the people to learn to communicate among themselves. Every life form that is here on Spring Farm—the people, the horses, the dogs, the cats, the birds, the frogs, the deer, the trees, the rocks—has come to learn or relearn that great gift of communication. I am very proud to be a part of that.

If there is one complaint that I do have with Dawn, it is that she is sometimes difficult to motivate. She doubts the material she is getting from me. It has only been in the last few weeks that I have really been able to get some deep philosophical thoughts down on paper through her. She is continually growing, and to be honest, aren't we all?

our Healers, Teachers, and Guides

I NEED TO WRITE *when the rain blows cold*
And the wind is whistling free
I need to tell of the love I feel
For the friends surrounding me.

Ginko, wise chameleon, resting on your fern
Pirouette, bright cockatiel, your song sent to the world

Heyoka, medicine cat, leading me through dreams
Chico San, hugging purrfully, sharing deepest schemes

Yoda, feline alien, watching silently
Winky, cheerful parakeet, pulsing intensity

Pasha, brave and wondrous friend, deepest joy revealed
Rana, softest goddess, deep, gentle love congealed

Finches, Sunrise canary, pouring piping mirth
Chiminy, shining rooster, crowing for the Earth

Hens, alert and masterful, in your gracious dance
Bunnies four, your lives just so, melting at your glance

Brothers, Nutmeg, Gingerbread, guinea boys so sweet
Ratties' curiosity, all the world's a treat

Fishes, salamanders, too, happy in your pond
All these friends so dear, so free, beauty does abound

In gratefulness, in soul connection
In love for life, in joy's direction
They lead, they follow, they nurture, they share
No matter the form, we'll always be there
Friends unbound but blended together—forever.

I wrote this paean to my animal family in February 1987. These friends of other species have been an unending source of inspiration and spiritual energy. They have helped to create paradise on Earth. I marvel at their beauty and truth and always am grateful that we are together.

PASHA

From the beginning of our relationship, Pasha was one of the most integrated beings I have ever met on Earth. Demonstrating a wonderful harmony of body, mind, and spirit, he totally enjoyed his identity and his life. People melted with his deep perception of them and his warm understanding. His charm won over most female dogs' interest, and male dogs often followed him around in reverence as their mentor. Full of fun and mischief, he believed life should be embraced with passion. He used his warm understanding to bring others toward the wholeness that he so richly exemplified.

Michel's parents, Jeannine and Claude, planned to visit us for the first time after we were married in December 1980. They were not animal lovers at the time and would not appreciate Pasha's exuberant nature, especially his special greetings where he put his paws on people's shoulders or bopped their noses playfully. I explained the situation to Pasha, that he would have to be very sedate and mannerly around Michel's family, sitting quietly and waiting for them to greet him. Like attendants to royalty, we rehearsed the proper sitting position and gentle presentation of his paw that would be appropriate.

As Jeannine and Claude arrived, I reminded Pasha about manners and hoped he would not get carried away with his abundant enthusiasm. When they opened the door, Pasha sat patiently and looked at them, exuding his princely charm. In all the excitement, he never jumped up or lost his composure. Michel's parents were very impressed, and in a short time they were enthusiastically greeting him and appreciating his company.

Michel, his parents, and I were in the car with Pasha on the way to a restaurant. Claude reprimanded Michel angrily about something. Later, Claude turned around to greet Pasha in the car, and Pasha, acting very uncharacteristically, turned his head away from Claude. Claude was hurt and asked why Pasha wouldn't respond to him. Diplomacy did not permit me to voice the reason, but Pasha had made it clear that negative behavior toward his buddy, Michel, was not okay. Pasha made a deep impression on Claude and seemed to help temper his impatience. Both Jeannine and Claude appreciated Pasha's friendship and often asked about him after they left.

Early in our relationship, I had worked with Pasha on matching his behavior to people's emotions—being enthusiastic only with those people who enjoyed his exuberance, being quiet and respectful with people who were fearful, and ignoring or avoiding those who were hostile. In Los Angeles, we had a cabin that served as our bedroom and office behind a large house that we shared with a few other families. A repairman had come to fix a faulty phone line in the cabin. He was terrified of dogs and asked if we could keep them away from him as he traversed the yard to the cabin.

I kept our other dogs at bay, but Pasha, then about three years old, sat quietly waiting for the man to come out. I assured the man that Pasha was friendly, and he cautiously entered the yard. Pasha looked at him thoughtfully, assessing his feelings. The man reached out and petted Pasha, who continued to sit quietly and looked into the man's eyes. While the man repaired the phone line in the cabin, Pasha sat near him. The man came out amazed and visibly relaxed, even though our other dogs were now milling around. Although he was afraid of dogs, he said he felt so different about Pasha. Pasha had worked his magic.

Pasha and I were attending a friend's party, when I noticed a young man who was very distraught. I tried to approach him to talk to him, but he avoided me and looked even more emotionally upset at the contact, so I withdrew. Pasha was wandering around having a good time, and I asked him if he would go over and help the disturbed young man. Pasha greeted him quietly, sat and looked into the man's eyes, and immediately the man relaxed as he stroked Pasha and returned his gaze. After about ten minutes with Pasha, I saw the man conversing with other people, although he had not been able to before. I found out later that he was undergoing treatment for a personality disorder.

Pasha was an unabashed chowhound. Where there was food or any kind of garbage resembling food, there you would find him. During a walk on a Point Reyes beach with Rana and Pasha, I saw some people having a picnic. I leashed Pasha, so he would not bother the people for food. The two women smiled at us and admired the dogs as we went by. On our way back, I saw that they were finished eating, so I let Pasha off the leash, and he led us over to socialize.

One woman lived in Berkeley, and the other was her cousin visiting from Kentucky. The cousin started explaining that she was a bit over-whelmed by the Bay Area lifestyles, especially all the metaphysical, New Age ideas, which were so different from her background. Pasha watched her and listened. Sitting near her, he reached out and put his paw on her shoulder. She looked into his eyes and after a few transforming moments said that she had never had an experience like this before, that she felt he understood her. She began to cry and stroked Pasha as he kept his paw on her shoulder. Tears released, she began to laugh, and said she would never forget this special time.

Counseling session over, Pasha took his paw off her shoulder and eyed his "fee"—the cheese and crackers in an open bag by her side. I was amazed that he had not tried to get them before. The woman laughed as she handed the food to Pasha.

A client doing spiritual counseling with me mentioned that Pasha's communications to him assisted in increasing his awareness of release and completion. He felt Pasha had awareness of basic truths above and beyond human analytical understanding.

We live on Inverness Ridge, sparsely populated with houses that are almost hidden in the woods. It borders Point Reyes National Seashore, with over a hundred miles of trails overlooking the Pacific Ocean. When we moved to the area and didn't know the people living nearby, Pasha acted as ambassador. When we went out for the dogs' daily run, it was Pasha's cus-tom to disappear for his own adventure before he came home. It was part of expressing his independent nature and enjoying life to the hilt. Our area was very safe, so we didn't have to worry about harm coming to him.

He had been gone for over an hour one evening, when we got a phone call from a neighbor about half a mile away, saying Pasha was there. They thought they'd better call for us to pick him up. They mentioned how he knocked at the door with his paw and came right in, friendly and without a care in the world. When I arrived, Pasha was lounging in their dining room and then happily sniffing in the kitchen as we talked. I told the people he wasn't lost, that he knew how to get home, but he just liked meeting people. They enjoyed his visit and mentioned how Pasha was introducing us to our neighbors.

Other neighbors have walked back with him or called to tell us he was there. Carole McFall, who laughed at all of Pasha's antics, several times sent him home reluctantly after he curled up on her bed for hours, watching TV, and eating snacks with her.

Pasha got bored during basic workshops on how to communicate with animals. He had no tolerance for people invalidating themselves or making telepathic communication difficult. He preferred to work with people when they were ready for deeper levels of understanding. Many people at advanced workshops have reported how he helped them to clear their own resistance and understand spirit on a deep level of communion. No one who looked into his eyes was unmoved.

CHICO SAN

Chico San, our fluffy Angora calico cat, has demonstrated her healing abilities many times. Her usual technique is to lie on the body area that needs relaxation or enhancement of energy. People experience suffusing warmth and healing changes throughout their body, with release of tension and pain. She loves being close to people, and she is very deliberate about choosing people who need her help. At advanced workshops, people have commented how she helps them to feel relaxed and increases their understanding and ability.

Once I had a very strong headache and went to Chico San for help. She told me to lie down on my stomach and she curled up on my lower back. I questioned her choice of areas to focus her healing for my headache, but trusted her judgment and cooperated. In a few minutes I felt the headache break up and dissipate. I realized that it was coming from a feeling of not being well-supported, hence Chico's choice of my lower back.

Another time, I was lying on the couch in severe pain after foot surgery. Our three cats were stretched over my body, and I appreciated their comforting. Chico San normally does not like loud noises; if I whistle to Pirouette, the cockatiel, or sing loudly while she is on my lap, she meows and asks me to stop. As the pain became intolerable, I cried and moaned loudly. The other two cats jumped off at the distressing sound and feeling, but despite my noisy cries, Chico San reached up and patted my tears and face gently with her paw. She has repeated that gesture at other times of sadness.

During that recovery time, Pasha came in and offered his suggestion on how I could feel better. He told me I needed a walk outside in the fresh air. Unfortunately, I couldn't follow his canine advice, but I appreciated his helpful intention.

Sue Goodrich was staying at our home while she participated in the advanced workshop. Chico San spent a lot of time with her. One night, Sue went to bed feeling ill, and Chico San went downstairs to the guest room to be with her. She told Sue to lie on her back, and Chico went to work, massaging her abdomen vigorously with her paws. This was something I'd never seen her do before. Sue felt a lot of energy in her bowels and had intense diarrhea after this treatment. This cleansing action eased her discomfort, and she was able to have a good night's sleep.

Animals often tailor their communication to our needs. If we are ready to hear them as profound truth teachers, we can journey and expand together. When we open up, they can give their gifts to us.

HEYOKA

Heyoka, our black cat who resembles a panther, has displayed intense, transformative power. Often, when I settled in for an afternoon nap, if he were not indoors, I would send him the thought that I was about to take a nap, and he would suddenly appear in order to take a nap with me. His shamanic ability to take me on journeys to other realms has helped me to expand and do my work better. Sometimes, when he slept with me, I have had a sensation of dropping, sinking deep into another realm, traveling and having vivid visions.

Heyoka has come here especially to assist me and often doesn't pay much attention to other people. Even so, he has sometimes been the main member of the animal family to lead advanced workshops and jolt people into recognition of their own power. He has a huge spiritual presence, at the same time being very sweet and affectionate. At one workshop he physically led people around to meet and meditate with all the animals, rolling on his back in front of people. At another workshop, we were talking about holistic health and nutrition for cats, when he appeared in the middle of the group of people to demonstrate. We laughed as he rolled on his back from side to side to give us the picture of a shining, healthy cat.

QUINCE

Quince and I met in the store where I picked up Chester and Molly. This beautiful black and silver chinchilla kept jumping out of his box and smiling at me while emanating powerful energy. As I researched chinchilla care to make sure I could meet his needs, his name came to me in a dream, and I knew he was meant to be with us. When I returned to pick him up, he let me touch him, but when the man tried to get him into the carrier cage he escaped and led a merry chase through the aisles and shelves. Unlike his initial friendliness, when we got home he bit me, frightened as I tried to touch him. He had been handled very little, and he asked me not to touch him. We transferred him to his habitat, a six-foot-tall, three-foot-wide, four-story condominium, where he would have plenty of room to play and lots of things to chew and hide in and around.

Although he did not want physical contact and leapt away when I gave him food or arranged his habitat, his spiritual power was intense and immense. He helped me with my book writing, giving me ideas for chapters, and joined in my meditations. Some advanced workshop participants have felt compelled to communicate with him, and he has given them deep insights into their lives. Other people have found him too intense or inscrutable, not feeling they could face or understand him. I felt his strength, his wisdom, and his intensity of purpose here. He came to help the people who came to him. His physical wildness combined with mystical power has provoked curiosity and inner searching.

SHERMAN AND THE ORANGE CAT CONTINGENT

I always wanted to have an orange tabby cat, and Sherman has been a special helper to me. When I was preparing to hold the first advanced workshop at our home in 1989, Sherman sat with me outside and suggested questions for participants to ask animal teachers. At most advanced workshops, he greets people when they come in and then vanishes for the whole day, only to reappear to give his blessings as they exit. He places a circle of light and helpful energy around us as we work through the day and stays in contact at a distance. His forte has been to appear in person when people are having a particularly rough time and he feels his penetrating skills are needed to open their abilities. We nicknamed him "laser beam Sherman" after he worked wonders in helping one person who was heavily invalidating her ability to ever get telepathic communication clearly from animals.

Groups of beings, such as species, often have a communication network with each other across time and space. They are aware of each other, their likeness, and their sharing of energy, and communicate across vast distances from one to the next. Animal, plant, and mineral groups have often shown me this long-distance telepathic connection.

An interesting group connection that I have found in my travels is among orange striped cats, which I call the Orange Cat Contingent. I have met various orange tabby cats separated by thousands of miles who tell me that they know each other and communicate with each other, even though they have never met physically.

These orange cats have certain characteristics in common, such as friendliness to people and many other animals, fascination with water, a passion for the outdoors, athleticism, enjoyment of physical contact, a playful sense of humor tinged with mischief, a sense of solidity and grounding, along with deep, spiritual wisdom. They seem to be a group of spirits with a mission to help people love themselves and to remind them, by example, of who they really are.

Not all orange tabby cats identify themselves as members of the Orange Cat Contingent. Those who do have a special quality. Their sense of humor provokes smiles and laughter when you are around them. While many animals are here to help us wake up to our true spiritual nature, the orange cats in this group seem to have their own way of doing it. They plant themselves in the middle of things, so you can't miss the point.

All cats have a species connection to each other, as do all dogs, horses, pigs, goats, etc. Cats with similar genetic backgrounds will have similar traits, but the Orange Cat Contingent has a spiritual mission unrelated to genetic inheritance. Other communicators have recognized this kind of grouping among the orange tabby cats and others, such as gray cats.

Groups of beings tend to reincarnate according to their common purposes and often reconnect with each other to assist and enjoy each other's company. The "OCC" is a special group to me, as I've always been attracted to golden (orange) animals—and, of course, Sherman is a member.

SULTAN

Sultan was a strawberry finch, born in 1983, who lived with a mate and with Frodo, a canary, for many years. When his wife died, he became good buddies with Frodo, but he was quiet and shy, happy to live anonymously as Frodo's friend. Sultan would only sing when Frodo was busy eating and would never interrupt Frodo's song with his own. With feathers of a striking red and black pattern, people noticed Sultan's physical beauty, but they weren't drawn to communicate with him.

In early summer 1992, Sultan underwent a metamorphosis. He began calling out to the wild birds outside and to Tommy Tunes, a bold green singer finch, who lived in the bunny cottage/aviary below Sultan's window. I was amazed at this change in Sultan's behavior, as he was always so unassuming, and Tommy Tunes is extremely dominant. For several months, Sultan bloomed, singing regularly, with Frodo giving him new respect and position.

Then, for the first time, he helped a person in an advanced workshop in September 1992. His conversation with Eva Kaye was very uplifting to her. It was fascinating to me that he advised her to be and do the things that he himself had just begun to demonstrate in his life. It was as if he had gone through these changes just so he could teach her about them.

Eva and Sultan were similar in being shy and fearful and now wanting to come out of their shells and help others. He advised her:

Let yourself be open. I will help you fly. I will be there for you. Overcome your fear by opening yourself up. The greatest of joys is at your doorstep. You are afraid of becoming who you are. It's the moving forward that matters, not the dwelling on why. Just recognize and acknowledge that you are afraid and move on. My purpose is to teach and be a catalyst. Your purpose is the divine communication of animals. You'll be a catalyst to bring about change in people. You can touch all animals. You will help the animals teach the people. You can have it all, everything I dream about. Just keep moving. This transformation is imminent.

As Sultan relayed the last part of his message, Eva felt she was breaking into "the light." When she asked him how old he was, he replied that he was one year old. Eva got a feeling of wisdom and age from him and wondered about his answer. Sultan was almost ten years old. When I checked with him, he said that he felt he was just beginning a new life, that this was the first year of his coming into being who he really was.

This example illustrates how animals can grow, just as humans do—in their own time, in their own way, even suddenly and drastically. We do them a disservice if we relegate them to sameness and underestimate their ability to transform spiritually and even change their whole way of being. Since the workshop, Eva had a number of long-distance telepathic conversations with Sultan that had deep meaning for her.

REGALO AND RAINDANCE

I have had a romance with llamas for many years. Their sensitivity and refined spirituality, plus their appreciation of aesthetic expressions such as music and dance, have held me captive. Seeing llamas in person repeatedly in my work infused me with "llama fever."

Meeting Regalo when he was five weeks old sent me researching how we could provide for llamas as part of our animal family. Months later, Michel and I went to meet our potential llama companions. All of Michel's doubts about having llamas in the family evaporated when Regalo leaned over to Michel's hand, checked it out thoroughly, and Michel heard him say,

"There is music coming out of your fingers." Michel is a classical guitar and lute player.

This was also our initial contact with Raindance, who was somewhat shy and uncertain of what he wanted to do with his life. After taking the young llamas for a walk with halter and lead rope, we were sitting on the ground as they stood near us. Regalo was munching grass when Raindance turned to him and asked, "Do you want to go with these people?" Regalo looked at him and answered confidently, "Of course, these are my people. I'm meant to be with them."

Raindance then warmed to the idea of life with us. Seeing Raindance's potential as friend and teacher, we decided to welcome him into our family. The people who raised Raindance noticed an immediate difference in him. Instead of merging anonymously with the herd of llamas as he usually did, he now stood out more confidently and became a leader of those in his group. He had found his purpose in life.

While I was preparing for the llamas' arrival by clearing fallen limbs, brambles and debris from the forested section of their run, the thought kept running through my head, "The dolphins are coming, the dolphins are coming," and I had a vision of dolphins leaping through our woods! I got the connection between dolphins and llamas in their roles upon the Earth as spiritual comrades and enlighteners. Our llamas, Regalo and Raindance, arrived at our home December 6, 1991. I wrote this poem after meeting both llamas on October 7:

Llama Love is bursting at the seams
Llama Love is filling all my dreams
I'm obsessed, I'm possessed
Oh, I'm really very blessed.

Llama Love—sharing life is what it means
Llama Love—knowing planetary schemes
We are One
We are Home
We are nevermore alone
Magic Makers

Silent Shakers
Ancient thoughts from ancient beings.

Thank you llamas for coming to this Earth
Setting stage for the hours of our rebirth
We are seeking life as lovers
Fathers, mothers, sisters, brothers
Tribal unity regained
Singing ancient, lovely strains.

Llama Love is dignity
Llama Love is grace
Sending blessings everywhere
Floating into space
We thank the gods for llamas.

At the beginning of the first advanced workshop that Regalo and Rain-dance experienced, they were at first repelled when the students' came to meet them. The llamas were not accustomed to the workshop participants' conflicting emotions, doubts, problems, and insecurities about themselves and telepathic communication. The energies felt too heavy or negative to the llamas. By the second day, when people had gone through and released much of their seriousness and lightened their emotional burdens, the llamas were more willing to participate. Regalo and Raindance quickly understood how to support the students' learning process, and for the subsequent advanced workshops, they came forward readily.

It pleasantly surprised me that Raindance was most interested in help-ing and teaching people. At the September 1992 workshop, he made a special connection with a participant named Dick. As two Libras, astrologi-cally, they matched energies, and Raindance helped Dick to extend his own sensitivities and abilities. Raindance mentioned his difficulty living on the Earth plane, and thought he felt the same in Dick. During their inter-change they strengthened each other. Raindance was so elated about this, that when Dick asked his age, he replied that he was four years old. He was just two at the time, but I understood from him that by helping people, he felt he was coming into his own maturity and had grown. At the same workshop he connected with another person and the healing process she was going through. He was surprised that someone could be apprehensive with him, as he had always been shy, and he was eager to help her because of that.

Llama silence is pervasive
Profound quiet
Cavernous connection to the soul.

Thought wave,
Mind vibration
Oceanic, galactic depth
Soft encompassing through the eyes
To the inner reaches of the soul
Warm, open, and cool
The sign of my people
Universal language
With nothing to be understood
Naked openness without boundaries
Contained within the frame of dark eyes.

The spirituality of all animals
Astounds, delights, and nurtures me
Llamas are spiritual caretakers
Of the highest order
Sent to take us home to ourselves
To the deepest regions of who we are.

Long lost brothers, from the same star
Sirius—whence come dolphins, wolves,
    Afghans, Arabian horses
With dignity, grace, and keen seeing.

The human form remains
A complex entryway for many vibrations,
Languages, modes of communication, and mental processes
We need the others so we don't lose our way.

JENNY

Marian Silverman referred to her experience with Jenny, a female black and white rat, as her "rat breakthrough." She wrote:

To Jenny—my friend and teacher

Sweet precious angel,
You touch my deepest self,
I feel your presence in my life,
A gentle reminder of my best self through you,
Seeing that you are perfect in every way,
What you are and what you do,
So too must I be perfect,
What I am and what I do,
You teach me how simple this is.

What I affectionately call my "rat breakthrough" occurred in 1990, when I met Jenny at my very first advanced workshop. I have been coming back every summer since, and it has become a sort of summer retreat and continuing education for me.

I began the workshop relating only to animals that I had some experience with: the cats, dogs, birds, and rabbit, and staying away from anyone I considered "foreign" and less than intelligent—the rats, fish, and chickens. When I arrived early Sunday morning, before the workshop had officially begun, I learned that there was a "ratty playtime" in the bedroom for anyone interested in visiting with the two rats: Jenny Boppers and Kiri Blossom.

I shuddered! The rats are out? But always curious, I opened the bedroom door and cautiously stepped in. People were sitting on the floor around the periphery of the room, and the rats were running around near the opposite wall from the one I hugged. I carefully slid down the wall and sat in the corner as close to the door as possible, pulling my knees up under my chin and trying to look inconspicuous.

Rats? Rodents? Embarrassed at my own aversion, I apologetically announced to the enraptured group, "I'm not really into rats. I've only had negative experiences with rats, and mice." I barely had the words out, when suddenly, the larger one came scurrying across the room. Without hesitation she ran up my leg, hip, onto my shoulder, kissed me on the cheek (an unmistakable kiss), jumped around my neck to the other shoulder, and ran down the opposite side of my body, leg, and off the same way she'd come.

The room froze in silent awe. I was not repulsed at all. I was completely thrilled, from the tips of my toes to the top of my head. I felt "blessed." The message was loud and clear, and no one in that room at that moment missed it. The message was "love," without fear, misunderstanding, bias, and ignorance.

Jenny kissed me, and in that moment of universal truth, all barriers dissolved forever. I was chosen because I clearly needed guidance. The gift she gave was given freely and lovingly, without reprimand.

What a lesson there for all of us. Never again would I be able to return to the position of negatives. Never again would I be able to say, "I'm not into rats or snakes or any beings." She kissed me, and I knew everything I needed to know. We are truly all connected. The connection is love. Thank you, Jenny Boppers, friend and teacher.

When I arrived at the August 1992 workshop, Penelope related to me that Jenny had been ill and preparing to leave her body, but she had stayed in order to be at the workshop, especially to see me. She had asked to visit with me, and Penelope put her in my hands, my arms, and my heart. She seemed to purr at me, and as I held her with tears in my eyes, she kissed my open hand, and I gently stroked her, silently thanked her, and told her how much I loved her. She loved me, too. I think she loved us all. I said my good-byes to her, with grief and joy and gratitude.

Jenny's physical condition deteriorated rapidly after making her special connection with Marian. It was obvious she had stayed just for that purpose. She let go after that mission was accomplished and went deeply into the dying process. After the workshop was completed on Sunday evening, Michel gave her a final concert on his classical guitar, and she left peacefully on Monday morning.

I found her body dead when I awoke, and as I cried, she filled the space, air, and universe all around us, the house, our land, and called to me, "I'll be back, I'll be back to you soon. I have to be at the next advanced workshop!" My tears were mixed with laughter. My Jenny Boppers—what a friend! We looked forward to seeing her again in charming rat form.

YOHINTA

Yohinta has specialized in emotional clearing with people at advanced workshops. She has singled out people who need special help releasing emotions and stayed with them until they do. One student was deeply moved when Yohinta lovingly rubbed against her and counseled her through the loss of her former cat companion.

There is a special place in our garden called the Fairy Ring, surrounded by trees and high on a hill, where the nature spirits gather and heighten smells, visions, and other perceptions for those who quietly sit there. Yohinta often made this her workshop counseling center. Sometimes she has not liked to come into the group gathered in the living room. It has seemed too serious and heavy to her, so she summoned people individually to the magic aura of the Fairy Ring. When we all gathered in the Fairy Ring for our opening invocation to the spirits, she has gone to each person, rubbed against them, and let them know that if they need her help anytime during the workshop, they are to go there. People have been delighted when she appeared as she said.

Her nature is normally soothing, with rubs and purrs to help clear people's blocks, but she has also used forceful methods when that is needed. A student called Stacy was struggling with what she referred to as a metaphysical "thorn" in her foot. Yohinta mirrored her by tugging at her own foot, then played with Stacy and grabbed her hand with her teeth and said, "Pay attention; get the point." When people are drifting or becoming confused, Yohinta has whapped them with her paw, pushed on their backs, or bit them lightly to center them, like a strict Zen master.

IGOR

Lizards and snakes have long been revered as ancient, wise ones by Native Americans. They respond to humans who are quiet, noninvasive, and attentive. While sitting on rocks near the ocean or walking through sagebrush paths, I have enjoyed hours of communion with lizards who, patiently and with interest, listen to my expositions.

An anole lizard (also known as a chameleon) named Igor graced our home. At an advanced workshop, Igor gave a sense of having a clean slate, of totally living in the present. He taught us that worry is feeling indecision or hesitation. For him, worry had no purpose. If there is danger, you run and hide or you live in peace, enjoying the moment and who you are. He is a master of crisp, uncluttered living. Wisdom pulsates through every pore of his body, in motion or stillness.

SOPHIE

Valerie Stansfield shared this discovery about her cat:

I have learned a great deal from Sophie, my long-haired cat roommate. She gave me an eye-opening revelation one day, when I watched her from an upstairs window as she was jumping between roofs. I watched how she focused her attention, moved her eyes and other muscles, obviously calculating, and made a perfect jump from one narrow edge to another! No human I know could ever do that, yet it was clear that she was using intelligence to calculate her moves. Since then I have watched her many times, studying how her intelligence works, and marveling at her genius! In doing this, I have learned a lot about calculation in physical activity, and my own coordination has improved. She is very proud of having taught me this!

She has also taught me much about perceiving directly what is going on with another person. In my work as a healer and therapist, I often have clients lie on a padded table. If I am unsure of the priorities, Sophie will gently jump up to the person and put herself exactly where the trouble is! In studying how she does this, I have been able to duplicate it. Then she only verifies my insight, like a good consultant!

TOBY

Nancy Sondel lived with Toby, a very special parakeet friend. He combined hundreds of words to make original, intelligent, verbal statements. To encourage Nancy's budding telepathic abilities, he nodded his head to indicate agreement or affirmation. She related episodes from Toby's lifetime:

I often reflect that Toby is a master: he teaches me patience and wisdom; he brings me laughter and pure, sweet love. Frequently as I'm thinking this, Toby nods his head subtly. "That's what I'm here for!" he communicates.

Toby delights in music, art, and literature; he demonstrates this through speech and action. One day he stopped eating and flew straight to my shoulder as I was reading a poem aloud. I recited a line about fairies dancing on the grass. From the corner of my eye, I saw Toby bobbing his head vigorously.

"Then it's true!" I thought. "Wonderful guardian angels and other loving spirits surround us. My little bird sees them; why don't I?"

At that moment I experienced a great truth: Our eyes simply show us life's veils; our soul permits us to see through them.

NORMAN

I had the honor to communicate with Norman, a Barbados black-bellied sheep, in a demonstration consultation at a lecture sponsored by the Ohlone Humane Society. Norman said he loved people and had a mission to make them laugh and enjoy life. His person asked why Norman liked plastic and had to butt it with his head. Norman said that he started this habit as a way to entertain people. Plastic objects were easily accessible, and playing with plastic got people's attention.

His person related how Norman's mother rejected him, and he had to hand-feed the baby sheep at the workplace—while fulfilling his role as certified public accountant, during tax time! I saw that his sheep mother thought Norman was very odd and pushed him away. Norman had arranged to start his life being close to people. Full of joy, he often looked at me directly, with a gleam in his eye, as he talked. He explained that people think he's a sheep, but he's not; he just looks like one. He's himself—a special being, a master.

JARVI AND THE ANIMAL COMMUNICATION NETWORK

Marcia Ramsland had this mind- and heart-opening experience with her master teacher/sled-dog companion:

I first became aware of Jarvi's compassionate nature before he was a part of my household. Friends of mine with a sled-dog team had called Penelope to have a consultation with the dogs. When Penelope tuned into the kennel, one dog came forward immediately saying, "If you want to know about anybody, just ask me." That was Jarvi. Penelope said Jarvi was an extremely gentle, compassionate being and was apparently somewhat surprised to learn that he was male.

While a part of this team, Jarvi had been known to stop the team, or refuse to start after a rest. We all assumed he did so because he was getting older and was unable to keep up with the younger dogs. But, months later when he was living with me, I asked him about this behavior.

He stated, "There were times that someone in the team needed to stop or was not yet ready to start again, and I was strong enough to stop the team, even over the musher's wishes." That startled me, and I did not initially believe that Jarvi had actually said it, but it fit with Penelope's comments regarding his concern for the other dogs. It was just the first of several things that Jarvi would say to me that I would not initially trust, but which I would eventually come around to believing.

I was thinking about dogs that are destroyed if they don't make the team. The thought came through loud and clear, "Sled-dog puppies are an easy entry point for dogs who want to get back into body. Because there are so many bodies bred, there are lots of bodies to choose from and enter. But dogs know what the deal involves. If you're choosing to come as a sled dog, you had better be willing to run. If not, the consequences are known. Some dogs hope that, even if they don't want to be sled dogs, they will be given away to someone else, but they take their chances." Since I had been sitting with Jarvi when this thought occurred, I accepted that the comments were his.

I returned from three days of house-sitting at Jarvi's previous kennel. While there, I had an unexpected communication from one of the dogs, and it prompted me to talk to each dog and record their answers. It was a good thing I did; little did I know that there was going to be a quiz. Back at home, all the dogs were complaining about my prolonged absence except Jarvi, who said, "Tell me about the dogs." That surprised me until I remembered these were "his" dogs that he had formerly been watching over, and of course he would want to know how each one was and what they had to say. My first comment to him referred to the unexpected communication, and I said, "You know, Noah is *very* telepathic." With that, Jarvi literally got a grin on his face, turned away laughing at me, and said, "I know that." In retrospect, it was a bit ridiculous for me to tell Jarvi that a dog was telepathic, but at the time, receiving unsolicited comments was still a new and thrilling experience. I will never forget the expression on his face and in his voice. It makes me smile every time I think about it.

In 1991, I was seriously considering getting more sled dogs. I was debating this in my mind for some time when I happened to ask Jarvi what he thought about the idea. He replied that getting more dogs would do what I wanted to improve the speed and strength of the team, but he added that Trapper, my lead dog, would not be able to keep up the lead position if the team were any faster. He added that it would break Trapper's heart to be taken out of lead or, worse yet, to be left behind.

In the weeks that I had been debating getting more dogs, I had never given that concept a thought, but I immediately realized he was right. Trapper was getting older, and an old injury was also hampering him. As a result of Jarvi's comment, I decided against additional dogs. The interesting thing about all this is that Trapper frequently harasses Jarvi in various subtle ways, yet that didn't stop Jarvi from expressing concern for Trapper's emotional well-being.

Jarvi's concern for others was expressed at the vet's last spring. With too many bodies in the small examination room, the plan was to take each dog back to the car when done. Jarvi was the first to finish, but he refused to leave. I was surprised at his behavior, but after a minute or two it became perfectly clear why Jarvi had refused. He had to watch over everything. With every move the vet made, Jarvi was involved. He placed himself next to each dog as the blood sample was taken and each shot given. He'd look at the needle, he'd look at the vet, he'd watch the dog, and he'd look at us. He wasn't willing to leave until the only dog left was Trapper, who, as far as Jarvi was concerned, could take care of himself.

I was thinking recently that I had only been scratching the surface of what was possible to receive telepathically. I mentioned this to Jarvi one day as we were out walking. I told him I felt there was some new area to develop. I didn't know what it was, but I was willing to entertain any ideas he might have on the subject. A day or so later I sat down with each of the dogs and the cat to ask if there was anything they would like to talk about. I recorded these conversations in my telepathy journal.

MAY 18, 1992

Jarvi: You said maybe you would ask me some new questions and that maybe I could tell you how to get to a new level.
Marcia: So okay, is there something of a different nature you would like to talk about?
J: YES! The world today.
M: The world today? [I asked somewhat unbelievably.]
J: Yes, it is in great turmoil. I am worried about the fate of people and the animals.
M: How do you know about the turmoil?

J: There is a network within the animal kingdom. (With that he showed me a picture of him sitting out in the yard by himself.)

I ended the conversation immediately. I did not believe that Jarvi could know about the world turmoil, and even if there was an animal network, what animals could he have seen? He may have learned information from other sled dogs during the major races, but that is not what he showed me. He showed me sitting out in the yard by himself, so where was the network? I felt I had to be making it all up.

The next day, when I got home from work, I picked up the cat and casually said (I was not asking nor expecting an answer), "Jarvi says there is an animal network." Without blinking an eye, Archer said, "Yes, the migratory birds bring in new information, especially the crows and ravens."

That stopped me dead in my tracks. I was struck by the immediacy of his reply and by the unexpected content. What was most startling of all was that it all made sense. I feed birds all year and have a tremendous number of birds coming through the yard, spring and fall. There are also a family of crows in the yard and several ravens living in the area. It also gave credence to the picture of Jarvi sitting out in the yard by himself. He was listening to what the birds were saying. I hadn't seen the birds in his picture, but he probably doesn't see them either. He just listens.

I was at war within myself. I just couldn't believe that there was an animal communication network relaying information of a global nature. There is a line between open-mindedness and gullibility which I felt I'd stepped over.

After a day or two of puzzling over this, I called a friend and told her what had been happening. She very matter-of-factly said, "I don't know why you are having trouble accepting this, Marcia. We both know Jarvi is Mr. Compassion. It fits perfectly with who he is and what he's all about. If telepathy is real, and we know it is, then of course animals can communicate with each other. So what's the big deal?"

Somewhat taken aback by her easy acceptance of what I was struggling with, I allowed her comments to settle into my thinking.

She was right, of course, but at some level I was still skeptical. About this time, I opened one of my favorite books, just to see what would jump out at me. The book was *Kinship with All Life* by J. Allen Boone. As fate would have it (obviously fate was working overtime to see to my enlightenment), on the very page that I opened was a description of Mojave Dan, a man who was known to be telepathic with animals and who lived in the desert with his family of dogs, burros, and an occasional wild animal. In that description were the following sentences:

"Dan never reads books, magazines, or newspapers, never listens to the radio, never watches television, and seldom asks questions of other humans; yet he is amazingly well-informed at all times about practically everything that interests him, either nearby or afar. This information comes from his dogs and burros, from wild animals, from snakes, from insects, from birds, indeed from almost everything that crosses his trail."

There it was, in black and white: outside confirmation that animals know information about events happening afar. It was as if the whole consciousness shift I had been struggling with finally clicked into place.

Some time later I was talking on the phone with Penelope, and at the end of our conversation I relayed my recent struggle with the Jarvi information, and in a roundabout way was looking for more confirmation from her. She laughed very gently, saying, "Is Jarvi expanding your consciousness, Marcia? I want you to ask him more about the network, and I want you to record his comments uncensored. I also want you to ask all of your other animals about the network. We will call it the Jarvi Journal."

Jarvi was very excited about this new turn of events, but I delayed for two days. When I finally sat down with Jarvi to discuss, as requested by Penelope, Archer (cat) immediately joined Jarvi and me on the couch (a very unusual behavior for Archer) and snuggled in so tight that Jarvi was uncomfortable but tolerating it all.

JUNE 12, 1992

Marcia: So, Jarvi, tell me about this network.

Jarvi: Well, it is the birds, just like the cat said. The migratory birds bring it, but the crows and ravens disperse it.

M: That's very interesting.

J: The reason you are so attracted to crows and ravens is that they are very high beings. It is no accident that one of your guides is a feathered friend.

M: But you killed a crow once when you were first here.

J: Yes, I was still operating as a sled dog, so to speak, experiencing freedom and letting my dog hunting instincts guide me. After I saw how you disliked my hunting and killing of others, I began to rethink things about being here with you and your expectations that I would respect other life forms. I was able to step into a higher aspect of being.

The skunk incident was one of the worst times in my life—to have you so mad at me for so long. [Jarvi killed a skunk and left it at the front door. I was mad at him for three days before he finally got a chance to tell me his side of the story.] It really made me stop and think. As it turned out, it was a turning point in your telepathic growth, so it was worth it. It was a turning point for both of us.

M: I am very impressed, Jarvi.

J: Thank you. I wish we would do this more often. I was so glad when you told me that your teacher had asked that my viewpoints be written down. I have so much to say.

Jarvi pictured himself going with me on consultations, saying that he could help the more disturbed animals in ways that I could not, and that he could do so while remaining in the car.

JUNE 15, 1992

M: So, Jarvi, tell me more about this network.

J: There is some difficulty in describing it because it is not exactly like how people communicate and also you are still experiencing some doubt about the whole subject.

The birds, particularly ravens, are registering a sense of worry, that things are not "right." Loss of habitat [Jarvi pictured a bird returning to a home base to find that area so changed as to be unusable] is causing confusion in some species, and their confusion and fear are picked up by other species. There is a growing sense that something is going to happen—a general unease.

There are too many people. It is getting out of balance. Not only loss of habitat, but a fouling of the air, making many areas unlivable.

There is a certain order to things that we animals understand. Even the hunter–prey relationship is fully understood by all parties. We have to eat. But even the prey understand that all is in order and that it is just a play, so to speak. We understand that all things die, yet nothing dies.

People do not understand how it all is and therefore threaten the entire process by their lack of understanding. One more thing tonight: It is of the utmost importance that people reconnect to the plants and animals. We can teach them what they have forgotten. [With that Jarvi got off my bed and went back to his.]

JUNE 21, 1992

M: Okay, Jarvi, and what would you like to talk about today?

J: I would like to talk more about the network. You should record what the crow told you this morning. [I had forgotten, but I did talk to a crow regarding the network.]

Crow: We are not so migratory, but rather, our territories are almost everywhere, and we overlap and so send information from one to another to another. We also are able to adapt more easily than other birds to the presence of people, so we are surviving. Because we are around people a great deal, we are very aware of what is going on with the human race.

J: Remember, Penelope asked that you talk to all the dogs regarding the network.

M: Okay. Do you know more than just the fear and confusion from loss of habitat?

J: Yes, the animals know about fighting and disasters. The animals pick up anything that disrupts people's lives. It is not just animal fear and confusion that is easily picked up telepathically. Also, warfare and natural disasters generally affect the air, food supply, and water.

All of the animal kingdom is concerned. Those of us who are companion animals are worried for the safety of our people. Other animals will be glad if many people die, because there are too many people. It's not that they wish ill on people, but people in their vast numbers, plus their lack of understanding, are the source of the problem.

GOLDFISH ENCOUNTER

Yvette Dubé called this her "Goldfish Encounter of the First Kind":

We were doing a meditation at the advanced workshop, in which animals choose whom they want to communicate with. When we came to that point in the meditation, the goldfish appeared. I instantly became judgmental and thought, "No, not goldfish. What could they have to say?" Little did I know.

A little disappointed that the chickens or llamas didn't choose me, I headed with my list of suggested questions into the pond enclosure. A circular fence surrounds the pond area, which is very nicely landscaped. I settled on the chamomile growing on the ground and determined to do my best.

As I began to relax and observe, I realized what a magical and active world into which I had just stepped. So I started asking my questions, and to my surprise and delight, it was so easy. It was almost as though they cleared this vibrant path to me. I could feel a clear, vibrant, flowing energy, as though they just swam through any blocks I had put up.

What a joyful experience I had! The goldfish are so clear and bright, attentive, and tuned in. They answered my questions so quickly, and some of the answers were contrary to my preconceived ideas. A good example was when questioned about their greatest joy and their environment. They expressed their joy in sunbathing, which I assumed I had misunderstood, since I thought the sun would cook them. Penelope later confirmed that the goldfish spend a lot of time in the sunny spots, not hiding under the lily pads as I had assumed they would.

They loved their environment; they have many friends that come by and visit; there are many hiding places; they feel very safe. It is such a lively place. The water amplifies everybody and everything.

I perceived their water as murky, and I suggested that it might be nicer if their water was a bit more clear. They said they were comfortable in this water, that it was clear and bright. Again, I assumed I misunderstood; when I mentioned this to Penelope, she explained that the pond environment is very balanced and so their water is clear and clean enough to drink, that the pond has a black liner, and the shade from the plants makes the water look dark.

The goldfish even gave me some good advice when I asked them what their viewpoint was about me. First, they mirrored my confusion, then explained that I make things too confusing. The suggestion was to clear things away, rather than accumulate more; humans already have too much extra stuff.

It is somewhat difficult to convey their answers using just words. It is impossible to be as eloquent as they were. The goldfish communicated using more than just words and pictures. Everything was conveyed with the feel of the experience, blocks of ideas and concepts that can't really be translated. When I asked about their past, it was more of a spiritual experience for me than just an answer. The best interpretation I can give is that this is a very special place, where light came to flow into physical form, and it encompassed more than the goldfish. It also included the environment of the pond area, which created this magic circle!

LLAMA REBIRTHING

Sherry Charlton wrote of her experience after the llamas at Bobra Goldsmith's ranch in Colorado helped her gain more awareness of who animals really are:

On arriving Friday in Denver, I was overwhelmed with large-city stress and energy. I decided to go straight to the llama ranch (the location for the workshop). Upon arriving, I was feeling a pounding in my head and an uncontrolled, ungrounded whirlwind of energy running through my body. Getting out of the car and greeting Gaucho, the dog, then strolling down the lane greeting the llamas along the way, I was amazed at how fast the combination of country air and llama energy grounded and absorbed the stress and excess energy. In a very short time, I was feeling in touch again.

On Saturday I quickly realized that what little I did know about llamas was incorrect, except for one very strong fact: this amazing species of life is very intelligent. I totally underestimated their amazing healing abilities.

I have never experienced a meditation so intense as the one on Saturday in which we each became an animal. I was trying to become a small Vietnamese pig, to learn about them. I was having difficulty when, all of a sudden, I straightened my back in my chair and *zap!*— instantly I was a llama. My neck grew long, my ears were tall, and my nose began to move and sense. I remember, when I arrived on Friday, telling the llamas that I did not know anything about them and would appreciate it if they would teach me. Well, "Ask and ye shall receive."

Sunday morning, after learning the lesson of becoming the birds instead of blocking out their voices, I was very emotional and started to cry and cry. I knew I was going through some kind of rebirthing or healing and kept hearing this voice telling me to come out now, that it was all right now, and I didn't have to be afraid anymore. It was time to come out now.

Except for my exchange with Gaucho, Bobra's dog, that morning I felt so plugged up, I didn't feel like I was getting anything. Just before I left that afternoon, I was talking to Bobra, and I realized I had all this knowledge of llamas. I realized things were beginning to process, especially when telling Bobra about Gaucho becoming a llama, to blend in so he could come to the workshop.

When telling her this, he started hitting my leg with his paw. I told him I didn't mean to tell her his secrets, but I really admired him for his abilities. It took me most of the following week to process everything that happened that weekend—so much, so fast, it was overwhelming.

I now realize than one aspect of llamas is to heal and offer the experience of rebirthing. I really had not wanted to be here this life, and, after being pulled out with forceps, I have spent a great deal of time and energy trying to rebuild a womb in which to hide.

The llama encounter and all that healing energy of the workshop weekend has really helped me with the process of peeling off the layers. I had not realized that this womb was made up with so much fear, hurt-betrayal, and mistrust, until now.

What I have come to know about llamas is that they seem to ask for a balance to be found. They share their essence with you, but in doing so, it makes you look at your own being and essence of who and what you are. Never have I met an animal who asks nothing of you, but asks so much. Walking with a llama is like walking with your higher self, so balanced and connected. They are reflections of what we can truly be as a spiritual connection. When with a llama, we are the ones doing the training and changing. They are a spark which lights the flame of change. We may smolder awhile, but we will change if we stay in the presence of a llama for any length of time.

CHICKEN TALK

I love being among my chicken friends. They are such lively, beautiful, curious, and loving individuals. When first introduced to the chickens at advanced workshops, many participants have never known a chicken as a fellow being. They bring the usual preconceptions found in our society that chickens are stupid, disgusting, dirty, or have nothing much to offer other than their eggs or flesh for human consumption.

Most people do not appreciate the communication possibilities with the chickens until they are more receptive on the second day of the workshop. We do an exercise in which people are to seek communion with an animal to whom they are not initially attracted, or with whom they feel uncomfortable or unfamiliar. This helps people to cast aside their inhibiting expectations and to receive profound, surprising, and delightful communications from otherwise avoided animals.

A medical doctor had an unforgettable chicken experience at an advanced workshop. He shared with the group afterwards that he looked at the chickens as ugly, unintelligent animals that were just fit for eating, but when he opened his heart and mind to them, he found something totally different. One hen in particular, whom he regarded as the least attractive, singled him out as he sat among them. She screamed at him to wake up, to see the beauty in all of life and in himself, and gave him very personal and specific advice about how he could improve himself and spiritually progress. His surprise and the directness of the information, complete with unusual sound effects from her, confirmed for him that he had genuinely received her communication, and he was moved to tears.

ROOSTERS AND THE RISING SUN

After raising a number of baby chicks one year, I ended up with nine roosters, each of whom had a distinctive crow. Before I found other homes for most of them, I decided to tape-record their crows at the best time to hear their chorus—before sunrise. In the 4 A.M. chill, I sat in the dark near their roosts, just outside the open door of the chicken house, and held out the microphone.

As they crowed in a series of rounds with each other, I became aware of magnetism around them stretching out to the sky, a field or aura generated by their crowing. I connected with all the roosters around the planet and knew, at that moment, that they were responsible for bringing up the sun. I realized that many folk tales were true about the animal's different functions, no matter how bizarre it seemed to our Western analytical mode of thinking. I knew totally that without the roosters crowing, the sun would not rise. It was their duty, and that's why they started a few hours beforehand, to prime the sky and the turning of the Earth to prepare for the sun's appearance. They were both the heralds and precipitators of the sun's arrival.

This glorification of the rooster's role may sound farfetched and be scientifically unverifiable. Nevertheless, when I sat there in the magic of that early morning hour, it resonated deeply within me as innate truth and as an aspect of the mystical connection of all life on the Earth. It explained to me why, when our first rooster joined the family, I felt a deep fulfillment on hearing him crow—as though a piece of the puzzle of life on Earth had been found.

The rooster crows
The day dawns
And all around me
Though darkness is deep
The day is growing
I may not see the light
But it is there
The darkness has seeped
Into my soul
I am dying
Slowly
I am reborn
Though I cannot see the light yet
The rooster crows
The new day dawns
All around me
The light is growing.

WILD BIRD GUIDES

Wild animals often come as guides during workshops. Deer appear when people do exercises of becoming one with animals. Insects quietly land on or around people, transfiguring human conceptions of connection and aware-ness with other life forms.

Birds often play a prominent role, following or leading us as we move along, checking in to see how we are doing, and encouraging us in our heightening of energy and joy. They have landed in the middle of the circle of humans, telling us to move on, to follow their lightness and their lead.

At the end of one advanced workshop, the group was gathered outdoors on the deck of our home when, above us, a pure white dove settled in a large pine tree. Two unusual features marked her appearance: I had never seen wild doves or pigeons of that coloring, and the dove sat where the tree's branches formed a large heart shape around her. We were very moved and felt her message to spread our love and peace, a beautiful closure to our workshop experience.

In the spring of 1992, a pair of scrub jays came to nest near our home. They followed me around in the garden, as my digging and weeding unearthed and flushed insects out of hiding. They were especially adept at catching grasshoppers. I thanked them for their help in maintaining the balance in the garden and appreciated their cheerful, competent presence. The female was missing her tail feathers, and I asked her what happened. She told me a neighbor's cat had pounced on her. I urged our cats to leave the birds alone. She felt our area was safe and protected, besides having an abundance of insects.

The blue-feathered pair foraged daily, flying back and forth to their nest. When nesting was done and fledglings gone, they disappeared to other territories. In early summer I was meditating outdoors, and I heard a unique and beautiful bird song. It was soft and chortling and sounded like our parakeet and finches, who lived in the Beatrix Potter Bunny Cottage.

Searching to see who could be singing, I spotted a young male scrub jay fifteen feet from me on a branch, half-hidden by leaves. He continued to give me a repertoire of interesting song and talk picked up from our bird family. Then, when he noticed I was looking at him, he told me he was sent here to make this his home base. His mother and father had told him that he didn't need to be afraid of me, and that I needed help with the grasshoppers in the garden.

Whenever I meditated in my favorite garden spot, he gave me a serenade or sailed overhead, calling to let me know he was there. He liked all our animal friends, bathed in the llamas' automatic watering bowl, talked to our birds and rabbits, and visited the chickens. At the advanced workshop in September of that year, he came around at the opening meditation and told us he was glad we were all here and that he would oversee and guide us. During the workshop, he called overhead to tell people they were doing well. Others didn't notice him, but I got his communications and felt his presence and purpose to heighten, spread, and focus energies.

At that same workshop, as the participants were busy in various areas of the Floating Island of Peace, communicating with the animals, I sat quietly in the garden, surveying the scene. I always ask the nature spirits for whatever weather is appropriate for the group, and we were having a sunny, mild, glorious day.

A male Allen's hummingbird appeared in front of me, alighted on a branch, and addressed me with an incredible song. He sang about how beautiful the day was, how glorious it was to be here. He told me how he loved our garden, so beautifully filled with flowers. He sang with rapture on his branch, took a few drinks from the flowers, and sang again. Then, after a longer time than I've seen a hummingbird sit in one place on a branch, he buzzed off to explore other areas. In a short time he returned and told me that this was the best place in over a mile. There were more flowers here, and wonderful energy encircled our land. He wanted to celebrate his day here. I felt uplifted by his presence. Later, he buzzed by the window as we were eating, and for many days afterward, he greeted me in the garden.

Dawn Hayman tapped into a playful sparrow conversation one afternoon when she was busily mucking out stalls in the barn at Spring Farm in Clinton, New York:

"Go ahead, it's your turn."
"No, I can't. I just can't do it."
"It's easy, go ahead."
"No. I can't. I can't. I just can't."

I looked up on one of the trusses and saw seven sparrows, all lined up, looking down at two of our horses. This conversation carried on, and I decided that I didn't have time to stay and find out what they were talking about. I went back to mucking.

About five minutes later, amid this flutter of activity, I heard this joyful yell: "I did it! I did it!" There was great cheering and laughter. I looked out and saw one bird standing on the neck of one of our horses. The other six all looked down and cheered. Then she flew back up to be with the others. The conversation continued, and this time I stopped to watch.

"I did it. Now it's your turn again. What will you do now?"

"Well, watch me," said one determined fellow. He flew down and tried to land on the horse's head.

"That's enough already! That's enough," said Bo, the horse.

They all laughed and flew away. What fun they were having! About ten minutes later I heard this: "How about this animal? He's big."

"No, he looks grumpy; maybe we should go do something else." And out of the barn they flew.

DOLPHIN DREAMING

Nora Star visited a dolphin named Misty in a lagoon in the Florida Keys:

The first point she made to me is that we are just as endangered as dolphins by the way we are polluting the oceans of the world. Her liver was not fully functioning, due to all the things it had to filter. I asked her why she was fighting so hard to stay with us. She said that she loved the people who worked here so much and also all the people who are "called here" for classes. I took notes during the precious dock time I spent with her. I quote some of her thoughts verbatim here:

We offer ourselves to humans to help them find happiness. Most of us love to teach, each of us in our own way. We have been here on this planet and other planets, so many millions of years, that we know beyond any doubt that expressing love and joy and harmony and health are the only things that matter to your happiness and your evolution. We are supreme examples of this and want to teach by example. We have no material possessions and certainly don't yearn for same. Many people now are beginning to let go of their materialism. Materialism was only born out of insecurity and fear. When all of that goes, the real life and love and growth begin.

We have been here so much longer than you have that of course we have had a head start to accumulate much more wisdom, but we want desperately to share it. We have been waiting so long for this time which is now here, when you are opening your hearts and minds to us to let us teach you all that we know. It is only now that people are becoming sensitive to and appreciative of our teaching and healing skills. We have been waiting for this for centuries, talking about it often among our own species. We are no less excited than you are about our future together.

LOST CATS

Judy Meyer had this experience with finding lost cats after she began to use her ability to telepathically communicate with animals in the summer of 1992:

I have done several consultations in which people are trying to locate their "lost" cats. I seem to be able to get in touch with the cats, but they don't seem to be lost.

The first cat that I tried to find was my own cat, Taos. We knew she had been doing spiritual work in the form of holding the feminine energy for the land. After she had been gone for a day, we got in contact with her, and she informed us that a dimensional window of feminine energy had opened up just below my property. Taos told us that she would be merging with it for three days and then she would come home.

Three days came and went. The next time we spoke to her, she said she might come home in a week. Finally, she let us know that she found that doing her energy work was so much easier out of her body that she had decided to leave it and continue her work in spirit.

This was very hard for us to accept. We missed her very much, and we wanted her to come home, but we had to respect her wishes and the work she is doing. Equally as important was the lesson I learned that I can only help to bring animals home who wish to come home.

After that, three other people whose cats had left home wanted my help. The cats have all said they were doing energy work for the planet. The first one told me and her person that she was not very far away and that she was helping to ground the energy all around her person's house. The cat had been gone for six weeks, and yet she said she was still in her body and intended to come back to the house when she felt the work was through.

The next person I spoke with reported that her sixteen-year-old cat, Kats, had been missing for a week. It was starting to get cold, and her person was getting quite worried. When we spoke to Kats, she said that she had some work to do with the Earth and the sky, and she would be home soon. One week later we communicated with Kats again. This time she informed us that she had decided not to come home, even though she was still in her body. Kats said that since her person was moving to Colorado, she would stay in Santa Fe, finish her work, and once her person got settled, she would come back to her in another body.

Another cat, Quincy, had been "lost" for one week. Quincy's person wanted to know if he was okay and if he could come home. Quincy said that he was not very far away. In fact, his person told me that two people in her apartment complex had mentioned seeing Quincy in the past week. After I asked him what he was doing, he said he was doing work for the planet. Quincy informed us that he was holding energy for an unstable part of the Earth so that it could continue its normal rotation around the sun! His person asked Quincy's sister, Isabelle, if she missed him and was that why she went out on the balcony and meowed so much since he was gone. She replied that she did miss him, but she was telling everybody in the neighborhood how proud she was of her brother.

All four cats taught me an even deeper level of respect for our animal companions and for the work they are doing for the Earth. Taos taught me, among other lessons, humility and a sense of letting go. I was once again reminded that animals can and do change their minds, and this is a planet of free will.

CAREER GUIDANCE FROM THE ANIMALS

As part of a career guidance assignment, Lora Steiner had to take an attribute from each of four animals and have each animal tell her how its attribute could serve her, particularly related to her "calling" or career:

BIRDS—PRIDE

Be proud of who you are, for you have been given the likeness of God, and we are all the likeness of God, connecting, interlinking to make up the universe. The only true sin is not loving who you are. Any other darkness comes from that point.

FELINES—KNOWINGNESS

What is knowingness, after all, but connecting with oneself, self-confidence, self-love, the connection to our inner strength, inner god—inner and, therefore, outer universe. With such connections spring forth an independence to own who you are and follow your heart. Climb trees or catnap. You can always be in charge of your destination. Your eyes will gleam; you will shine from your own inner light. As Buddy, your feline friend, has said, "Never underestimate yourself."

HORSES—ABUNDANCE

Everything can be on our side. Time to graze, roll, and nap. We take time and turn it into what is needed then and there. If we're left tied for long, we can nap. If we're left in the field for long, it's a play-day of eating, playing, rolling, or more. Our size and stamina carry us to whatever our goal may be. Bring the abundance of the universe inside you. The answers will come, the energy will follow. Abundance can mean whatever you want, or need. That includes patience, also. Use your abundance in strength and intent. It is here for you.

WHALES—EASE AND POWER WITH GRACE

Grace has power without force. It is power with ease, with presence. Own who you are, the Grace that you are, which is within you. In doing so, there is power. With power comes ease, the ease of being who you are. The ease of just plainly and simply enjoying life. Your life.

DEETEZA'S MESSAGE

In 1987, Deeteza came to Spring Farm in Clinton, New York, to be with Bonnie Reynolds and Dawn Hayman. Despite her impressive Arabian horse lineage, her person had to find a new home for her due to financial difficulties. Deeteza was staying at someone else's farm when Dawn and Bonnie were asked to take her because she was a "renegade." They wondered what they were getting into, but it turned out that Deeteza was misunderstood. After a trailer accident and then a consultation with me, Deeteza began teaching and sharing stories and poetry with Dawn. Her role at Spring Farm Cares was teacher and author. She intended to reach as many people as possible with her words and observations.

Dawn transcribed this message from Deeteza on October 13, 1990:

From the Heart of All That Is

What was once flame turns into ash.
What was once light turns into darkness.
What was once time turns into space.
What was once life turns into living.

It is from the heart of All That Is that keeps us safe in the darkness. Warm in the cold. Nestled safe in the all-loving knowingness of God. As we took that first breath of life-giving air that energized our physical bodies, so did we swear an oath to our higher beings. This is true of all living things. I pray now that we remember that oath. Hear its words. Sing its songs. And live its melody. It is from the heart of All That Is and resides in the souls of us all.

Hear ye now the call of the spirit. As I enter into this physical realm in search of the answer to the question of my being, let not the torch be dimmed by the darkness of uncertainty. Let not my quest be stopped by the ignorance of my own unforgiveness. And let not my questions be few. As I step lively down the path of my self-created destiny, let my feet wander freely. Let my soul search out its every whim. Let my heart beat deep from my soul.

As I travel the path I have chosen, let me not forget at any time that though I myself may never walk this way again, it is certain that someone else shall. Let me be sure to leave them markers of light and love to guide them along their way. Let me not forget to share my findings freely with all who wish to share, for as much as they are mine, they are also theirs. Let my treasures be that of the universe, and then I shall be rich and fruitful.

As I am an integral part of All That Is, let me also recognize that everything else I shall meet is also an integral part of All That Is. Let me never forget the importance of the single cell, the single atom, the single molecule. Let me always remember that I am one with the universe. The words I hear can be heard by all. The words I speak can be spoken to all. And the visions I see are shared by all who see them.

Let my voice be heard. Let my heart be open to all who wish to browse. Let my soul be free to explore. Let my message be clear to all. And as I peruse the vast dreams and landscapes of time, let me not ever forget its beauty and importance. Let me never take any part of All That Is for granted. For it is here by the same token that I am and we all have taken this same oath. Let this oath be spoken from the soul, stored in the heart, and remembered by us all.

With this I pledge my spirit to find the answers to the questions we pose in the heart of All That Is.

My dream is that we shall all remember this pledge that we made to be here. We are all guilty of ignoring it. We need to be reminded. Just one message will reach thousands. Let your lights shine to us all, for we have lost our way. Many times we reach others through the stories we tell. What may seem important to me may not seem so to you. And by the same token, what may seem important to you may not seem to speak to me. The important thing is that we speak it. This has become my goal.

matters OF LIFe anD DeaTH

RESPONSIBILITY AND OWNERSHIP

HOW MUCH RESPONSIBILITY do we have regarding other animals' lives? What about their choices?

Barbara called me in distress over a hound dog that was tied on the other side of her fence by her neighbor next door. Her dogs would bark at him through the fence, and she, her cats, and dogs were all upset by the dog's mournful howling.

The man had a number of dogs, some kenneled and some tied. Their food needs were supplied, but they were not given exercise and human companionship. Barbara said that the man appeared hostile to any suggestions. The hound howled so often and so plaintively that she was thinking of going over the fence to steal the dog and take him to a shelter where a new home could be found for him.

When I got in touch with the dog and found him lonely, I described to him Barbara's plan of taking him to a shelter to find a new home. He was terrified at the prospect and pictured that he would become totally panicked and appear unadoptable if he were taken away. Her plan would backfire. Even though the circumstances of his life seemed miserable, he did not want to go. He just wanted his current person to see him more.

Since Barbara could not directly change her neighbor's ways, and the dog did not want a new home, I proposed that she and her dogs and cats join together to send him warmth, love, and healing to keep him company and help his life to be happier. Barbara then joined with her animals in silently sending this positive energy. Instantly the dog was quiet and peaceful, and remained that way each day as they repeated their transmission, although the other circumstances of his life were not changed.

I don't believe we ever own animals, so I don't use the word *owner* in referring to human relationship to animals. Along with the roles of guardians, caretakers, caregivers, companions, friends, partners, kin, or just "people" to animals, comes the aspect of honoring the sense that they have their own lives and their own paths. These don't necessarily match human design or desires.

In 1991, I raised a number of bantam chicks, ending up with a number of roosters. It is difficult to have too many roosters in a confined area. Their crowing contests can continue through the entire day and begin again hours before sunrise, straining our neighbors' tolerance. Many roosters fight with each other over territory and hens, and it is hard on the hens to be jumped on for mating so often. It is also hard to find good homes for roosters, since most people want just one rooster for their flock. The rest are surplus to be killed and eaten. Fortunately, purebred bantams are more valued, and I found out about a Junior 4-H Poultry Show at the Santa Rosa Fairgrounds, an hour's drive away. I could attempt to sell my roosters there and find good homes for them.

The night before the show, I was struggling with my feelings about giving them up. They were all such special, personable characters. That night I had a dream about the fairground's show. An owl's hooting outside my window penetrated into the dream with the clear message: *"They belong to the universe; let them go; they belong to the universe."* I thanked brother owl for the assistance and felt myself able to let go of the little roosters with a clean conscience and a peaceful heart.

The next day at the poultry show, I was so pleased to see the loving care the children lavished on their chicken friends, carting them around on their shoulders and showing off their qualities. Michel and I were able to sell four of the roosters to very good homes.

Once before, when faced with a surplus of roosters, I hunted around for homes to no avail. I went to the roosters and told them of my plight, that somehow they were going to have to find homes for themselves, or I would have to take them to be killed. The next day, as I was reluctantly calling a person who knew a chicken butcher, I found out about a dairy farmer who didn't mind the crowing of extra roosters on his large ranch, because they helped keep down the number of insect parasites around the cows. The roosters had plenty of room to roam, so they didn't fight, and they could roost in the rafters of the cow barn. Although I was sad to drop them off, I was relieved for them to have a better alternative than the knife and thanked them all for their help in finding a better situation for themselves.

Rose lived in a cluster of houses where no dogs were allowed. She let her rabbit companions come and go outside, where they could take shelter under the houses when needed. Rose asked me to communicate with her rabbit, Larissa, whom she thought was angry because George, her rabbit friend, had been in the house and she hadn't. Our communication revealed just the opposite. Larissa said, "I'll never go back to that house again! I have always done exactly what I wanted, and you kept me a prisoner."

Rose respected her wishes, though she felt sad that she might not see Larissa as much. Later, after enjoying her liberation, Larissa and George appeared on Rose's porch. George did a dance to let her know he wanted to go into the house, and she waited to make sure she was not imposing on him by bringing him in. He then grabbed her pants leg and threw himself on his side and kicked furiously at her leg while he looked up at her, asking, "Do you get it now?" At that point, Rose opened the door, and both rabbits ran in. Given a choice, they chose to come and go and enjoy her company, also.

Some people think having animals in any cage, enclosure, or habitat other than their natural, wild environment is cruel or against their rights. I have struggled with this, and would like to give my animal friends the world, literally. However, there are the practical considerations of safety from predator animals, cars, hostile people, and harsh weather that a guardian must consider.

I have found that most domestic animals choose to be with people and generally accept their living situations. Obviously, you want to help your animal companions to fulfill their physical and emotional needs for space, freedom, and exercise by your choice of habitat for them. I have worked to create as close to natural habitats and enclosures for my animals as possible, and most of the time they love their homes and are very happy in them. If they are not, we communicate to find an agreeable resolution.

Pirouette, my cockatiel composer, was in the Bunny Cottage for several years, where he could fly around and be close to the elements and trees and wild birds. He had formerly been in the house with us, confined to a cage for most of the time. He became extremely vehement about wanting to be back in the house to be able to hear Michel's guitar and lute playing daily instead of the infrequent times Michel came down to play in the cottage. Even having a radio in the cottage with classical music playing for half the day did not placate him.

I thought it was healthier for him to be with the other birds and fly around. But he wanted to be in the house in a cage, and that was that. He began attacking me when I came into the cottage, because I didn't respond to his request. As soon as I returned him to the house, he was ecstatic. Though I would try to get him out for flying exercise, he preferred to stay in his home-base cage, happily whistling and dancing to the music and contributing to Michel's musical inspiration and compositions.

Ellyetta requested to be able to run free in the great outdoors, even though she had the spacious, multilevel Bunny Cottage. The dangers were so many outside of her habitat that, while I have tried letting her loose, it was too risky for her life and health. Ellyetta got plenty of exercise in her cottage, and I brought her lots of wild and domestic plants to munch. She also enjoyed the close company of Perky Pete (cockatiel) and Winky (parakeet), who often sat with her on her wooden box. Occasionally I took her out to the fenced pond area, where she raced around, and I've thought of training her to go out on halter and leash. I also reminded her that most domestic rabbits live in small cages, and then she was more grateful for the space, freedom, and loving company that she had.

When we moved to the woods in 1984, several of my finches and Pekin, a Chinese nightingale, wanted to fly free in the trees outside of their large aviary cage. I communicated with them about the dangers they would face and the likelihood of living only a short time outside, but they persisted in their desire to go. They arranged their own way to freedom. I was out of town when Michel rolled their cage on the deck for fresh air and sunshine, and, somehow, the cage door popped open without Michel noticing until he went to bring them back indoors.

Only those who wanted to fly free left: a pair of orange-cheeked finches, Pekin, and his buddy, a Cordon Bleu finch. About a dozen finches and one canary stayed in the aviary cage. The Cordon Bleu finch was spotted at a neighbor's bird feeder for a few days. The orange-cheeked finches lived in bushes near our deck for a few weeks. I heard Pekin's song for a few months off a trail within a half mile of our home. I was at first saddened by their departure, but I knew they had done what would make them happy, so I was able to accept their choice to enjoy their time of freedom.

Domestic animals can be happy in a variety of situations that their wild cousins would not like, because most of these beings have chosen to be the companions of humans. As the fortunate recipients of their love and devotion, we owe it to them to help provide for their needs and enable them to grow and expand as spiritual and physical beings. They, too, delight in our friendship, so our interspecies relationships can be healthful, balanced, enriching, and a joy for all.

HUMANS AS SAVIORS

Alice called in a panic, grieving and desperate. She was a nutritional consultant and healer who worked with animals and normally communicated well with them. This time was different. She and her animals were drowning in confusion and pain.

Three months earlier she had rescued a neighbor's cat, named Punch, after an encounter with a coyote that left him very torn up and nearly dead. The veterinarian did not think the cat would live, but Alice was determined to nurse him back to health. She had been friendly with Punch before the injury, but afterwards he was inseparable from her. The neighbors did not want him back, because he fought with his brother, although before the accident they had been buddies.

Unfortunately, he also terrorized the rest of her six cats and turned her harmonious family into disarray. Punch injured several of her cats in his attacks. Her favorite female cat, Zola, who used to sleep with her and give her healing energy, now would not come in the house. Several others were ill with urinary and digestive disorders from the stress. She herself was suffering severe headaches since he came, which she thought were recurring from an accident she had had over a year ago.

She had tried to place Punch in another home, but it did not work out because the person was afraid of him. Now she had him back, and the situation in her household was worsening. She didn't know what to do with him. She loved him.

At this point she called me for a consultation. After talking to Punch, it was apparent that he had suffered some head or brain injury in the coyote attack. He had severe headaches, which at times almost blinded him. It made him feel very aggressive toward other cats, and he didn't want them near him. He told me that after the coyote's attack, he had gone out of his body and to the spiritual dimension, but he had wanted to return to Earth. He fought to live and succeeded with the help of Alice's ministrations, though his body was damaged. While I was listening to his story and gathering his emotions and images of what had happened, I kept hearing the words, "Mistake . . . mistake . . . mistake."

In Alice's zeal to rescue and save, she overlooked something. This became obvious as Punch destroyed her harmonious household. The overwhelming desire to continue life no matter how bad it is may not be the wisest option. Sometimes we don't know until the damage is done.

In communicating with each of her other six cats, it appeared that three of them felt they would die if Punch stayed. They were ill or planning to disappear because of the chaos he created. Punch's condition was also deteriorating. As much as he was attached to Alice and felt happy around her, he wanted no one else around, and the headaches were almost intolerable and becoming more frequent.

She could keep him and lose her other cats and her health. She could try to find him a home with a saint, who would devote his/her life to Punch. She could have him live in a cage (she had already tried confining him to one room, and he didn't like it). Or she could have him euthanized.

Of course, Alice felt terrible about having a cat killed whom she had worked so hard to save. Who wouldn't? She loved him, but the love was destroying her. As we talked, she realized her headaches started when he arrived and were very much like the head pain he described. Alice had gone to her doctors, who ordered CAT scans (they didn't find Punch inside her head!), and even taken painkillers, which was an extreme measure for her as a natural healer.

After much discussion, any decision seemed painful, and the only path available seemed to be to kill Punch. She agonized over it, and he fought it, making it hard for everyone. But as soon as she decided to make an appointment with the vet to have him put down, her headaches disappeared, and Zola and all the other cats reappeared in the house and were peaceful, even though Punch still attacked them.

She had always communicated with animals about impending euthanasia and did it only when they were ready and peaceful about it. This was different. Punch reacted badly to the tranquilizer, hissing and growling and fighting, which made it difficult for Alice, but they went through it. Alice felt Punch was very angry with her, and she felt awful.

When I contacted Punch, after his body was dead, he indeed felt angry. He was a fighter. Again, I got the chant, "Mistake . . . mistake." I realized that Alice had made a mistake in saving him in the first place, he had made a mistake in fighting to come back to a permanently damaged body, and he had made a mistake in hurting everyone and fighting to stay.

We learn from our mistakes. As I communicated with Punch, his anger dissipated, he relaxed into peacefulness, and he allowed his spirit guides and other friends to help him into his wholeness as a spiritual being. Instead of clinging to a life that had to end, he let go into tranquillity and harmony. Whew! Alice had a lot of healing to do from all this, both toward herself and her family. I felt the relief of her sweet cat family, and the desire of several of them to help her and the others heal.

There is no set procedure to follow in a difficult situation like this. This example may remind us that we need to attune with spirit and the harmony of all. It may not be wise to assume the role of savior or have the attitude that bodies must live, no matter the circumstance. Life and Spirit go on. Sometimes it's better to let go and give beings a chance to begin anew. It's a hard decision.

Janet was heavily mourning the loss of her old Doberman, Cheeta, when her new dog, Rasha, arrived. Janet felt Rasha helped her through her pining. The new dog proceeded to knock the box of Cheeta's ashes off the shelf, looked at Janet and said, "Get out of it. I am here. Stop this nonsense."

When Rose found a lump on her rabbit Larissa's belly, she wasn't sure what to do. She had had a number of conversations with Larissa through me and was recovering her own ability to directly communicate with animals. She didn't want to take Larissa to a veterinarian to be treated unless that was what Larissa wanted. She felt George was communicating that Larissa was not feeling well and wanted help. When she checked with me, Larissa made it clear that she wanted help, and Rose took her to the vet to have the tumor removed.

The diagnosis was uterine cancer. Through the process of nursing Larissa and seeing the veterinarian a number of times, Rose became very close to her rabbit friend and developed her telepathic and healing skills. Months later, when Larissa left her body, Rose experienced a peaceful feeling of oneness with her friend—a deep communication and understanding that she had never felt before.

BEYOND DEATH

In every death there is life
In every life there is death
In every joy there is pain
In every pain there is joy
If these things are mingled
If they are one
Is there joy, is there pain?
It is all the same
Oneness and the breath of living.

Jean Mahoney rescued cats and dogs and tried to find homes for them. She called me about various animals, asking how they were adjusting in a new home or whether they wanted to live despite pain, illness, or psychological suffering. She kept a number of animals herself. Due to lack of space, some who could not get along with others lived in the bathroom or bedroom, with as much time and attention that Jean could give them. Jean died after a long period of combating stomach cancer. She was a very loving and spiritually aware person and obviously cared very much for the animals.

I thought of her after she left her body but did not try to contact her, as she seemed very much involved in her own "business" in the spiritual dimension. One morning in November 1991, just before arising, as I was reviewing my dreams, I thought of her, and she tuned in clearly. We conversed, and she told me that she was in the process of healing. She had wonderful friends on the other side, who were helping her to let go of the pains and frustrations that ate at her when she was on Earth and caused the stomach cancer.

She realized that she "overcared" for the animals. She bled for them and tried to keep them alive when often it would have been better for them to be peaceful and happy in another realm. She'd been immersed in her perception of the suffering and pain of animals and trying to save creatures of all kinds for many lifetimes. Becoming bitter and judgmental of humankind, she harbored a feeling of hatred—even for herself, who never could do enough for the animals, who never could right the wrongs. It ended up consuming her body.

She told me not to worry about the animals, that all beings, even unto death and through great suffering, can really take care of themselves. She advised me not to let people's needs and demands for help with their animals drive me to deny the true purpose of existence, to fully enjoy and appreciate each moment of life.

The contact with her supported my own philosophy of life. Do what you enjoy, even if others judge you. Don't stop yourself from doing what feels right as your own unique expression of Spirit. If we think we're indispensable or our efforts are never good enough or we must keep on even if we drive ourselves to illness and death, we spoil our joy in living. Each phase of existence, in whatever form or realm, is ours to create as beautiful and happy or filled with misery or suffering. We can get caught in emotional patterns filled with guilt, sadness, anger, or resentment that trap us into thinking we cannot change. We can change even abject circumstances if we know that we are good and worthy of joy.

Jean let me know that her healing would be slow and savored, that time did not matter in the spiritual realm. She could take care of herself and become whole so that she didn't repeat her destructive pattern if she did reincarnate. I could feel her gratitude, her peace, the nurturing from herself and others, and her gentle help and friendship.

We are all part of each other and share the effects of everyone's choices, whether we're dealing with pollution, greed, and war, or laughter, aesthetics, and friendship. We all share in the "soup" of creation of everyone in our sphere. The universe is malleable; it flows and changes constantly. We add our flow, our energy, our pictures, our creation, and influence everything, especially for ourselves.

Attitude, more than circumstances, determines how you enjoy or appreciate life. Obviously, if we desire beauty and harmony, we seek to change what feels disharmonious or get out of ugly circumstances that bring our spirits down. In some times of our life we seem to have less choice, as in childhood or episodes of illness. Even then, determination and visualizing what you want can bring your dream into existence. On the Earth plane at this time, "reality" doesn't usually mirror thought immediately or completely. You have to persist in channeling energy toward your dreams to materialize them.

For creatures who are dependent, such as most domesticated, captured, or food animals, it seems particularly difficult to change their circumstances and fill their physical, emotional, and spiritual needs without the help of their human guardians, protectors, keepers, or captors. We are all responsible for our own actions toward others, and it is natural to seek to end suffering, injustice, and disharmony. The trap comes when a being gets too caught up in the physical game and doesn't see the spiritual realities behind and through it. Individuals make their choices, somewhere, to get into or create the circumstances of their lives. Though some feel relatively helpless now, for myriad reasons they did choose to try that life or form, and they can choose to change their circumstances, by communicating to those around them for help and visualizing change for themselves. They can even choose to die, if they see no other outlet for having the life they desire. Death is not the end. It is a change from one realm and form of life to another. The innumerable beings I have communicated with have taught me this.

Hector was a cat adopted from the humane society seven months before his person called me for a consultation. The person asked where Hector had come from, and the cat's answer made me laugh. Hector was so direct, so bright, so untraumatized. He said that he was born, he lived awhile with other kittens, he was taken to a place where he would get a home (the shelter), and then his person came, and he was very happy. Hector never expected life to be painful or to suffer and be killed. He just knew he would find a person and have a good home and life. His attitude smoothed the path ahead.

I have met many animals who, like Hector, definitely and consciously create their own lives as happy and full of pleasure—even in the most abject circumstances, where people project that they should be miserable and must be saved! I have met other animals who expect to suffer and be killed, who fear and dislike human ways and their own animal identities. Some animals do not want to be saved. They want out. Well-meaning, over-solicitous, perhaps even over-controlling people who try to save them can cause endless misery to themselves, the animals, and others. That's why it's so important to communicate with the animals themselves, to learn what they want out of life.

Jean even felt, from her perspective in the spiritual realm, that most unwanted animals would be better off being put to sleep. The fact of being "surplus" often means there is no place for them, nor any life for them in that body or at that time as a domesticated animal. I feel that efforts should be concentrated on those who really do want to live with and be helpful to people and come here for that purpose. Why fight to save those who find existence with humans miserable?

I was called to the Hollywood Dog Training School to consult with a very unhappy Rottweiler dog. When I approached him, as the trainer held his leash, the dog warned me that if I put my hand out, he would bite. He had been treated well by people since he was a puppy but was a very unhappy, vicious dog who tried to attack almost anyone or anything that came near. He did not want to cooperate with people. Instead, he said that coming into this body was a mistake, and he would continue to attack people until he was put down. He wasn't at all afraid of being killed, as he wanted to be out of contact with human society.

A formerly prominent human inventor and philosopher showed me an image of himself in the spiritual realm lounging on a tropical isle by the water. He told me that his life now was effortless and he could have whatever he wished, such as harmony among species, beautiful forests without stinging insects, or tropical drinks. He could communicate with the masters of the ages and has experienced many ecstatic moments exchanging ideas with them. No time constraints, hierarchies, or other barriers inhibited sharing knowledge and discoveries. He felt that his biggest mistake on Earth had been his feeling of indispensableness—that his ideas and discoveries were more important than anyone else's and had to be kept intact. This had made life frustrating, and he had longed for change. He now saw life as a river of spirit, in which we all contribute our flow or expression of self as co-creators in the macrocosmic master plan.

SPIRIT CHOOSES

What is life—
It is the flash
of a firefly
in the night.

It is the breath
of a buffalo
in the wintertime.

It is the little shadow
which runs across the grass
and loses itself in the sunset.

—Crowfoot

During their earthly existence, animals are usually conscious that they are spiritual beings as well as physical. They generally accept death naturally and will often go off to die quietly and relatively painlessly, if they are allowed. Dying gets complicated, especially for domesticated animals, when they or their people do not want to let go of their life together. This can make their transition to death a painful, prolonged experience. They may feel obligated to stay in their worn-out or malfunctioning bodies for their people's sake.

Harriet called about her aging standard poodle, Jacko. He had refused to eat for a week after a series of veterinary treatments for various ailments. Harriet realized that her dog was dying and she could probably do no more for him physically. What most concerned her was that for several months, her formerly affectionate canine companion avoided her and seemed morose.

Jacko told me of his frustration in communicating with his person. He knew that it was his time to die. He didn't want any more veterinary treatment, nor for his person to hover over him worrying. Harriet's desperate attempts to medicate him and her pleading for him to get better made the whole process very painful for Jacko. He felt he had no choice but to distance himself from her.

After I acknowledged Jacko and relayed his feelings to Harriet, and while we were still on the phone, her poodle companion came over to her. For the first time in months, he put his head on her lap and nuzzled her affectionately. He was so grateful that at last his person understood.

One of Elaine's five cats, Ralph, was severely ill when she called me for help. Ralph told me that he felt he was dying. He wasn't able to tell me more about any emotional factors involved in his illness, but communicating his feelings to Elaine seemed to perk him up a little. I also sent him some healing energy, long-distance, after the phone consultation. I advised Elaine to get whatever treatment she felt would be good for Ralph, but also to prepare to let him go. She needed to let him know that, while she would like him to get well, she would not try to hold him back if he really felt it was his time to go. The thought of her cat dying was definitely not easy for her.

In a surprising turnabout, Ralph slowly started to get better, allowing another person to do some gentle bodywork, and he responded well to more veterinary treatment. Then another of Elaine's cat companions, Mandy, also became ill. It turned out that Mandy was trying to absorb the emotional stress in the family and was taking on Ralph's illness to help him get through it. While she appeared even worse than Ralph, Mandy assured me that she would get well. She survived a fever of 107 degrees through willpower, good veterinary care, and healing energy from all involved. Elaine felt that this ordeal was a test of her own willingness to let go and emotionally "clean house," allowing death to be a part of life.

Michael called me about his fifteen-year-old arthritic dog, Panda. He felt that his dog was suffering so much that she should be put down. Panda told me that she was not in severe pain, but only felt stiff and sore when she first got up. She wanted to be her person's good companion as long as she was able. Panda would let her person know when it was her time to go. It was quite a number of months before the dog, then almost unable to move, did tell Michael that it was the time to help her along. They both had time to prepare and to consent to the departure.

Each case is individual, and it's vital to regard what the animals think. If they are fighting to live, want to get well, and are willing to undergo potentially helpful treatments, then that's the way to travel. Some animals who can't even move without human assistance, still want to go on and feel they are being of service to their people. The inspiration, love, and growth the animals and their people derive from each other can't be measured.

Other animals will say, as they see their bodies deteriorating, "Let me go now, help me along, before I lose my dignity." Senator, a large German shepherd, had lost bowel control and was losing rear-end coordination. His person, Marsha, wondered when she should have the vet put him down. In discussing the alternatives with Senator, he decided he did not want to continue to wake up lying in his own excrement, and he knew his body was getting worse daily. He was not afraid of the injection that would release him from his body. I told Marsha to have a great outing and celebrate with her dog the wonderful life they had together and his upcoming release into the spiritual realm, before taking him to the vet. Senator was very grateful for this opportunity and had a peaceful, happy departure.

Carolyn Blakey, a holistic veterinarian practicing in Indiana, had consulted with me about a number of animals when she decided to sponsor a workshop in June 1989. While I was at her veterinary clinic, she asked me to see a hawk who had recently arrived with an irreparable wing. She felt the hawk was very unhappy with being in captivity and wanted to hear his point of view.

The hawk was angry with being kept in a cage. He realized that he would never be able to fly again, but felt he would rather take his chances and die in the wild than be a prisoner in human surroundings. He was adamant about being released, regardless of his survival prospects. At least he would die in dignity, he felt. Carolyn felt his relief and gratefulness when she later released him in a rural area. She saw him one morning on her way to work, as he caught mice on the ground by the side of the road.

Sitting quietly with your animal friends, listening as best you can, making peace with them, going over the life you've had together, and being willing to let them go—these are the best things to do when it's obvious that life cannot be sustained anymore. Many animals then go quietly and happily. Even with the sadness of losing their physical presence, it's possible to experience their joy in being a free spirit when the body dies. You can learn to maintain a spiritual connection and communication with your departed friends, which also helps to put the whole process in perspective.

It is natural to seek the best treatment you can to help restore health. If you also are willing to view death as a natural, profound, even beautiful part of life, it becomes easier for the animal to relax—and either get well, or have a peaceful departure. Be willing to accept your own and your animal friend's emotions as they come, but don't put the burden on your animal friends to handle your feelings by their hanging on. Listen to your animal friends, and keep in touch with their spiritual nature. Understand their viewpoints, and let death, like life, be a growing process.

Soe Hut, a sixteen-year-old Burmese cat, died while his person, Joyce, was on a trip away from home. Joyce was devastated and worried about her other Burmese of the same age, Khin Su, who had been crying ever since.

When I contacted Soe Hut, he was distraught, as he seemed to be held in a limbo state by his family being so upset about his departure. Khin Su needed to release her anger about being left. Joyce needed to calm her distraught state and connect with Soe Hut as a spirit, thus showing her willingness to let him die in his own way, even if she wasn't there at the time. I communicated with all of them and helped to discharge the painful emotions. Soe Hut could then be released from "duty" into the spiritual realm, where he could still communicate with his family, but was free to follow his spiritual path.

In more ways than we may think, we are connected with each other through life and death. Jack was in the living room with his girlfriend's tabby cat, Luella, watching television. He called out to Martha that there was something wrong with the cat.

Luella was in her usual position across Jack's outstretched legs, but her limbs were spread out, she appeared not to be breathing, and her body was cold. She hadn't been sick, and Jack said she'd been fine just moments before. Martha called Luella's name, over and over, and after agonizing moments, she slowly opened her eyes! Her body relaxed and once again felt warm.

An hour later, Jack's sister called to tell Martha that his mother had died of a heart attack. Later they found that his mother's death had coincided with Luella's "death."

While staying at the home of a couple who were sponsoring a workshop, I was asked to consult with them and their animal friends about various issues. They were concerned about their collie dog, Sam, adopted a few years before, who always seemed sad and somewhat distant. While I communicated with their other dog and cat, Sam lay behind the piano. I could feel his suppressed emotions and contracted energy, even though he was hidden from view. He wanted to talk to me but was too reclusive to ask. When his turn came, I told him he could stay where he was if that was comfortable for him, and perhaps he could tell me what was burdening him.

Sam relayed that his person, an elderly woman, had died a few years ago, and he mourned for her. He felt that he could never be happy, now that she was gone. His people confirmed that his former human companion had died of cancer before they adopted him. As Sam and I communicated, the departed woman contacted us. She had loved Sam dearly, and they agreed that they couldn't be happy on Earth without each other. This "pact" was first made in a previous life, where they had known each other in human form. In reviewing this decision and getting Sam and his departed human friend to connect with each other in the present, something changed. I felt Sam's emotional burden lighten, and he came out from behind the piano. He said he would talk to me again later. I could feel that there was more emotional releasing to be done.

The next day, Sam came and sat quietly in the guest room where I stayed. He let forth a stream of emotion and images connected with his loss and his life in general. In a short time, visibly more cheerful, he left the room. After that, he grew more outgoing and playful, quite a change from his morose and overly quiet state.

Animals have their own unique histories and reactions to life and death. I have met other animals of various species who respond differently than Sam did to their person's death. Some die in order to follow their person to the other side. Some feel close to the person in spirit, but make a new life for themselves. Others are confused, frightened, saddened, and have a hard time adjusting. The whole range of emotions and responses is possible.

For those of you who care for animals who have experienced the death of people close to them, explain to the animal what happened to their person, in case they are confused. Help them to feel the connection in spirit if you can, honor their mourning time, and help them to extrovert their attention with favorite activities so that they renew their participation in life. We can all help each other to understand, accept, and learn from the constant death and rebirth of life on Earth.

I was browsing through a pet store in October 1986, when I zeroed in on a terrarium full of anole lizards (popularly known as chameleons). All were quiet, except one small fellow who wildly leapt at the glass and called to me, "Take me home. I'm meant to be with you." I felt a deep connection with this being, but I knew nothing about the care of his species. Finding a book in the store about anoles, I turned my back on the terrarium and proceeded to read. The lizard's strong intention pulsated at my back. This was one high-powered being! When the salesperson came to catch him for me, he climbed out and jumped into the box to go home. His name came to me as Ginko. I enjoyed making a fern- and stone-filled terrarium habitat for him and totally enjoyed his presence. I wrote this poem six days after he arrived:

Ginko, so wise and still, godlike
Ancient teacher
In your woodland home
The plants, rocks, soil, and bark helped me fashion
Spiders, worms, flies, moths, and crickets
Sharing your sacred, glass temple
Cats and humans admiring from outside
So wise, so beautiful in your chameleon form
Shifting color with your mood and state
Physical and spiritual transforming
Watching, I learn stillness, joy in patience, quiet communion
Even with those you need to eat to nourish your lithe life.
I've overheard your conversations with the spiders and the flies
Understood your friendship and the pact between predator and prey
Love—complete sharing
Felt your beauty and truth
The deep well behind your eyes
Your joy, your peace
Seen my father, years gone from Earth, resurface through your eyes

And connect with Earth and me physically for a moment
Time dissolves
Deep peace reveals the simplicity and union of all life
Thank you for calling to me
Giving your breathless soul beauty to all.

I caught many flies and other insects for Ginko in the time he dwelled with us. I began by asking permission for each insect to be his food, but then made a general announcement that any insect who entered our home was prospective food for Ginko. They could make their choice to stay or leave. Even normally speedy flies were surprisingly easy to catch. Their deaths were swift and smooth, with one graceful vault and open-mouthed snatch and gulp from Ginko.

Ginko would sometimes spring up and out of his terrarium when I opened the lid to put insects in. He wasn't easy to rescue from behind furniture, so I got into the habit of quickly snapping down the lid after releasing an insect into his habitat. On March 14, 1988, the lid caught Ginko as he leapt to the edge and squashed his body hard as I snapped it down. His small, lithe form was bent, and I painfully watched his shiny green color turn to brown and then black as his life force ebbed.

After his death, Ginko appeared to me in spirit as a tall Amazonian Indian figure. He communicated that he came here to be a special guide to me. Although his time in lizard form was finished, he would be with me to help me spiritually.

I felt his presence over the years, among my many spiritual guides and helpers. In September 1992, on the Hawaiian island of Maui, I was seated in a hotel restaraunt next to the garden, when a tiny green anole nimbly hopped onto a plant at eye level. I experienced Ginko, communicating through this lizard to let me know he would help me in my approaching talk at the American Holistic Veterinary Conference, which I was excitedly anticipating. I was buoyed as the anole looked me in the eye, offering his lightness and encouragement.

After that, the idea of getting another anole lizard as part of the family began to take hold. I put it aside, as I remembered how much time I spent looking for a variety of insects for Ginko. Being very practical and organized about having new animal members was a necessity, since we already had a variety of species and individuals. Nevertheless, when helpers have had a strong purpose to appear here, they have sparked a passion in me for their arrival. Igor, the new anole, arrived October 9, 1992, bringing his wisdom and grace to our lives.

Sherman, our orange cat, came in one day looking ill. When I questioned him, he said he just wanted to rest. He didn't eat and was sore when I touched various places on his body. He didn't want to talk about what happened, but merely wanted to be left alone. Later, he relayed to me that he had fought bitterly with a neighboring cat. He had things to work out and wanted to do it on his own. Although he didn't eat for a few days and mostly slept, I kept my motherly instincts from taking over. I didn't override his wishes by trying to give him herbs or taking him to a vet, but instead gently offered healing energy every now and then and asked the angels to help him heal.

He appreciated the respect I gave him as an aware spirit able to heal himself. When Sherman was feeling better, he shared his realization that he had been getting too involved with cat behavior patterns and conflicts and losing sight of what he was here for—to bring harmony and enlightenment to all beings he met on Earth. He decided to meditate on it more and restore himself.

After a day of improvement, he began to look ill again. I remembered that Sherman, as an emissary from the angelic kingdom, had a time line on his incarnate mission. When he first came to us in 1988, I felt that he would be here for a short time. He was three years and five months old. It appeared that he was going back to the spiritual realm. The energy was draining from his body for no organic reason. He couldn't eat without throwing up. Michel and I and our animal family sent him healing energy. We respectfully asked the Higher Powers if he could stay with us, as he was such a help here on Earth, and we loved him so much in his cat form.

When I did a healing with Sherman that day, I perceived a giant angel form behind and around me, giving him energy. There were numerous smaller angels all around us. He had been given permission to live longer.

That night, Sherman ate again with no difficulty, and his energy field had changed. I witnessed an energetic swirling, whirring, and clicking in his body, as his internal time clocks were reprogrammed to continue for years more of healthy life.

Later, when I was drawn to hold him, we united with a rare, mystic quality. Our bodies flowed together in energetic harmony. We knew each other physically and spiritually, as one form and spirit.

From that moment on, Sherman dedicated himself to be my special assistant. As close as we had been before this episode, we were now tightly bonded in our mission for interspecies and universal harmony.

Heyoka, our shiny black panther cat, has always been a paragon of health, smelling like herbs, pine trees, and fresh flowers, even when he lived indoors in Los Angeles. However, he had several bouts with cystitis, which would not clear up with vitamins, homeopathic remedies, or energetic healing. Urinary problems usually have an emotional or stress-related component causing or prolonging them, but Heyoka wasn't ready to face and release that aspect. Despite being neutered, he was having conflicts with a feral tomcat in the area. It wasn't something I could counsel him through immediately. He had to unfold his own drama and learn how to balance his male energy and spiritual power through his cat body.

In the meantime, he had to go through catheterization and eat a special diet to ease the physical manifestations while he came to terms with the emotional and spiritual roots. To fully enjoy and appreciate the bodies we have and all the patterns of our particular culture and environment without getting lost in sensations, impulses, instincts, hormonal patterns, habits, or conventions is quite a balancing act for individuals of any species. For domesticated humans and animals, this task may be either complicated or facilitated by human-made environments and rules altering natural checks and balances. The challenge is to be conscious of how we wish to "be" in our bodies, and to integrate body, mind, and spirit in a fashion that is harmonious for us.

I trusted Heyoka to resolve his internal conflict, and he did. I communicated with the feral cat and got him to leave our area.

Elfie, a white dwarf rabbit with dark gray ears and tail, had helped many people who came to deepen their telepathic connection during advanced workshops. Her death on September 10, 1991, was very soft and magical. I wrote this tribute to her the day after she departed.

Elfie rabbit died today
Left her matter form and flew away.

We knew this day would come
Ever since Georgie, her dear mate, left her alone on Earth
Things had not been the same.
She loved him dear but more they shared
Both from the fairy kingdom had come
To dwell on Earth in soft rabbit form
And help spread the word
That all Spirit, all spirits, are the Same
Kingdoms, forms, bodies all are games
Sparked with divine grace
Expressions of the Same Being—Infinity the name.

Elfie knew that wisdom could incarnate in any shape
That evolution was not linear
But spirit encompassing more of life.
She shared her power and beauty, her grace
She taught those who came
To know themselves
And honor beings of any face.

When she yearned to be with Georgie in the spirit realm
She would become ill
Then decide to stay and heal again
A thing unheard of in rabbitdom.
Now she knew this was her time
Seven years of life—a cycle ending
She would go to return no more.

Quietly she left
In a day her body's clock wound down
And left her free to go
A beautiful death, a peaceful transition
Her breathing slowed
Her head become heavy till it rested on the ground
The life force ebbed
But yet, amazingly
The light grew.

I covered her gently to her chin to ease the chill
She welcomed my gentle caress of her head
Then I left her to peace
And when I returned, I knew she was gone
Yet strangely, her body was transformed.

I'd seen many die and when they go
They leave a cold and stiff form unyielding
Obvious that the spirit has severed the bond.
Elfie's rabbit form was surrounded with light
Her open eyes were like pink crystal jewels sparkling
Her body was supple though cool
Her fur felt softer than ever in life
The luxuriousness of some other world
She looked like a gentle, young rabbit—a sprite.

Georgie had not died so
His form was smashed and stiff—so lifeless
Elfie was transformed
Pale, translucent lights of pink and orange
Floated all around her
I felt her as spirit in a whirlpool of light
With Georgie, entering her chosen place.

I was moved to place her body deep in a new garden bed
Her soft and supple form glowed as she lay in the rich dark earth
Accompanied by lettuce and calendula flower—favorite foods
I sensed if I had held her body longer
It would have melted into liquid light
The fairy friends, her family, would have taken it away.

I feel the glowing as her body dissolves in the ground
Doing fairy work of helping plants to grow
I planted broccoli, cabbage, cauliflower, spinach, and lettuce above
Those friends she ate now eating her form to live again
Round and round it goes.

The next day she showed herself in spirit play
Hopping, leaping, dancing with Georgie in the dream meadow
Surrounded with freshness and dancing lights.

The fairy lights follow
Helping, transforming, bringing magic to us all
Elfie—rabbit translucent—spirit glowing
Thank you for coming our way
May Georgie and you be part of our life
And shine your light on all of us forever.

While attending a workshop at our home after Elfie's departure, Carol Landsberg communicated with Gingerbread, the guinea pig. She asked him if there was something he thought she needed to know. What he told her and the feelings she had while he was talking to her changed her point of view about death, which was a very painful issue in her life.

I want to tell you about death. It is wonderful. It is something to breathe into and love yourself for. It is a transition and a change, and I know you must look at it as an opportunity, not a threat. It is going to happen to you, so you might as well use this point of view. Security is inside, not with outside things. In order to do the best job in your life and have the best time, you need to relax and trust your process. You are very close to realizing this, and I know that it will be very helpful to you because how you live your life is important at death.

Death is wanting to be peaceful; it is knowing that your work is done. There is no struggle because it feels right. It is a letting go of ego/personality/persona stuff. It is tapping into a greater whole. It is releasing tension; it is getting off the treadmill. It is relaxing into warmth; it is going to source. It is being held by love itself. It is a giant sunset. It is complete trust; it is joining a larger force. It is welcome; it is going home. It is all senses balancing and harmonizing in a perfect way. It is not hearing "mind chatter" any more. It is delicious; it is chocolate pudding bubble bath. It is a gentle implosion of all the senses; it is being All at once. It is beyond words. It is sinking into heat. It is truth in a way you don't know. It's aligning all things; it's seeing the connection of all things and being the connection of all things. Its magnificence is Knowing. It is the feeling I'm sending you right now. Every time this "issue" comes up for you, feel the feeling I'm sending you now and you will be okay.

I'm looking forward to my time to depart. I'm not there yet because I have work to do for Penelope. Soon I will have the company I need to help take over and learn how to hold the space. It is a very powerful space here, and I love doing this work. People relate to me because so many of them have had a guinea pig in school. It is the main reason I chose this body. I can do very deep work because of the positive memories people have of guinea pigs from school. I remind them of being students, and it opens them up so I can teach them about connecting with other species. I love this work so much. I am so peaceful inside because I am fulfilling my purpose. I love my home here and enjoy my cottage. I love working with the beings that come here and am happy to see how much you've grown since you were here last year. You will continue to grow rapidly if you give yourself peaceful time like I'm giving myself. Feel how good it feels.

When Michel and I went to Maui for the American Holistic Veterinary Conference in September 1992, our coastal area had an unexpected heat wave. We did not think to caution our house-sitter to watch our rabbit family if the temperature ranged above eighty-five degrees. Even though the Beatrix Potter Bunny Cottage is in the shade and well ventilated, if the heat stresses the rabbits, I normally put a fan in their cottage and spray them gently with water. The weather had been below seventy during the week before we left, and we hadn't had high temperatures for so long, so none of us anticipated the heat.

When we returned, I found our mother rabbit, Molly, in horrible shape—disoriented, with severe pains in her head. Her son, Periwinkle, came up to me and told me that she was very ill, and he was glad I was home to take care of her. He licked Molly's eyes and was very concerned. He also did not look well. I gave all the rabbits Bach flower and herbal remedies, but it was too late. Chester, her mate, kept close by Molly. She died overnight, and I found her in the morning of September 26. It was a blow to all of us, and Molly felt surprised and shocked at being separated from her family. Periwinkle quickly deteriorated and joined her that day, in the late afternoon.

It was very strange to have them gone, and Chester and his daughter, Velvet, looked lost. Chester was solemn, and each day he grieved more. He had so loved Molly and his dear son, Periwinkle. He and Velvet at first stuck together, but then they became more separated. I was very concerned about Chester when I left to do lectures and a workshop in British Columbia on October 1. On the morning of October 2, Chester joined Molly and Periwinkle. When I returned home in the evening of October 6, Velvet was on her way out, and she left during the night.

I felt so bad when Molly and Periwinkle left, especially because Chester and Velvet felt so incomplete. They were such a close-knit family. When Chester and Velvet joined Molly and Periwinkle, I felt a relief. These beautiful spirits were now together, sharing their universe. Each one said good-bye to Gingerbread, their "uncle" guinea pig companion, before they left. Molly's departure was the hardest for Gingerbread, as she took daily care of grooming his eyes and ears and letting him know how much he was appreciated.

Molly at first was surprised at her heatstroke-induced departure. When all of them were together in the spirit realm, we all realized that they were meant to be on Earth for just a short time. It was a special time, and I will always be enriched by the thought of all of them lovingly together in the Beatrix Potter Bunny Cottage as a beautiful family. Chester and Molly were here for one year, and Periwinkle and Velvet lived for less than nine months. We had carefully arranged for all of them to be neutered, so they could live together without sexual rivalry and a population explosion. It was a joy to see them all in a row peacefully grooming each other, or racing around their cottage together.

On the physical level, Molly and Periwinkle seemed to have a predisposition to be especially sensitive to heat. After Molly went, the group fell apart spiritually. They all had to be together in the same realm.

A week after Velvet died, Michel saw the man who had adopted one of Molly and Chester's sons, Benny, and this man reported an amazing occurrence. Benny, brother to Periwinkle and Velvet, had suddenly and inexplicably died about the same time as Velvet. He had always appeared healthy, and he played and snuggled with his person just before he was found dead.

This family was a soul group that had to be together. I recall how Chester was angry with me when anyone came to look at his baby bunnies and take them to new homes. Molly was more independent about it and almost pushed each one out the door. She was definitely the leader, and carried about three-quarters of the energy of the soul group. They couldn't be without her.

Deep, deep it runs
The feeling
Riding on the absence
And the presence
Gone from one realm
To another
A family
Of beauty light
So deep, so bright.

A family
A soul group
Graced our life
Brought their beauty into Earth
For such a short time
But a time
To cherish forever.

A family
A soul group
Whose comings and goings
Are not under my control
Or anyone's
Perhaps not even their own.

A profound silent grace
A warm quiet comfort

Fills the air
Each molecule of matter
Touched by their love.

Such a family love
A soul group play and harmony
Is a treasure forever
In all our hearts.

We dwell in bunny love forever.

Having many animal companions with short life spans has given me the challenging opportunity often to face and grow with the transitions of dying, death, and rebirth. The year 1992 contained a series of animal deaths and my own mother's passing.

Gingerbread, our guinea pig friend, had mentioned in his "treatise" on death, as told to Carol Landsberg, that he was looking forward to his time to depart. He still had work to do with me, but soon he would have the company to help take over and learn how to hold the space. How much I and all who have come to workshops here have learned from this sweet and wise being!

On December 1, with the sun shining brightly, Gingerbread left this life gently and peacefully, in the manner he had lived. A powerful, expanding energy surged from his body as he lay dying. It was remarkable to witness that as his body energy ebbed, his spiritual force welled up in vortices of light to fill the space of the cottage and beyond.

Ellyetta rabbit raced around, almost in glee, saying, "Gingerbread is going to a higher state." She was literally beside herself in excitement. Even when she jumped around and on Gingerbread's body lying on its side in the hay, he didn't mind. He said that she was experiencing his energy and the joy of his transition.

After Gingie left in the early afternoon, he shared with me his experience in the spiritual realm. He visited Elfie and Georgie in their magical kingdom and Chester, Molly, Velvet, Periwinkle, Benny, and all their friends. He showed me how the spiritual realms are a faster, finer vibration of this realm, and are all around us, outside of our physical space and time, but present to finer-tuned perceptions. He showed me how the recently departed bunny family was still present in the bunny cottage, giving their light and love, at the same time being fully in the spiritual realm. He flashed an image of his sparkling eyes and lovely guinea pig nose and mouth turned up in expectation, and shared his exhilaration with the lightness, harmony, and universal connection that he felt. He could go anywhere, be with anyone, and have endless laughter and light. He was himself totally—a sparkling, free spirit.

From my many contacts with beings who have left the Earth plane, I am aware that there are infinite "places" or dimensions in the spiritual realm. Sometimes the dimensions seem to coexist with the Earth plane, with just a slight veil or difference in vibration separating them. The act of perceiving them is like shifting your awareness to lighter forms or tuning in to different television or radio channels. Other times, beings seem a long "distance" away, in other realms or planes that are not very accessible for communication. This distancing is created by choice of the beings who have departed and according to the "rules" of perceiving or purpose of entering into that realm.

Beings can all know each other in the spiritual realm, but they seem not to be in touch with every other spirit at all times. They go to realms, "departments," or dimensions according to their purposes and visions. It appears that anything can be created in the spiritual domain. Infinite peace and love are available, although not all dwell in that state unless they allow it for themselves.

It became clearer to me after getting Gingerbread's perspective that the Chester and Molly bunny family had to exist in the spiritual realm. They vibrated themselves out of the physical universe. Together they had manifested an "unearthly" beauty and harmony that kept increasing in vibration until it eliminated the physical forms.

People often strive for the ecstasy that they experience as free spirits dwelling in a divine state. They may not have yet mastered the experience of being and knowing themselves as eternal, infinite beings, while still enjoying life incarnate. They may think it's an either-or proposition: i.e., either I dwell in a body and be miserable, lost, and in pain, or I leave my body and the physical realm and be a free, happy, and infinite spirit. As humans, they may feel dissociated or alienated, especially in our culture, which has lost most of its deep spiritual connection to all of life on Earth. Other species can teach us about harmonious integration of spirit and form.

Permanent maintenance of a state of ecstasy, like a drug or out-of-body high, does not usually lead to a harmonious integration of body, mind, and spirit, or full functioning on the Earth. The Earth plane requires indwelling in form and following the consensual rules to create and learn from this game, with its hazards and fulfillments. If you dwell too much in the spiritual, you can lose the experience of the physical.

I have had the experience a number of times in my life, when I focused so much in finer, faster vibration realities, that I almost slipped out of the physical—literally, almost vanished with my body. At those times, I have been reminded why I was sent here and the need for my presence by the beings on Earth, and that my job in this body has not been completed. I have been cautioned not to perceive and focus on other realities for too long, or I risk losing my grounding in the physical.

A balance is struck in knowing who you are in your fullness as spirit, while consciously creating an identity and a purpose to live your life happily on Earth. Allowing awareness of the spiritual nature of all things to be the foundation and to permeate your life, as you also consciously live the game that you and others create on Earth, can help make life a harmonious, joyful adventure. There are as many potential life adventures open to us as there are choices!

The same day Gingerbread left, a student named Patricia, who had done the November 1992 advanced workshop, left a message on my answering machine to ask for healing for her cat Sweetie, who was gravely ill. As I focused on sending healing energy to Sweetie, I clearly got that she was in the hands of the angels and would be going soon from this world. I also got a message from Gingerbread that it was a good day to die.

Patricia called the next day to talk about Sweetie's passing. She was grateful that her cat had gone peacefully, but was worried that she had let Sweetie down because she was not holding her cat when she died. She thought it was odd that she had spent most of her time with her cat for four or five days, and at the end, she was not with her. She had cut her hand with the syringe needle while giving Sweetie fluids and had been occupied with trying to get the cut to stop bleeding.

Sweetie needed the space and lack of pressure from a human holding her to make the final break and die with dignity. I explained to Patricia about Gingerbread's death, how there was a tremendous energy buildup and that I left him undisturbed while he was dying. It is not always easy to make the break from your body; there are many energetic connections, attaching you to the body and vice versa, that enable you to operate and function in the physical realm. It can be even harder for the body to let you go. Each cell is alive, a physical and spiritual entity, working in groups of cells for cooperative functioning and survival of the whole.

Bodies are programmed to survive, and when they determinedly keep pumping blood and breath, it can be difficult for spirits to depart, despite their intentions. Holding animal companions and giving them energy, or constantly ministering to their bodies, can make it more painful or impossible for them to leave. The person's emotions and thoughts may also be distracting. Each case will be different. Some animals want you to be there and comfort and hold them as they go. It is also very common for animals, including humans, to die when everyone leaves, in their own quietude. They often need that space in order to focus on the spiritual realm and make a peaceful transition.

It's important to honor your own emotions, but also to clear yourself to listen to and honor the other's emotions and wishes about their dying. When I first found Gingerbread on his side in the morning and knew he was going, I made sure he was as comfortable as he could be and checked if he needed anything from me. Then I went off to cry and tell Michel, who went to spend time with him. I left Gingerbread alone as his body twitched and the energy rose, and I felt his peace. I returned to check on him a few times, but let his body be. After his departure, I went to take his body away for burial. I ensured that Ellyetta understood, and held his body for her to see. She told me that she didn't need to see his dead body; they had already said good-bye, and she understood what had happened.

Patricia mentioned how, just before Sweetie died, the cat had wedged his body in an unusual space that Patricia couldn't reach, so she couldn't hold him as she had been doing. I recalled how I was told that my father, when he was dying with lung cancer, got out of bed and lay on the floor naked. When my brother-in-law tried to put a blanket over him, my father shoved him away in an uncharacteristic, altered-state communication that he wanted to be left alone. Shortly after that, he departed.

Patricia also noted how unusual it was that she had cut herself and had to spend a long time handling the profusely bleeding wound. I saw how Sweetie and her guiding angels had arranged for this break in Patricia's vigil. Sweetie took her final breath peacefully alone, sending her blessings, gratitude, and peace to Patricia as she left. There was no need for Patricia to blame herself for not being there. It had all happened as it was meant to be, harmoniously.

Gingerbread was six years and eight months old when he died—a very ripe old age for a guinea pig. He led a good life, the first four years choosing to quietly enjoy his earthly pleasures, and during the latter three years adding to his repertoire by working with people and expanding his abilities to know and impart wisdom to others. I felt his incredible, sparkling presence all around me on the day after his death.

Each transition of a friend moves me through another transformation and deeper understanding of all realms. It is magical how this earthly plane is one of transformation and rebirth, never stagnant, always giving us surprises, to be enjoyed as delicious fruits, or to greet with the full range of emotions, according to our perspective. I give thanks for spirits' sparkling majesty enlivening all forms and energies. Thanks for all the animal guides who have come and gone and are always available in spirit. I wouldn't live without them.

Most communications with animals reveal their joy, love of life, patience, and generally refreshing perceptions. Life being what it is, you will also have to face pain and sorrow.

After communicating with people and their horses at several farms in Ontario, Canada, I discovered that there was a lot of neglect and abuse of horses in that area. Many of the horses had been rescued from abominable situations and had much trauma to heal.

Just before a lunch break, and after I had spoken with her current horse companion, Francine asked me if I could contact a pony that she had ridden as a young child. She described her pony, Tara, who had a son with whom she lived for years. They shared the same pasture and deeply loved each other. Francine felt badly because, as a child, she looked at the horse as existing solely for her pleasure, and her parents regarded the horses as commodities. When she and her sister were too busy in school to ride the ponies, her father sold Tara's son and left Tara alone in the field. Heartbroken, Tara stood forlornly in one place, gradually stopped eating, and died after months of sorrow.

As I listened and tuned into Tara's life, I broke down and cried. Inwardly congested with tales of animal abuse and physically tired and hungry, I could hear no more. These patient, loving beings who give so much to us can be so misunderstood and mistreated. They deserve much more.

Francine sought absolution from Tara. Contacting Tara in the spiritual realm, I found that she had long forgiven all the people who had contributed to her sorrow. She was reunited happily with her son, and Tara acknowledged her life path as her own choice.

We might wish that the ones we care for could always be happy on Earth, but that is not the way of experience and growth here. Perhaps we would be bored if we could not experience contrasting emotions and feelings that help us to appreciate the pleasant and beautiful things of life and make life interesting and challenging. We live and choose our course of adventures.

Here are a few stories about the life-and-death choices of spirit that people have shared with me. From Jeri Ryan:

Soul determines choices. One of my favorite soul experiences with animals came from rescuing snails on a rainy night from annihilation on a city sidewalk. On my way out to dinner, I was a snail myself, gently tapping each shell so the snail would withdraw, and patiently moving one at a time off the concrete to the grass. There were many snails; it took a long time to "rescue" them. On my way back, their soul was spotlighted in their persistence, for they were out again, taking their chances on life by braving the dangers of heavy, sometimes soulless, human feet. The snails were determined to follow their respective paths. I have since been enamored of snail soul.

Leona Troese:

I have your *Animal Death* tape, and I have to say that it's helped me a lot. When Diamond Girl died (actually it's starting to feel much more appropriate and accurate to say "left her body") the opening poem kept going through my mind. And, when she did leave her body, at first I felt her strongly in my heart, but then went on with my usual depression and grieving. I think now, again, I'm settling back into our togetherness. I really hope people can come to bridge that gap more readily at times of "loss." I have exceedingly strong emotional attachments to my animal friends, but hopefully am turning the intensity of that love into a more balanced and equally intense insight into *life* and our relationships with nonhuman animals.

Sue Goodrich:

Starting about a week after Hawk (Siberian husky) left his body, I started getting a huge white light coming in. I thought at first it was the next being waiting to come in. Turns out it is a group of beings, including Hawk, giving me the most wonderful support and messages to help me on my way. Numerous times now, Hawk has come in to guide and help me with distant healings. Incredible! And always with humor and joy!

Kathleen Huston:

Saddened, but relieved, I am bringing you the news that on January 31, 1992, at lunchtime (of course!), Julie, the world's most notorious dachshund, left this life to go on to her next adventure.

It's hard to imagine that a little dog could touch so many hearts, even in a life that lasted twenty-five years. Of course, you can imagine that she's all around us, and most assuredly grateful that she doesn't have to go out in this rainstorm to go potty!

I thought if I waited a week or so, it would be easier to write this, but I really do miss her, and it's hard sometimes. But I also want you all to know that she was always Julie. She never lost her ability to scope out a spilled treasure. She slammed the cabinets at mealtime until the last two weeks, bit the mailman regularly, and loved company to come in large numbers so she could beg mercilessly.

During the last two weeks we made lots of visits to her vet, who was terrific. We speculate, based on her diagnosis, that Julie had internal bleeding from a tumor on her spleen. She became more and more uncomfortable and then couldn't eat. Well, we all knew what it would mean if Julie couldn't eat! Penelope confirmed that Julie was really ready to go to sleep. She was through with her old body, but her spirit was "happy, almost lighthearted." So that was it. She was cremated, and her friend, Kirby, suggested that perhaps we should spread her ashes near a large smorgasbord!

I think we were lucky she picked us. Just beware. If you get hooked up with a bright-eyed, button-nosed little waif, it might be Julie on her next go-round. I told her to slam the cabinets, and we'd know for sure!

Nancy Sondel:

If I ever had any doubts about the awareness of animals, Scooter laid them to rest.

He was a yellow-faced, green parakeet, like those native to Australia. Now five years old, he had been one of the first born in my aviary. With fifty birds, I couldn't tame them all, but Scooter had always been friendly.

He lived cheerfully until a long illness took hold. I watched patiently for several months, until he reached the point of no return. I knew he might hang on another few days, but it would be cruel to let him. To euthanize him would take all the courage I could muster. To drive to a vet's office, then watch as the needle was inserted, seemed cold and impersonal. It would be blasphemous to put him in a paper bag and force him to breathe toxic fumes. Other alternatives were even less acceptable. If it must be done, I wanted to do it myself, gently and with love.

I had faced this on other occasions; the irony confused and infuriated me. I expended enormous energy to nurture and preserve life. Why must I be the one to end it? Why me, I kept asking. Why do I have to make this decision, to commit this mighty act; why again, why now, why me?

Instead of getting it over with quickly, I decided to try something different. I would focus on (not fight against) the process. I lifted Scooter out of his cage and took him to a quiet place. I told him I was going to release him from his body, and asked if he wanted to fly one last time. I felt the thrill of communication as he lifted off.

He flew a few yards and flopped. We tried again. Then I cupped him in my hands and reminisced, telling him how happy he'd made me. I explained exactly what I was going to do. He looked skeptical, even fearful. I said, "You'll be uncomfortable only for a few seconds, and then you'll know no bounds." I stroked his head and finally said, "Okay, are you ready now?"

Scooter closed his eyes and lay still. He clearly understood.

Turning my consciousness inward, I took a deep breath, closed my eyes and slowly pressed his diaphragm. "I love you," I cried, until all his breath was gone.

For a few moments there was only the stillness. Then I felt him floating, soaring, as he became living spirit.

"Farewell, little angel!" I thought. His presence filled the room and beyond. I realized I was smiling.

Scooter didn't fear death; he knew it was a natural transition. He communicated this peaceful acceptance, as well as his trust in me.

With an easier method of euthanasia, I never would have known these moments of incredible closeness and truth. I felt immensely grateful, and lighter than I had in ages.

And then I understood, "Why me?"

THE PREDATOR–PREY DANCE

Kate lived in an area where deer were hunted. She loved seeing the deer and was very upset when hunting season began. During a break at an advanced workshop, she and another student were talking about hunters and deer. Their voices escalated as they talked of how they would booby-trap the hunters or interfere in violent ways with the hunting. I could only take so much of this before I interrupted.

What about the deer and their life choices? They were forgetting that the deer could think and choose. It wasn't just up to humans what happened in their lives. I recommended that the students concentrate on telepathically communicating to the deer about the hunters and where they would be safe, instead of angering the hunters and causing more resistance and violence toward the deer and themselves. The deer could make their own choices about their life and death. Kate could also visualize a white light of safety around the deer and ask their guardian angels and the devas of the land to protect them.

In nature, there is a balance between predator and prey—an agreement, and a love between them amidst the struggle for survival. Humans are part of the predator–prey agreement. It seems that the odds have been overbalanced with the introduction of high-tech weapons, yet humans remain a part of nature and the whole scheme of things. We can exert a positive influence, without violence, by communicating directly to the animals, even praying to the guiding spirits of the animals for the good of all involved. Sending peaceful thoughts and harmonious images to hunters could help them learn a balanced way of relating with the animals.

Anne had a similar situation with hunters and ducks on the pond on her land. She tried various methods of scaring the ducks away and interfering with the hunters, with mixed results. Her most successful method was communicating telepathically to the ducks and to the devas, or spirits of the land, to guard and guide the ducks. After she did that, the ducks didn't land when the hunters were there, or the hunters would miss the few that did appear, or the ducks wouldn't take off into the air to be shot.

Dawn Hayman relates her experience of hunting and deer:

In this section of New York state, the safe serenity of our farm is rudely interrupted every fall for about six weeks. The cause is deer hunting season. It is very difficult for my partner, Bonnie Reynolds, and me. Our Spring Farm is a haven for animals of all kinds to expand, grow, and be safe.

Although our land is very visibly posted against hunting, we have had hunters in our horse pastures, shooting. Our horses are afraid to go out during that time. There are stories told to us by policemen who have stopped cars with unbelievable things tied to the backs, like a donkey shot and gutted. The people thought it was a deer! This whole territory becomes a shooting range, and we become prisoners within our own lands.

Each year, just before hunting season begins, Bonnie and I broadcast to our deer friends to stay within the posted areas for maximum security. We have several does that love to hang out with our horses.

One day, I was starting up the road when I heard a series of gunshots. They seemed awfully close. I looked over our pastures and saw a buck laboring heavily across our hay field. I turned my truck around and went bombing through the fields. I put my vehicle between the buck and the direction the shots came from. The buck immediately slowed to a limping walk. He knew I was trying to help him.

I asked him if he had been shot. He said, "No, just exhausted from running." I told him to follow me, and I carefully led him over to a wooded area where he'd be safe. I told him to jump the fence and stay in there. Instead he turned and came within twenty-five feet of the truck. He was a gorgeous animal. He thanked me, and I told him not to get this close to people. I explained that if I had a gun, I could just shoot him.

He told me, "You wouldn't do that because you talked to me. Hunters never talk. They just kill. If you were to kill me now, you'd never be able to hear another animal again, and I know you'd never do that. I am safe in your trust." Then he turned, gracefully jumped the fence, and headed into safety. I'll never forget him or his words.

Hunting ends at dusk on the last day of the hunting season. It was just dusk, and I was doing some work in an area parallel to the highway past our farm and our hay fields and the wooded area. I suddenly heard, "We came to thank you." Out of the wooded area stepped a majestic buck. My mouth fell open. Then, as if in a well-rehearsed chorus line, other deer began stepping out and standing in the open field, all in a row. We lost count at thirty-one, and there were more behind them. I heard cars stopping on the road. Hunters poised for their last chance. But there I stood in the way as darkness fell and hunting season ended. Once again they were safe.

A woman called me with concerns about the pigeons being killed by cars in a heavily trafficked area of a city. She had tried to communicate to them about the danger, but they continued to return to the street despite her warnings and didn't seem to listen to her or understand.

Tuning in to the pigeons, I felt their lack of concern over the traffic danger. They had their own world; they were accustomed to surviving independently of human direction, and had no need to listen to the woman. Their flock was a group of beings who worked together, and they each seemed to survive as a member of the flock, even if their bodies were killed on the street. The idea of being "saved" was totally foreign to them. In order to communicate well with them, Margie would have to assume their viewpoint; by attaining harmony with their lives, her communication would be appropriate.

Nature has carefully engineered the predator–prey cycle. Animals (as spirit) generally leave their bodies as soon as a predator pounces. Even though the body keeps functioning and may struggle to get away, often the spirit will not return and take over conscious control unless the predator has gone away for a while. The body may be in a state of shock, with a dazed or faraway look, until the spirit decides it's okay to rejoin the body. When I have interfered with my cats' hunting escapades and rescued chipmunks, rabbits, mice, or birds, the little animals need some coaxing to return to their bodies, even though uninjured physically. Nature also takes care of prey animals by triggering a release of endorphins into the body as the predator attacks, so no pain is felt after the initial blow.

Yohinta, our tortoise-shell cat, is a skillful huntress. We have a rule in our household that the cats must kill and eat their prey animals outside, not in the house. My office windows faced the pathway that Yohinta regularly took when she was bringing critters back into the yard. Sometimes I became involved in the life-and-death struggle.

I have tried to rescue chipmunks and release them before Yohinta or the other cats kill them. Often, despite my good intentions, they would run away from me, their rescuer, and scurry back under the nose or legs of the cat—expecting, almost asking, to be killed. It appears that a smaller cat predator that you know is preferable to a giant human predator that you don't know! The predator–prey ritual is programmed into the species and agreed upon as part of natural living for those involved. Human rescuers may seem like an anomaly in the natural process.

Instead of interfering physically when Yohinta parades past my window with a chipmunk in her mouth, I have found that working telepathically eliminates a messy struggle and is much more effective.

Cats often drop and pounce on an animal a number of times after they've made their catch. Chipmunks are often in shock after a cat attacks, and don't try to run away when the cat releases them. I have concentrated on helping chipmunks to stay conscious, sending them an image of running up a tree to get away as soon as the cat drops them. The result has been that I have seen Yohinta walk away disappointed and heard chipmunks chattering from high in the trees after their escape.

Nonhuman companions have also taught me to look at the relationship of predator and prey in a totally different way than my human-acculturated viewpoint. Sherman also hunts and eats a variety of animals. Once, while I was walking in the yard, feeling emotionally exhausted after a hard day, Sherman ran up to me with a bird in his mouth. He placed it at my feet, backed away and said, "Here, this will make you feel better." Instead of trying to pounce on it again, he sat calmly watching me as I picked it up. I thanked him warmly for his gift and his thoughtfulness. The little bird, scared but unhurt, quivered in my hands. As I opened my hands to let the bird fly away, Sherman watched quietly, blinking a smile to me. My spirits were definitely uplifted by his gift.

Another time, I was roused from my desk by the high-pitched squealing of a baby rabbit. Sherman was flinging the rabbit up in the air and leaping on it. While I knew that the spirit was disconnected from the body and this was the predator–prey agreement, I couldn't stand watching or hearing the scenario. I tried to get the bunny away from Sherman as he tossed it, only to have him snatch it more quickly than I could. I asked Sherman to release it, telling him that he didn't need this rabbit. As I reached to take it from him, he growled at me and told me it was his rabbit. I then stood quietly, asking him to release it. He looked at me, with the rabbit in his mouth, and said that I didn't understand. He loved this bunny. It was his friend, and he loved him. He let go and caressed the rabbit to graphically demonstrate his affection.

As he did that, I experienced, right through the core of my body, the love that exists between predator and prey—the agreement that is as old as life on

Earth. I walked away with a new comprehension as I heard Sherman complete the ritual and eat the rabbit.

On a television program called "Wild America," a mountain lion was shown with a deer he had killed. The big cat lay next to the deer's head, fondling it and purring. The commentator, Marty Stouffer, mentioned the same thing that Sherman had taught me—how much the mountain lion loved the deer.

Present in most predators is an unspoken gratitude to the animals who nourish them with their lives. This same sentiment is celebrated in the lives of native peoples as they speak to and honor the animals and plants that they kill. Modern, urbanized people, who are remote from the life and death of the animals and plants that they eat, or hunters who do not communicate with animals and kill for "sport," lose out spiritually when they put aside this connection.

In my family there are a number of animals who would normally have predator–prey relationships, such as cats with birds and rats, or dogs with chickens and rabbits. The "prey" animals are assured that they are safe in their habitats, or that living among the "predators" is possible. The predator animals are coached to guard and take care of the other family members, looking at them as fellow beings rather than as prey.

When I got Igor, the anole lizard, Chico San became very interested in him and would jump next to his terrarium, which frightened Igor into the corner. Chico persisted, despite being chased off when I spotted her. I told Igor he was safe and Chico could not get him, and I felt them develop an understanding with each other. I could see from one angle how it created a more natural environment for him, where there would be predators, and of course, he was safe and could hide behind his bountiful potted ivy plant. But he couldn't keep running or hiding in safer places, as he would in a wild situation, and this was stressful.

At Igor's first advanced workshop, several people learned from Chico San and Igor about the love and friendship they felt for each other. As the people talked about it, Chico San rolled over, meowed upside down with her mouth open, batted at the person near her, and asked, "Can the lizard come out now?" Later, I put Igor's terrarium in a place where Chico could not jump up next to it, as he was being chased from warming himself on the bottom heater and wasn't relaxing enough to eat well. Moving his habitat to a cat-proof area created a better balance in our domestic predator–prey relationships.

Igor had a peaceful kinship with the flies, crickets, and other insects that I gathered for him to eat. They watched each other and communicated, understanding and accepting their relationship as predator and prey. It is a natural but remarkable connection. Obviously, all creatures try to survive, but there is also the understanding of how we are to exchange with each other, even unto death.

Jim Dietz wrote this poem during an advanced workshop, as we communed with wild animals and plants next to a stream in a forested valley I call the Alder Cathedral:

In the Alder Cathedral
In silence the word
Read not by a priest
But by a large black bird.

Learn and read
Your lessons of culture
And the lessons of life
From a turkey vulture.

His lesson is simple
Yet also profound
Whatever may fall
Stays not long on the ground.

He flies treetops in quiet
In air that is sweet
All death holds new life
The circle complete.

VEGETARIAN OR CARNIVORE?

A person who was writing a magazine article about communication with animals called me. She asked if I was a vegetarian. Her righteous, demanding tone created a feeling of being invaded, and I asked her why she wanted to know. She said that she would not interview any animal communicator who ate meat.

I immediately thought of all the people I knew, those who came to lectures and workshops or read my publications, who loved animals but still ate animal flesh as part of their diet. Even though I was vegetarian at the time and could have left it at that, I felt that this interviewer might benefit from understanding more of what animals felt about being eaten, and some discoveries from working with human nutritional testing.

As I tried to discuss this with her, she became very frustrated that I could think there was any other possibility but vegetarianism and hung up. She called back in a few minutes to apologize and said she felt this discussion was futile and could go on forever. This shows how intense people can become about the subject of eating or not eating animals. I'd like to offer my own experience on the subject, and most of all, I'd like to put forward the animals' viewpoints.

I was born and raised in Chicago, Illinois. We consumed meat from various animals daily. No one ever thought about eating any other way, as this was the standard American diet at the time. I, like most urban dwellers, never thought about where meat came from, only vaguely associating it with real, living, breathing animals. I remember, as a teenager, being appalled when I realized that the "liver" that we ate was the actual bodily organ, the liver. I had just thought of it as another piece of meat, that food of ambiguous origin.

After I left home at age eighteen, my meager income lessened my consumption of meat, but it wasn't until I was twenty-nine, when I began to study nutrition and learn Touch for Health and other body balancing techniques, that I considered changing my diet drastically. After reading extensively about the nutritional properties of foods, I decided to become vegetarian. I felt it was more wholesome, of a higher vibration, and more ethical than a nonvegetarian diet. For years, I experimented with fasting, cleansing diets and colonics, fruitarianism, and even breatharianism (not eating anything but air), which was a disaster in the Los Angeles smog! I continually learned more about my body and how it functioned.

Along with doing animal communication work, teaching body movement and dance, being a performing artist, and doing spiritual counseling,

I worked for years in a holistic health center, doing applied kinesiology, nutritional testing, and body balancing. There I learned firsthand how the dietary requirements that might provide energy and good health varied widely among individuals.

Humans appeared to function well on a wide assortment of diets, with diverse vegetable and meat combinations. Their dietary needs changed as they and their life stresses changed. Some people never needed to eat meat and functioned better on plant food alone. Others did much better eating some meat, and even developed nutritional deficiencies and energy loss if they abstained. Sometimes these people would need to eat little or no meat, sometimes more. I tested hundreds of people extensively with applied kinesiology muscle testing and found that their health and energy levels visibly improved on various diets. It appeared that humans were not carnivores or herbivores, but omnivores. The human digestive system combined meat- and plant-eating capacities, and obviously, people all over the globe had survived on a variety of plant and animal food combinations for millennia.

To argue that humans are herbivores by nature, and hence should be vegetarian, did not seem to be the case. More to the point is that a meat-laden diet derived from unhealthy animals who are loaded with antibiotics, steroids, and pesticides and who suffer in mass animal farming conditions needs reforming for both human and animal welfare.

Research by nutritionists has shown that people have different body types, evolved over centuries from the climates and foods of their ancestors. Tropical people could exist on a fruit and vegetable diet that wasn't available to northern peoples and wouldn't supply the necessary energy for living in a harsher climate.

My recent ancestors were Slavic and Germanic—people who ate a vegetable, grain, and meat diet. In our family, the women tend to be borderline anemic. I had always handled that by eating liver or other red meat once or twice a month when my body seemed to ask for it, and generally felt much better as a result. As a vegetarian, for years I tried a multitude of iron and B-vitamin-rich vegetable foods and nutritional supplements, and included eggs in my diet, but my body seemed unable to utilize these sources of iron and other nutrients that I had previously derived from meat. After about seven years as a vegetarian, I found myself growing weaker and more irritable. I also found I was developing a righteous, judg-mental attitude toward nonvegetarians—a sure sign that something was out of balance in me.

Eating vegetables is necessary for health, but eating certain kinds in too great a quantity, while good for cleansing the body, may lead to imbalance, just as eating too much meat or too much of any one thing can. A person on an imbalanced vegetarian diet can be too delicate and oversensitive, feeling their own and others' pain and emotions in an exaggerated or intensified way. Eating too much meat can cause clogging of body functions and too much density, leading toward a lack of sensitivity to others' feelings and to lighter vibrations, emotions, and spiritual realities. Finding what works best for each person requires communication with one's body and one's food.

I asked my guiding spirits and the spirits of the animals and the Earth to assist me in finding my dietary balance. I got a clear message to eat from the sea, both sea vegetables and fish. When I did, I felt much calmer and stronger and able to do my work better, and the rigid, righteous sentiments disap-peared. In times of severe stress or spiritual transformation, images of cows planted themselves in front of me, and I was invited to eat them and share their grounded energy. When I ate meat from cows who were fed organically, I felt strong and restored, like someone saved from starvation. Instead of feeling guilty and berating myself for killing and eating the cows, I felt a lov-ing gratitude and communion with them from sharing their substance.

For several years, I was directed to eat beef about once a month, usually right before I began menstruating, and to eat fish from one to four times a month. I wished I could be vegetarian, as it seemed "purer," but I didn't thrive on it. Gradually, the need for meat became less, until my diet was vegetarian once again. After a hiatus of two and a half years, my body's demand for meat resurfaced. I pushed it away for months, trying to substitute beans, tofu, grains, or anything that might calm the desire. When I finally allowed myself to eat beef for one meal, I experienced again the feeling of full nourishment, relief, and grounded balance, in harmony with the cow and the world.

So, because I must take care of my body properly as my most intimate animal friend, I cannot join the wholly (holy!?) vegetarian group, about which the person who called will write articles! For most people, including myself, whole grains and organic vegetables can be the bulk of a healthy diet.

But, like other omnivores such as ravens, coyotes, raccoons, and rats, humans are made to survive by eating just about anything, depending on where they live and what's available.

I give thanks to all the plants or animals who give me their energy to nourish my life. I always feel the energy coming back and the joy of the plant or animal, body and spirit, in consciously exchanging with me. They never seem to blame or get righteous, as humans do, about the subject. Being raised as an urban dweller, I am not geared to kill my own animals for food, although I remember how much it was a natural part of the cycle of living in other lifetimes. If it were necessary, I could probably adopt Native American ways of killing by first asking the animals for their lives and honoring and revering their gifts.

In one of my "have to be vegetarian" times, naturally, I wanted Michel to do the same. To avoid offending me when he occasionally felt his body needed meat, he would eat out in a restaurant. Once Michel came home, admitting that he had a chicken taco. Chiding him, I asked if he would kill and eat any of our chickens. I was raising bantam chicks at the time, and among them was a very small, frail, Silver Sebright hen called Spinky. Michel quipped, "Yes, I'd have a Spinky sandwich." I instantly visualized dainty Spinky, with her head and feet poking out from between two slices of bread, and we rolled with laughter at the picture. It helped us to put humor into an all too serious subject.

Raul was part Native American, and had been raised in a traditional way to hunt deer and other animals for food. When I met him, he lived with a vegetarian woman, who felt that hunting was unacceptable and that Raul should become a vegetarian. Raul felt a communion with the animals that he killed, and hunting was an important part of his life. As this was a major issue for both of them, he meditated deeply upon it.

He asked the spirit of the animals to give him a sign, whether he should hunt again or not. He took his gun into the forest and sat quietly on the ground. A large buck appeared about ten feet away and stared at him directly for a long time. He clearly knew that he was meant to kill the buck, and did so with the deer's full consent. He had his answer.

Darren raised some geese, which his father intended to kill for Thanksgiving. Darren communicated to the geese when and how this would happen, and they did not object. When his father approached the chopping block, the geese, one by one, calmly laid their heads down to give their bodies.

Peter Caddy told me that when the Findhorn Garden community began raising animals for food, people who were versed in animal communication would ask the goats or chickens for permission before slaughter. The animals' answers varied. Some felt it was okay now, and others felt they needed more time on the Earth. The people honored the animals' wishes and waited until they were willing to move on from their bodies before killing them.

My experience communicating with animals who are raised to be killed for food is that most of them accept their finale, as long as they get to lead a good life, and their death is not traumatic or filled with confusion, fear, and suffering. Most spirits who incarnate understand and accept the type of life that is experienced by their chosen animal form, whether they are wild predator or prey, domestic companion, or food animal. They are generally willing to let go when it is their time to die.

I have also experienced the suffering of animals in factory farming situations whose lives are unnaturally confined and deprived. When animals around them are crying in pain and fear as they are roughly transported and pushed along the assembly line for slaughter, they, too, are often filled with confusion and terror. They do not deserve a death like that. It is up to us to evoke attitudes of dignity and gratitude when killing the animals who nourish us. We are responsible, as caregivers, for the quality of the lives and deaths of the animals and plants that we raise to eat. This is part of our communication and communion with fellow beings of other species.

Death is part of the natural cycle of life on the Earth. Our own bodies continually kill millions of microbes and other living beings, such as parasites, to enhance survival. We unavoidably trample insects and other life forms under our feet as we walk and carry out our other activities. As animal guardians, we have to control or exterminate parasites or pests of our animal companions, such as ticks, fleas, and flies.

Many people are very disconnected from the plants and animals that they eat. They are not aware of the consciousness of animals and plants, or the vital sharing of energy fields that occurs when you raise plants and animals and kill them for nourishment. Both animals and plants can suffer at the hands of insensitive humans. They can also willingly give of themselves when you honor their lives and thank them for helping you. I have experienced this with vegetables in the garden, that they grow abundantly with loving care and give their heightened nutritional energy to our family. They are always willing to be picked if I explain that we need them for our nourishment.

Eating is a form of becoming one with others, sharing their qualities and their lives. Honoring their gift creates a continuance of positive energy, and evokes smiles among the spirits who gave their plant or animal forms for sustenance.

People have asked me if eating lighter, vegetarian foods doesn't raise consciousness and help you to be more in tune with animals. It depends on the person. If people have accumulated toxic waste from eating improperly, a lighter plant diet cleanses their bodies and clears their mental and spiritual energies so that they can be more sensitively attuned to others' communication. Other people would do well on a fruit or vegetable diet for only a short time and then need to be grounded and supported by eating some animal food. Eating meat doesn't automatically make you dull and insensitive to telepathic communication. For me, eating meat sometimes, when my body needs it, clears my mental focus, grounds my energies, and helps me to be more connected to animals and sharper in my telepathic abilities.

Some people act as if prey animals, who are herbivores, are more ethical, evolved, or just nicer than predator animals, who are carnivores or omnivores. This is not a realistic view of how the Earth actually maintains its balance. We live in a great recycling center, where life forms eat other life forms in a continual cycle of death and rebirth. Death and killing have to be faced and accepted as a part of life, if one is not to become emotionally disturbed. A woman once told me, proudly, that she was coaxing a robin that she had rescued to eat vegetable food instead of worms, as if the robin's consumption of worms was a crime and being vegetarian was the only acceptable way. Prey are not holier or more worthy to survive than predators. It is good to accept who you are, even if that means that you are a part of the rest of nature and kill for survival.

With more consciousness of what we are eating, whether animal, plant, or mineral, we might change our approach to the growing and harvesting of our food. Instead of the widespread practice of loading plants and animals with pesticides and other chemicals, or confining animals to cages and inhibiting their natural patterns, we would tend to farm organically and care lovingly for the animals we eat by providing a good life and clean death for them.

Plants and animals that are nurtured well, and that understand human actions through good communication from their guardians and caregivers, live and grow better and give their bodies with love. Animals and plants are aware of their spiritual nature and know that they continue after death. While they are alive, it is important that we honor their right to be and choose, even if they have a short life, as do most of their wild prey animal relations.

In all the ways that people benefit from animals' lives, the answer to the questions of ethicalness is to ask the animals. Find out their purpose for being on the Earth, and learn whether they are happy living alongside and relating to or serving humans. In dialogue with our animal friends, we can find mutually beneficial courses to take together. In the course of evolution, it may come about that we do not need to eat or depend on other life forms to survive. But now, we need to balance the factors in the predator–prey dance, as they exist, and intimately share each other's lives in the symbiotic circle of life.

WHen a GReaT one DIes

A PRINCE.
Bringing light to a world of confusion.
Life is the composition of musical notes of the spirit,
He was a symphony.
Once touched by his musical performance,
Always remembered and carried in your soul.

Feeling his presence was like coming home to yourself.
In times of confusion, when direction was needed,
He would offer his light for help.
Sharing came as easy as a heartbeat,
And as freely as the wind.

A free spirit in a land made more free by his presence,
He slipped through time like a feather through the air
Gently moving on.

His body now distanced from our touch,
His breath now distanced from our skin,
But the symphony plays on as purely as before,
There for all who wish to hear.
Gone, but not far, a true prince and guide,
His resonance lingering in the souls of all that shared with him.

What a beautiful sound.
What a beautiful soul.
What a beautiful memory.

—Dawn Hayman, January 25, 1993: In Memory of Pasha

Pasha, our beloved Afghan friend, was always a strong, passionate, noble individual, straightforward in his self-expression. His love for life and people was intense and exuberant. As one of the people who knew and loved him, Nancy Sondel described Pasha as "so unforgettable, so full of soul/love; open, expansive, majestic, evolved to such a fine state and, like Toby [her parakeet friend] and other wise beings, never too refined to *play* joyfully." His death was very difficult.

He loved to leap tall fences in a single bound. At age twelve, though very healthy, he had slowed down and now took rests when we ran on the beach, instead of racing nonstop for hours. He felt the changes in his body, and he didn't like it. The late summer weather was hot, depressing his energy and usually ebullient outlook, and he let me and a few advanced workshop participants at our home know that he was thinking of leaving his body soon. He felt a lot of the fun had gone out of life as his body aged.

Since I first met him, Pasha was the most special friend in the world to me. Even in his youth, I thought how difficult it would be to have him leave this world, and it took me years to reconcile myself to his eventual death. When he became dissatisfied with his aging form, I honored his feelings and got myself as prepared as possible. Rana, his daughter, who adored Pasha, became anxious about his potential decision to leave. So I started to take her on special "sister" walks alone, to get her accustomed to doing things without Pasha, and I talked to her about how it would be. She began to exhibit more independence and acceptance of what Pasha was planning.

One afternoon of that year, I found Pasha in the yard, covered with leaves, shaking, and unable to move. I called Michel, and together we did some healing energy work with Pasha for about ten minutes, until he was able to get up and walk around. The aftereffects of this stroke were that he walked around shakily that day and did not eat, but after a few days, he returned to normal.

Then, a pea-sized nodule in his scrotum that I had noticed for months began to grow and become hard and sore to the touch. It was dark on the outside and, on scanning it internally, it appeared to be a malignant tumor. After weeks of keeping an eye on it, Pasha began to yelp when I examined it. He didn't want me to apply any healing herbs or touch it at all. We discussed what this meant. I did not want to have to take Pasha to the vet for surgery if I didn't have to. I told Pasha that having cancer could be a very protracted, painful way of leaving the body.

I asked him to let me do some healing work on the growth, which was now as big as a golf ball. He agreed and allowed me to transmit healing energy without touching his body. In a few days, the growth burst open and, unlike an abscess draining pus, it exuded a foul material that smelled like decayed flesh. For days it drained, and Pasha let me spray it with a healing mineral and herbal spray. After a few weeks, the growth shrunk to the size of a raisin, and Pasha let me move it around without any protest. The closing of that avenue to death brought relief to us all. This incident helped us to be ready, as much as anyone can be, when the inevitable departure time came.

I meditated on Pasha's situation and got from the angels that Pasha's body had the potential to live to age sixteen, due to his strong genetic inheritance and good health. It was up to Pasha to decide whether or not he wanted to continue life in his current body. That winter, Pasha decided he would stay, as long as the following summer was cool. That next summer, in 1991, was the coolest and foggiest we had known in our time here since 1984, and Pasha looked and felt great. At age fourteen, he acted livelier than he had at age twelve, despite having lost his hearing and being stiffer in the rear end.

In his last year, as dogs who are approaching their departure often do, he slept very deeply and looked groggy when he woke up. He also wanted to be close to us more frequently and desired more affection, something an independent Afghan doesn't usually have much time for when they are younger. We both appreciated the abundant massage and hugging sessions. For the last month of his life, I cautioned Michel to look after Pasha more, both around the yard and on walks, to make sure he wasn't in trouble anywhere, as sometimes he acted a bit confused. I felt he might have a stroke.

I made the three-hour drive home on Sunday, January 17, 1993, after giving a workshop in San Martin, California. At 9 P.M. I arrived to the greeting of Pasha and Rana. I fished for two liver bars to offer as a coming-home treat. When I gave one to Pasha, he had a hard time finding it. The outside light shone on his beginning cataracts, and he was a bit disoriented. This was the last food this inveterate chowhound was to enjoy on Earth—a moment now stored as a poignant memory.

On Monday morning, we found Pasha moaning and shivering on his side on the driveway, unable to get up. We took him indoors to warm him and do healing. Unlike Pasha's first stroke several years before, this time he lay immobilized, despite our healing ministrations—including the Bach Flower tincture called Rescue Remedy, and a homeopathic remedy.

After a short time indoors, Pasha struggled to get up and wanted to be outside. He found it hard to breathe. We placed him on a cot on the deck outside our living room windows and covered him with a blanket. For six hours he didn't move from the spot. Periodically, I squirted water and homeopathic remedies into his mouth and administered healing energy. Finally his shivering stopped, and he closed his eyes and slept. That afternoon he struggled to get up, and with our help, he managed to go off to pee and defecate, falling on his face several times. The effort was painful and exhausting as he fought to regain control of his body.

Sue Goodrich's former canine companion and our very good friend, Hawk, who had departed from his Siberian husky body over a year previous, appeared with his group of Indian spirit friends and said that Pasha would be gone within twenty-four hours. They would help him make the transition. It was not to be so. Pasha was not ready and struggled on, and later Hawk revised the estimate to forty-eight hours, which came to pass.

The next day Pasha had yet more difficulty moving. I consulted with our friend and holistic veterinarian in Virginia, Joyce Harman, about the prognosis. She thought that while it was possible he could slowly recover, in her experience, this severe of a stroke in an elderly dog usually led to more strokes and eventual death. She recommended another homeopathic remedy to alternate with what I was already giving him.

We helped Pasha back to the large dog cottage, prepared with extra soft cushions and blankets. He did not like us having to assist his movement, but without it he fell on his face with pain and indignity. A storm was pounding the rain down, so we tucked him into his dry, safe house for the night. The specially built cottage, which measured 3-1/2 feet wide by 7 feet long by 6 feet high, was on the deck right outside our bedroom. The large windows facing our sliding glass door allowed us to remain in view of each other. Rana accompanied Pasha and bravely stayed with him through his painful transition.

Pasha loved his body and the life he shared with us. It was hard for him to believe that this was the end of his life. We told him that we did not want him to suffer so and spiritually released him. I reviewed our life together, but in his struggle, it didn't seem to help him to leave. Michel played him a concert on his classical guitar while I sang, prayed, and worked with a special healing crystal. Michel and I both saw Pasha running in the sky and in meadows on the Earth that he had loved. I asked all the angels and powers to help him to leave.

Black wings of night
White wings of death
Storm raging, dark moon
Pasha dying
Meeting his Gethsemane
I wait
I let him go
The love of Earth
Tugs at the spirit
Strings must be detached
Slowly
Erratically
He meets his friends
Of other realms
We wait
We watch
The black wings of night
Meet the white wings of death.

January 20, 1993; 3 A.M.

That night Pasha suffered a number of strokes. Michel and I visited him often to soothe him and administer remedies. When he screamed in agony and his body stiffened against the wall in a particularly severe episode, I called Michel to be with Pasha as he departed. Pasha pulled through, despite the pain and shock to his body. I cried, and Michel had to leave, as he felt he was going to vomit and faint. Pasha did not deserve this suffering. I was amazed that the intensity of the brain cells exploding did not kill him. Pasha's vitality and will to live kept him going. It also felt as if the pain trapped him in his body as he struggled against it.

The sun, just moving from the sign of Capricorn to Aquarius, and the moon being in Capricorn, with its strong Earth energy, seemed to accentuate the attachment to Earth and the tenacious struggle to survive. The moon was almost new, its waning energy echoing death. I knew that if Pasha were not dead by morning, I would have to call the vet to help him depart. During the night, I talked it over again with Pasha. We faced the reality that even if he continued living, the strokes would probably continue, and he would stumble and fall. This was not a life for our noble, passionate friend.

I lay on the floor in earshot of the dog cottage, fully clothed so I could go to Pasha quickly if he needed me. At 6 A.M. on Wednesday, January 20, I was amazed when I heard Pasha get up. The rain and wind, howling ferociously through most of the night, had abated. Pasha walked without falling, managed to take a drink on his own, and went to the garden to pee. He wanted to be outside, but the rain began again, and I urged him back to his cottage. With great effort, he made his way in and collapsed on his pillows, breathing with great labor, never to rise with his body again.

I prepared to give him the Bach Flower essences, Oak and Walnut, to assist him to make his decision to let go. I wanted Pasha's release approval before I called our local vet's office. When I went in to see him again, he had thought over our whole dialogue about his life and purpose and his deteriorating body. He already had received the balancing vibrations of the Bach Flower essences I was going to give him. He was now ready to go and needed help. The vet could come at 2:30. As Pasha's bodily suffering became more intense, all of us were more than ready for the end of this.

The storm raged with fury. It was the windiest yet, in a season of severe storms. The large pines swayed and bent toward the ground. It rained heavily in the two days of Pasha's passion and death. I felt strongly that the Spirits who loved Pasha were hailing Pasha's life and his imminent death. I felt the Earth would rift with his presence being taken away.

Our local veterinarian, Bob Fisher, was very gentle and kind. We carried Pasha on his blanket to the cot on the deck underneath the eaves. After the vet administered the sedative, and we held and kissed Pasha good-bye, his soft groans quieted, and his eyes closed as he slipped out of his body. Pasha's struggle ended. With the final injection, the last strings attaching Pasha to his body were severed, and he sailed into the sky to the south, through the veil of this dimension to the welcoming arms of his spirit friends. As he sailed past my face, I heard him say, "I didn't realize it was so easy." Our strong bond, and his love for his body and life on Earth, had made his departure very difficult. Even when he said he was ready, all the ties did not unravel, and the merging of body and spirit would not dissolve.

We moved from Pasha's lifeless form, and Michel and I hugged each other and the vet. The reality of Pasha's death brought Michel to tears for the first time. We cried in each other's arms and then collapsed with the strain and relief over the conclusion of his suffering. We couldn't have taken another night of this torture, waiting for Pasha to be set free. Within an hour of Pasha's death at 2:50 P.M. on January 20, 1993, the howling winds and heavy rains calmed. As I thought about how the weather followed his transition, Pasha replied, "I'm a passionate person." He always was a strong, dramatic character.

Many friends awaited Pasha's return to the spiritual realm after his canine life of fourteen and a half years. Among them was my father, who left his body in 1984; he exclaimed what a beautiful, wonderful dog Pasha was and how glad he was to meet him. Shortly after exiting his body, Pasha reviewed all his lives, which have mainly been in human form. He had become an Afghan to be with me, and he lived his life as a dog to the hilt. From that point, he showed me his image as the human male form he had in a previous life. He said he loved us and loved his life as a dog. His potent energy required a life full of adventure and variety. He demanded it, and we helped provide it. He let Michel know what a friend and brother he was, always, and sent love to everyone in the family. He appeared to be at a party, a large gathering of joyful friends, which on Earth was his favorite activity.

During Pasha's agony, I could not feel where Pasha hurt, as I normally do with animals. I could see by his expressions of pain that his head and spine were affected, but I was shielded from experiencing it as it happened. After his death, I suffered severe head pains and nausea, and Michel had a sore throat, pinpointing the areas of Pasha's suffering. Sleep relieved my pains.

Michel battled the onset of flu symptoms brought on by the loss. We were exhausted and relieved to be through the suffering and so glad we could enlist our veterinarian's assistance.

Rana, Pasha's eleven-year-old daughter, stood by bravely through his struggle. She had been preparing for his departure since his earlier thought of leaving, more than two years before. She had always lived for Pasha, adoring his every step. During his struggles with dying, she stayed with him in the dog cottage—patient, sending him love, unafraid of the high winds of the raging storm, which usually would distress her.

Whenever I returned from the dog cottage throughout Tuesday night's struggle, Sherman sat in my lap, sending Pasha and me his blessings and love. Rana couldn't watch the departure. She had already given all she could. She would not gaze at or even sniff his dead body, as she passed it on the deck. It was done. Heyoka came to the window, shocked when he realized what was happening. Yohinta was anxious. Chico San focused on healing and comforting us. Sherman continued to offer his wisdom and support.

The void after his departure was accentuated by the sudden calmness of the surroundings, so long raging under storm winds and pelting rains. Pasha's body lay outside on the cot where he left it. I could not bury his body right after his death, as I did with most of my departed animal friends. I needed to see and touch and feel his soft hair and velvet face, and absorb the reality that his body, which appeared to be simply asleep, was truly dead. I had bravely let go of him as spirit; now I needed to let go of his beautiful form, graceful and noble even unto death.

Well, Pasha, here we are, left to grapple with our feelings and our memories and your absence—a vacuum, along with the unreal picture it creates. You were Number One, maybe always will be. I know as we keep in touch, we will all learn and grow. But what in life can ever prepare one for this loss? We take it as it comes. What a blow, after a life of joy together. But still *life is*, and we are never apart—friends forever.

At 10:20 P.M. on January 20, seven and a half hours after Pasha's demise, with his body still outside on the cot, I found my feelings change from a reluctance to bury him to a sudden repulsion: "Why am I keeping around a dead, stiff body?" Time to bury the dead and move on. We planned to have our burial ceremony the next day, with a few friends.

The storm that raged during Pasha's dying created flooding that came just short of disaster levels in many areas before it receded. Pasha's struggle and our feelings did the same. Tuesday night, before Pasha's death, Michel had a dream about carrying excess baggage. I had a similar dream on Wednesday night after his death. We got the message to let go of the physical form and emotional attachments and move on.

Why can't we go together, live and die at the same time, so there's not this pain and wrenching? Of course, that's not the game we've organized in this variety-store dimension. We come and go, meeting many different beings, to experience life's plentiful adventures.

When Pasha communicated to me from the spiritual realm, I wondered why he identified himself with an image of his former human form. He explained that he fully completed his life as an Afghan hound and left it, and he wanted to help me do the same. He said that he'd always be part of me. That I know.

Our relationship would have been so different if he had been human. I often said that if Pasha had been a man, I'd have had two husbands! Michel and Pasha were best buddies. Having an Afghan form made a wonderful, socially acceptable threesome. When Pasha was about seven months old, having been with me about a month, he looked at me very intensely, came over and began to breathe into my ear and lick it gently and passionately. Gently pushing him away, I told him then that he was not human, and that having a sexual relationship as two different species would not work. He would have to erase those feelings and behavior toward me. He immediately relaxed, and only once, a short time later, did those feelings come up again for him, to be quickly controlled.

Pasha's deep intensity, compassion, love for life, humor, and wisdom charmed all who met his gaze. From my first meeting with Pasha, I fell in love. His brightness, amiability, zest for life, freedom, integrity, and beauty bonded me to him forever. I loved him so much that when I met Michel in July 1980, I told him honestly that, as much as I loved him, I loved Pasha more than anyone. Michel gently, wisely, lovingly responded that one day I might love him as much. He was right, and Pasha was his buddy from the start.

On the morning of January 21, I dug Pasha's grave on a hill near the Fairy Ring. After I brushed Pasha's hair gently for the last time, I labored to carry his sixty-five pounds to gently lay his body in its final resting place. Michel had to be away that morning, but he and our friend and neighbor, Elizabeth, planned to attend the ceremony that afternoon. Rana slept in the dog cottage, wanting to be quiet and not see Pasha's body. I went to collect flowers from around the garden for his grave. My baskets were soon filled with flowers and sprigs of trees and bushes that jumped out and offered themselves. I discovered that some Shasta daisies and one agapanthus grew out of season for this purpose. I felt their spiritual knowing, unbound by linear time. I heard again and again, "Take me. I want to be part of Pasha's grave." When I asked a Douglas iris if I could pick it, she replied, "Of course you can take me. We loved Pasha." With that thought, I received images, from the flowers' perspective, of Pasha walking around the yard and lifting his leg. I felt the love of the plants toward their animal companions and the harmony and unity existing among them. They all contributed their life to each other.

The turkey vultures that sail over Inverness Ridge and roost in the trees nearby at night did not appear over Pasha's dead body. I thought of how they smell and see and know the smallest death, how they have circled over a dead shrew on our driveway, or the laid-out body of each of our family rabbits as they died, surging to their mission as supreme recyclers. I asked that none would come over Pasha's laid-out form. No vulture appeared in the sky overhead for the twenty-four hours of his waiting to return to the Earth, even when the skies calmed temporarily. They honored his wholeness and our feelings.

The rain began again, and I covered Pasha's body with a plastic tarp to keep his coat dry for the funeral ceremony. As I waited for Michel to return, I made cards to send to the people who had known and loved Pasha, with special photos of nature scenes, or of Pasha, chosen for each recipient, and variations of this inscription:

During a raging storm brought on by his passion, power, and grace

PRINCE PASHA PAZOO
born August 12, 1978

left the Earth
January 20, 1993

On Thursday, January 21, about twenty-four hours after he died, we gave Pasha's body back to Mother Earth. For the first time since we found him paralyzed on Monday, I felt joy—the joy of his release into the realm of spirit. I placed a walnut and a liver bar, favorite snacks, near his chin, and a few bones he had chewed, near his feet. These tokens helped to complete our lifetime nurturing of him.

We sprinkled flowers over his body and thanked Spirit for his life. I had searched for red flowers to rest near his neck and face, as red was his and my favorite color. I found a few small salvia blossoms, but the universe arranged to send a perfect red bloom for him. Michel had picked up my car from the Honda dealer after it was repaired that morning. The company's custom is to give people a rose after their car has been serviced. He brought a perfect, deep red rose to rest on Pasha's neck.

A deep peace and satisfaction suffused me upon laying Pasha's body in the Earth from which it came and which he loved. I felt, so profoundly, how our bodies are borrowed for a short time. They are Mother Earth's creation, made from her elements. We infuse them with our personalities and our purposes, and use them lovingly or otherwise in our sojourn on Earth. Even if bodies are neglected or abused, when returned to the Earth they are cleansed and healed—aligned freshly, molecules restored for regeneration—just as herbs and other elements from the Earth can cleanse and renew the body while alive. In the end, Mother Earth must take our bodies back, as they belong to her. Mother Earth will heal all and return life from lifeless form.

For a moment, the night before, when I was still attached to Pasha's beautiful body, I entertained the reasoning of freeze-drying bodies. Fortunately, that passed quickly. Then it felt good to love all our family and let Pasha's body rest. He had the most beautiful body with the softest fur, velvet face, wonderful sweet-smelling ears, and deep eyes, the memory of which I cherish.

There would be no more suffering for Pasha. All the effects of aging—the deafness, the slowing down, the aching joints, and the fading vision—are no more. Watching Pasha age, I wrote this poem on December 30, 1992:

Pasha
A once glorious King
Still glorious in spirit

Now the golden furred body
Loses its senses
Steering gone awry
Cutting off from Earthly grasp.

Once you ran and leapt
So recklessly and long
Nonstop drive and joy expressed
In glorious dance.

The feeling of freedom
Immortality of youth.

Sad was I to watch you slow down
Resting on the beach
Stopping to chew a bone
Of deer long dead.

Now you putter
Venturing a short streak of speed
Then slowing to one foot after another.

Where's the Afghan joy
Unbridled ecstasy?

Now deep ensouled
In every hair of gold
A dream of yesterday.

Here you are in dignity
Heading toward fifteen
Ripe years
Hearing stilled
Sight weakening
Earthly connection passing.

You seek comfort as never before
Your independent ways melting

Into cherishing
The closeness of our friendship deep.

Still the young dogs follow you
Recognize your leadership, strength, and wisdom
You offer them a smile
A prick of ears, a play bow and a jump
And on your way.

On your way
The golden light is strong all around you
Your days echo the sunset.

When it comes time
To lay your handsome form into the Earth
The world will shake for having known you.

Prince Pasha
Prince Pasha Pazoo
Leo
King
Lord of Universes Unending.

The earth felt so warm and loving as we blanketed Pasha's body with soil and mounded the grave. The feeling of being incomplete and torn vanished. I felt Mother Earth welcoming her child, her creation, Pasha. As much as Pasha had totally relished life on Earth and struggled in agony as he had to leave, he was now totally welcomed in the spirit realm and in bliss with friends. They had missed him while he was on his mission to assist us here. I felt how beautiful it will be when I, too, return—a soul reunion. Letting his body go, I felt how loving is the Earth, how beautiful the soil, how united we all are in life and death.

His death was not easy, but the experience was profoundly filled with gifts of revelation and deep compassion. I gained more of Pasha's wisdom, love, and understanding for all beings. We certainly had a good life together and shared much in our outlook on life and death.

All the animals offered their presence to give me hope, joy, and love. After the burial, Sherman followed me around and, after getting my thought of how much I would miss kissing Pasha's velvet face, he generously offered his soft, fluffy orange face and neck for me to kiss. Chico San nestled in my arms and comforted and healed my tears. Yohinta offered closeness. Heyoka saw Pasha die and spent a day being very quiet, as they were very close, then appreciated our usual strokes and play. Rana gave me gentle kisses, quietly enduring her loss. I marveled at the animation and beauty of my chicken family, so in contrast to the stiffness of death. Alive and curious, expressive and soft—how much that meant to me. I am surrounded by beautiful beings.

The day after Pasha's burial, the sky cleared and the sun shone brightly for the first time since the onset of his departure. The grave, sprinkled with flowers and sprigs of trees, looked beautiful, restful, and warm. The agapanthus cluster, stalk upright, bloomed freshly as if growing from his grave, and stayed that way for months! The flowers rejoiced at Pasha's return to Earth. They are born and relinquish their forms so gracefully.

How deeply I felt the love of all forms of life for each other and the intimate exchange of coexistence. On Tuesday, January 19, my body had felt the need to eat meat to balance and strengthen it through Pasha's struggle. On eating an organic hamburger, I felt so supported and loved by the cow who gave its energy to me. The vegetables also gave me their rootedness, strength, and vital connection to air, water, sun, and soil. Throughout this transition, it became crystal clear how we all need each other to be complete.

Pasha had played with neighbor dogs the week before. In his last few years he had more time for other dogs, as he slowed down and wasn't so busy racing here and there. All his life, even after he was neutered, Pasha would stand and look at male dogs with the erect pose of a challenger, not with the intention to fight, but to ensure they recognized him as King before he relaxed and gave them his blessing. Most dogs revered him and followed him around as leader and mentor. A golden one of Earth, full of confidence and vitality, nothing deterred him. The only time he was distressed was when aging took away his hearing and his stamina, and he adjusted with dignity to each.

Pasha always asked forthrightly for what he wanted. He expected life to be good, and it was. He deserved the best. When he was young, I searched for safe places for him to run free. How he relished his freedom, telling us of his adventures! Why would he be a dog, unless he could experience life to the limit of his capacities and be understood for who he was? He chose to be with me. I am honored and blessed for his appearance and his communion. We shared the passion of life in the world together. All the Earth celebrated Pasha's coming and going.

People often thought he was not full Afghan. His genetic inheritance harked back to the stockier, stronger build of the mountain Afghans of Afghanistan, not the refined thinness of many American show Afghans. In a book I found a photo of an Afghan imported to England from Afghanistan who looked exactly like him. When people asked about his breeding, I told them he was a kangazelle—his father was a kangaroo and his mother was a gazelle. He ran and sprang into the air like no other dog I have ever seen. He yelped in high hound pitch as he chased deer. Deer were the most electrifying. Rabbits and squirrels deserved a chase, but did not elicit the intense yelps.

In his last year, as he slowed down, deer did not even interest him. He'd look up, start to run, and turn back. Once when a deer crossed our path, and he appeared not to notice, I was shocked. In earlier times, if leashed, he would leap when deer appeared and almost pull our arms from their sockets in his trying to begin the chase. If free, he would race for miles, returning happy from the pursuit.

Years ago, Pasha and Rana frequently detoured at a certain place in the woods to gnaw on the bones and hide of a deer who had died there. After two years, Pasha brought me the whitened skull of a young buck that has since had a special place in the garden.

I don't think that I'll repeat the experience of having such a born-free, male Afghan. I lived to find places for our dogs, especially Pasha, to safely run free. When we visited New York City in 1979, I found an old deserted highway on the West End, near where we stayed, and let him exercise there. It went on for miles, and Pasha, as usual, ran off ahead of me. One morning, I caught up to him in time to see him race across an intersecting highway that was alive with cars. I screamed, and workmen caught him on the other side of the highway and brought him back to me. Afghans are like cats in many ways, and Pasha surely had nine lives.

When we moved from Los Angeles to the woods in 1984, my decision to rent the house was sealed when I saw the wooded trails at the end of our driveway. To walk instead of having to drive to parks to run the dogs was the ultimate luxury. We let the dogs run free on our walks. Pasha and Rana would sometimes go off together for many hours, coming back smelling like clams from the beach four miles away. Several times, people picked up Pasha and called us. I worried about his being stolen or mistreated, but he said he always checked out the people and knew they'd take him home or call me to pick him up. He never got lost, even when we traveled and he ran free all around the country.

We were careful to walk on the seashore trails around sunset, to avoid being fined by rangers for violating the "no dogs allowed" rule. The writing was on the wall when a caretaker for the National Seashore picked him up late at night. We then adopted a policy of alternating Pasha and Rana on the leash, as Rana wouldn't run off without Pasha, and Pasha didn't go as far or as long without Rana.

Pasha always had to have his adventures. Usually, he'd knock at the gate within an hour of our return from a walk, after visiting the neighbors, who loved him, or racing here and there. The advantage of his slowing down with age was that we saw him more often on our walks, and he'd often come home at the same time as we did. In his last few years, I rejoiced when, occasionally, he would still get that old independent gleam in his eye, and run off to visit a neighbor or explore for a while.

On Friday, January 22, Rana came out in the sun instead of spending most of her time in the dog cottage mourning. I thoroughly aired and cleaned out the cottage and bedding for Rana, as the storms had passed. It felt good to make a fresh start, as I sprayed all the floors and walls with cleansing herbal spray.

Grooming was a chore for Pasha. He had beautiful, soft, fine, silky, golden hair, which had been sparser and easier to care for before he was neutered at age six, but grew full, woolly, and easily matted after that. The hormonal change from neutering can cause profuse hair growth in Afghans. Rana, spayed at eight months, had a voluminous coat. Moving to a cooler climate and living outdoors increased their coats' density and made their grooming a difficult task.

Pasha's skin was extremely sensitive. He'd yelp, jump, paw, or bite if I pulled the slightest hair, or if he thought I might. His nails grew longer as he got older, since he didn't wear them down with as much running. I could handle his sensitive feet, clip mats, and pull burrs from between pads, but bringing those nail clippers near him turned me into a nervous wreck, as Pasha jumped and screamed in protest. I'd manage to clip one or two nails before it became too stressful for both of us. It became imperative to get them done, as they began to twist and impair his movement. A few weeks before his departure, a friend came over to help cut his nails. Not being as emotionally involved or subject to his protests, she managed with much discussion and grappling with Pasha to get them all cut, at least as far as the grown-out quicks allowed. It helped his walking, and we had planned to do it again.

All the signs were evident that Pasha would be going. He had lost his hearing gradually since the stroke at age twelve. In the last few months, his vision began to dim. Sometimes he became disoriented on the trail when he couldn't see us at fifty feet away and would run home and bark at the gate. What a change for Pasha, who always had the sight of eagles. During his last two weeks, he began an intermittent dry cough. Walks were slow meanderings, but he still enjoyed and demanded them. He slept very deeply.

It was sad to see his senses failing, but he accepted it and enjoyed life, charming people with his beauty and vitality. In his last six months, he asked for more closeness to us. He had always been independent but loving, allowing me to kiss his velvet face. We had special times, when he would tuck his head between my arm and chest and we would deeply commune. He was noble, balanced, and wholly full of grace and love.

From the experience of his passing, I felt myself swelling with compassion for all beings. On Friday, January 22, I felt happiness, a deep joy, emerging through the pain of loss. Tears still came easily, but there was so much I was gaining. The Earth felt more whole and full.

I have always felt that individuals make a difference to the whole world and the grand passion of life, especially if they live their greatness, not as conceit, but based in solid spiritual awareness. We are all connected and learn from each other. Call it communion, morphic resonance, or telepathic communication. Here we all are in a sea of life, reverberating with one another's changes.

I wanted to give Pasha a party before he died, to celebrate his life, including an ice cream treat, but his mode of dying did not allow it. After his stroke on Monday, January 18, he couldn't eat. His death on January 20 occurred at his usual mealtime, very significant for the chowhound who previously would have been demanding his dinner.

It's hard to imagine having to go through this again. I can understand why some people will not get another animal friend after a special one has departed. I was more prepared than most for this departure, having counseled many people through their animal friends' deaths and having experienced a number of deaths in the family the prior year. Past losses did not burden me as much as they might have, since I had benefited from the considerable hours of experience as a spiritual counselor, clearing my past traumas, including the losses carried forward from past lives.

At the time of Pasha's dying, I was spared the full impact of his suffering by my focus on being there for him and doing what I could to ease his pain. Afterwards, when images of his passion and agony welled up, I faced their painful, emotion-laden moments and ran through them mentally, to release the pain, grief, and heaviness of the memories.

I have no regrets, no guilt. Pasha needed to feel that he had no hope of recovery before he would give up his life. We all had to see that. Even when we fully let him go and prayed that he would die and end the suffering, he needed to experience his Gethsemane, his final passion, and his hell. He had to clear the path, breaking from his beautiful form and love for us, to the other side. Once released, he was flying.

Feeling happy and more detached on January 22, Pasha's presence was felt everywhere. I saw him ethereally sunning and walking around. I talked to him "above," asking why he was now appearing in dog form. He was free to enjoy us and make his presence known in that way as we moved farther through our process. Rana, feeling lighter, bounded up to go for a walk with Michel. It's been many years since I had had only one dog. I wanted Rana to enjoy her specialness. I groomed her well, and we planned an outing. Pasha's suffering was over.

The universe timed Pasha's death so that we could share our process and realizations with others. I was basically finished with the writing stage of the first edition of this book and was beginning editing. This chapter was added to convey this archetypal mystery. Birth and death are two of the most beautiful, deep, unique, mystical experiences of our lives. It serves us well to make the most of them and appreciate them, even if the heights and depths of emotions are plumbed to gain their richness and wisdom.

After meditating in the garden on the afternoon of January 22, I felt relieved, liberated, as though I had passed a very grueling test. I knew that I had not lost Pasha. I still had sadness waxing and waning like the tides, but I felt Pasha all around. His body was comfortable in the Earth. His grave made me smile. The flowers communicated that more of them were blooming, even out of their season, so I could put fresh blooms on his grave as I wished. The support from the spirits all around warmed me. They all loved Pasha's presence in Afghan form, and they all loved him now.

How clear it is to me that spiritual communion and communication save one from the burden of not knowing what is going on with a departed friend and the guilt of feeling you could have done more. I felt at peace, though profoundly moved, as if I'd been gouged out by a spiritual Earth-mover. I felt the spiritual vacuum being filled with the rich cream of awakening to new life and understanding—resurrection.

The suffering of the dying process was a section of the path that needed to be crossed. I gazed at Pasha's picture on my desk, and I was so grateful we had lived together. He was an integral part of me, which at first seemed wrenched away. Then, as acceptance and understanding arrived, he became fully a part of me again. How difficult it can be for people who live alone to lose their only animal friend! At the time and through it all, I had the support of my loving husband—Michel, who had shared the union with Pasha and with whom I could talk—and of my many animal friends, so vibrant, loving, and wonderful.

Taking a walk with Rana that night, I focused on her more than usual, because Pasha wasn't there. For the past year or so, she'd often not wanted to go on walks, especially if I stayed home, as she liked to take care of me. Sometimes she would balk, going slowly and hanging back. That night she was labored, and I realized she was having trouble with her heart. I looked internally and saw a white, fatty tumor, like a hand around her heart.

Other fatty tumors over her ribs had appeared just after Pasha decided that he wanted to leave at age twelve. I perceived then that Rana was manufacturing a way to go with Pasha. So I took her on special walks alone, and she became more independent of Pasha, more able to ask for attention, instead of always deferring to him. Rana has always kept things to herself, opposite to her extroverted father. She quietly grieved Pasha's passing, and we planned to take her on outings to help us all through it. I felt she did not have long for this Earth, but this feeling may have been a reflection of the grieving process for us all.

On Sunday, January 24, we drove up the coast to Mostly Natives Nursery to buy a special plant for Pasha's grave. A small coastal live oak had already offered to be transplanted from another section of our garden, and I placed it behind his body. Usually these native oaks, even when young, grow immense roots and resist transplanting. This one came out easily and proudly rooted in its new chosen home. From the nursery, I sought a plant with red flowers or leaves to place in front of his grave. A heavenly bamboo plant, wearing bright red leaves for the winter, volunteered.

As I meditated outdoors and thought of Pasha that afternoon, Sherman, in an unusual gesture, clawed my clothes and offered this comfort: "I can't take Pasha's place, but I can be here and love you."

Rana was quiet and somber, even with our attempts to lighten her grief. On Monday, January 25, we wondered if getting another dog companion might not be good for her and us. Rana had never liked any dog but Pasha, so this seemed incongruous. But as I went through the motions of talking to people about dogs who might join our family, Rana perked up. Our neighbor's two boisterous six-year-old Labrador/Australian shepherd mixes, Arrow and Gideon, came to visit, and Rana, instead of going away from them, acted interested.

Rana had avoided going near Pasha's grave or wanting to talk about Pasha. That day, I found her poop respectfully but pointedly placed at the edge of his grave. I felt her communication of resentment to Pasha for leaving her. The next day, I found another heap at a different edge. After clearing the leavings away, I went to Rana, acknowledged her emotions and thanked her for expressing them. Since we got the message and Pasha understood too, I asked her to not do that again. She felt satisfied and quietly complied.

We experienced the week of Pasha's departure as a disjointed blur of events. I continued to review and clear the grief and pain from parts of the dying episode that forced themselves to attention, bringing gradual relief in a seemingly long process. Sometimes I sang and played around as usual, and other times I felt heavy. I went from exaltation to hell and back—a powerful alchemy.

Pasha told me he was in a place of much happiness with enlightened beings, full of joy. I asked about my sister, who disappeared in a mentally unstable state in December 1992, and about my mother, who died in April 1992. He hadn't seen them, but said they were in other places, where they could work through their burdens. He had seen my father, who had died in December 1984 and who welcomed him as Pasha entered the spiritual realm, but he was not in immediate or constant contact with him. Spirits appear to group according to their task and their bonds with each other, as well as their stage of acceptance of spiritual realities and ability to be free and joyful.

Sacred splendor
A friendship so deep
Transects species, time, space
All bounds.
Eyes limitless look at mine forever
Soft, tender love
Closeness expressed but uncontained by bodies
Bursting through each molecule
Beyond death it reigns
Spirit rolling
Clasping invisible hands
Touching cheeks
Velvet fur connecting with warm skin
We feel each other close
A bond of unity
Forms' decay cannot erase
We go on.

In the evening of the January 25, I found myself in a hollow—a cavern, a sus-pended gloom that seemed outside of life—perpetrated by Pasha's death, but also separate from it. It was as if I were being called to something else, to somewhere else. Perhaps I was dying, or soon to go. I wondered if it was Michel who might leave. Since July 1992, I'd been impregnated with thoughts of death. Astrologers pointed out that the planet Pluto was traveling through the sign of Scorpio, saturating the earthly drama with death, threat of death, and transfiguration, renovating lives with its depth and intensity of transfor-mation. That certainly rang true for me.

My mother had died in April 1992. I hadn't seen her physically for seven-teen years. She had been an extremely paranoid, abused, and abusive per-son. My presence elicited insane tirades from her, so I chose not to be around her. I sent her occasional letters and photos of our family and a tape of her favorite old songs. We talked on the phone twice. My sisters, who stayed more involved in the family drama, provided an occasional commen-tary on her life. When she left her body, I felt her relief from suffering, as she went into a place of deep, healing rest and forgiveness.

Then a series of deaths occurred in our animal family. I felt more com-ing. I knew Pasha would have a stroke; the signs were there. I thought that instead of the very long life I always envisioned and others of psychic bent had predicted for me, perhaps I would die shortly. Perhaps, after writing this book, my work would be over.

Then the big one came, the inevitable—Pasha going. The big one was not an earthquake, but a taking back of one of her children by Mother Earth. Each stage of the loss or grieving followed its own pattern, its mysterious path. I felt I was recovering well. Yet there was a limbo, a creative state I had slipped into, a zone between life on Earth and death. Sometimes grounded by the animals and life around me, even singing and laughing, sometimes in the hollow, full of something else besides blood and bones, full of *resonance*. Resonating with all around me, all of life seemed to be understood in the moment. This state was so quiet, so sullen, so charged with mystery, like the eye of a storm. Something was about to happen: an insight, many insights, a historic change, a *moment*.

Much was given to me. I was hollow, but filled. New talents, new life emerged out of the understanding, out of the deep caverns of death—which were not despair, but the underworld from which all life springs, Pluto personified and demonstrable.

I felt the profound magic. Led to write and think and touch upon all hearts, I was propelled by the deep, sad yet ecstatic beauty of feeling all creatures' death and life, joined as brothers and eternal traveling companions. Our journeys have their intermissions where we are called to reassess our courses and to drink deeply of the chalice of truth and wisdom.

Pain is real. Loss is the tearing away from that with which you are so attached and so in love. Staying in the loss is hell. Coming through the torrents of the river of suffering and pain brings some kind of championship, a compassion so deep and rapture so ardent that you know it can only be won by the contrast—going through the depths to feel the heights. We cannot see or feel the vigor of life without willingness to experience all sides of creation, decay, death, and rebirth.

I am truly blessed. Thank you, all Creative Forces, all the faces of God. In accepting the gift of separation by death, I have been given the golden caldron of life eternal, beautiful and loved in all its shapes and forms, all its comings and goings.

Solemnly, a most sacred ceremony was being performed. I must be silent to witness its effects. Sacred is this ancient and universal rite. We all go through it if we love, and how we fare is a measure of our understanding. I accept the ebbs and flows of the river and dive in to join the water in its solid, meditative movement to the sea.

On January 26, my body tingled as I read in a magazine that many indigenous holy people believe when a great person dies, the universe acknowledges the spirit's departure by sending storms and rain. Pasha's departure storms were from the south. They signaled the final southward departure of his spirit and his body's final resting place with his eyes facing southward, the direction of the coyote on the Native American Medicine Wheel.

The sky opened up to let Pasha in and celebrate his passing. The Earth rumbled with the water passing, to let him through to the other side. You could see the depth of water unlimited in his eyes. Storms will ever remind me of Pasha's passion.

In these profound concluding moments of the life of one so great, one left on Earth is also made liquid, open, and vulnerable—lines softened and spongelike, so that everything said, done, smelled, or sensed leaves a deep track. Now that the grief had ebbed, the line was no longer blurred between dimensions. I saw the passion and joy of being on Earth more clearly—the crisp colors, the sharp sense of physical artistry and sensuality. I experienced the beauty of the Earth as Pasha had, and felt why it was so hard to leave, even with blood vessels bursting and forces exploding him to another realm.

So, Pasha, I feel you, I see you, and I know you as you are. As spirit, I can even cuddle you. No, it's not the same as form to form, sense to sense, but it resonates throughout my being.

Clearly, winter is the time of leaving, as the Earth revolves towards dying, from end of summer to start of spring. I, too, will die in winter, and rain it will—storming, as I scream my way through all of nature's mysteries, into the peaceful, joyful realm of translucent grace, mystical shapes, and glowing peace. Until then, I'll give my gift and live my life as Pasha did, fully, with passion and grace. May we all do the same, and dance in laughter, joy, and full communion someday.

On Saturday, February 6, during a Basic Workshop Instructor's course at the Floating Island of Peace, the full moon shone brilliantly. We all power-fully felt the energies of transformation, making us somewhat dizzy. I went to bed early. Oddly, Heyoka started yowling just before midnight. I was sum-moned to sit outside on the deck under the full moon, beaming down from the southern sky. I had never seen the moon so penetratingly bright, though I had sat and walked under many a full moon. Later, I discovered that the moon was in the sign of Leo. The moon was in Pasha's sun, crossing and combining the energies of the moon with the sun, which is the ruling planet of Leo. Returning to my desk indoors, I wrote these words:

Full Moon. Ancient Mother. Grandmother Moon calls me outside. I sit and feel myself a grandmother, one of the ancients calling me home. A gathering of friends in the heavens. Many great friends, masters dying, leaving the Earth. A gathering, a party, a big celebration in the heavens dancing over Mother Earth, sending blessings and mighty gifts our way. A gathering of ancients.

As many of my animal friends die, I feel the rending of the skies, the skin of dimensions broken. Powers come through from places unknown, yet so known. Homes, realms so dear, homes here and there on Earth. An inner experience of trembling, a giant rending, dying, transforming energies. Calling me . . . calling me.

As Grandmother Moon beams on me, full and clear, she lets me know the time is coming to join her and the ancestors. How, in what way, I do not know yet.

The clouds form slowly and deliberately into the giant eye of a whale. My people, my teachers call me. If they leave, I must go. They are here, so am I. We have the same mission—to bring us all back home together. The eye of the whale in the clouds formed in the sky where Pasha sailed as he left his earthly form, and I see him dwell. The South, the place of gathering.

I am moved to tidy my affairs, to ensure the safety and the life of the animals. Perhaps this is why they go: the work is done. Perhaps they all go with me.

The magic has been created and goes forth. I cry with so much power unfurled and feel detached from Earth. So strange, the Earth, the garden, the Isle of Peace—I'm so fond of all these. I can leave; I may be called. Carry on the work, all whose sparks have been ignited. Let the *fire of light*** go on and spread to purify the souls of humans, so that community, communion, and unity can be recognized, and joy may prevail, as all souls know who they are and share their beauty.

I have no part in their destruction, the mad ones racing to their doom. We who know come in peaceful harmony to grace the Earth with majesty, her natural state and gift to us. It's only right that we give it back to her.

The wind increases—my friend who sends and brings all things, all changes, all messages on wings from afar. We are the wind, we messengers of change—riding the waves, the forward crest. We come and go upon the Earth and skies and o'er the seas. We are the ocean's waves.

So, my dear friends, whatever end is near or here, carry on the beauty that has been revived. All souls seeing the oneness of us all and cherishing the beauty of the different forms, the many facets of the jewel, the many faces of God. Divine expression.

---

*During my initiation to the healing energies of Reiki I, Spirit gave me the title "Priestess of the Fire of Light." My job on Earth has been as a catalyst for transformation. In my natal horoscope—with three planets and the sun in the sign of Scorpio, and most of the other planets in fire signs—I often identify my energy with the Earth's volcanoes and earthquake zones. I loved the image of the "fire of light," so powerful and unusual.

And if I follow the Dancing Ones skyward, let me breathe upon the Earth, my planetary home, a breath of hope and peace; of fire and passionate life; of fun, of beauty, of joy, for all to know and share. I have been given much from all sectors of Creation, all corners of the Spirit World afar and near, permeating all life, and I give my joy to All.

May all of you remember the Ancient Song and rejoin in the chorus that has always gone on, singing in the hearts of plants, rocks, angels, animals, native ones. Humans have been the errant ones, so easily led astray and yet so fondly led back to their profound mystery of soul shared with all. May we all, complete at last, join the dance and song to mend the broken circle. These friends of ours have hummed the strains so long to keep the song alive, so patient and so loving. May the chorus rebound with full voice as ancient memories shake and stir. May we all love together.

On Wednesday, February 17, four weeks from the day of Pasha's death, a powerful stormy wind crystallized just before noon. The sky had been gently, steadily raining since the night before. Now the winds howled violently through the trees, just as they had on January 20. I watched the trees bend and pitch, checking to see that Rana was okay in her dog cottage. She noticed too, but was not afraid.

The day before, a bantam chicken named Pumpkin had died. She was a sweet and lovely member of our chicken family of twenty-five, but not a special friend to me. I had held her the previous day, giving her warmth and energy and wishing her well along her way, as she had been ill for several weeks. When I buried her gentle form and was aware of her flying joyfully as spirit, I could not help but think of Pasha, with body in the ground and spirit in another realm. That day was infused with a background solemnity. Michel and I talked in the evening about how the fact of Pasha being gone sometimes struck us with an unreal jolt.

I was relieved that the wrenching grief episodes ran their course in the first few weeks. Instead, I began to question the remnant sadness that surfaced, as I had integrated Pasha's departure as a part of life and didn't see a benefit in dwelling in emotions of loss. Life was renewed in each moment, full of waterfalls of changing colors. Balance. Rebalance. We are jugglers in life's circus. That morning I saw Pasha's realm as more distant and vague and his spiritual figure as smaller and fainter, although the connection with him was deep and unbroken.

During February 12 through 22, we dog-sat for Arrow and Gideon—rambunctious, loving, obedient, uncomplicated characters. We enjoyed their enthusiastic company on walks. Previously, Rana had expressed her dislike of their company by refusing to come on walks with them or avoiding proximity with them. This time, Rana went on a very long walk with them without protest or balking and even enjoyed their company. It was a nice breakthrough. The time with Arrow and Gideon may have helped to change her mind about accepting a future young canine companion. As I wrote this, Rana sat and looked at me from outside on the driveway, pensively considering my thoughts.

I received a card of condolence from a client whom I had met in New York the previous year. Her exceptional Afghan hound friend, Kalie, reminded me of Pasha with her deep gaze and playful warmth. The woman sent a photo of Kalie and added the note, "Please don't be sad long. You know they come back!"

Pasha had given me only a slight feeling that he might be back someday. The conditions were not ripe for him or us as a family. As I looked out the window and remarked to Michel how much this storm duplicated the one four weeks ago that ushered Pasha to the spiritual realm, I felt a message coming through. The dimensional veil rent with a scream of wind, and I whooped, "He's coming back! He's coming back!"

And I knew he would appear to us again soon.

Pavane for Prince Pasha

Precious Pasha
You couldn't leave us
even if you tried—
not while winds blow free
and rivers endlessly flow,
not while wooded paths
invite running and romping.
How you loved those trails!

Playful Pasha
You couldn't leave us
even if you tried—
not while good dogs
still snatch an occasional cookie—
Pasha, even well-mannered you!

Patient Pasha
You couldn't leave us
even if you tried—
not while so many remember
your willing assistance
and gentle, all-knowing
benevolence.

To know you on Earth
was to expand one's self,
to embrace the universe
through your noble
inimitable grace.

Peaceful Pasha
You haven't left us.
To deny it is a lie:
whatever form the body takes,
Love and Soul
refuse to die.

Prince Pasha Pazoo
I'll never forget you.

—Nancy Sondel

reincarnation

THE CONNECTING THREAD

AS SPIRITUAL BEINGS, we are free to choose the form of life that suits our own desire for experience in the physical universe. Those who have had human bodies may now have animal forms, or the reverse, for various reasons and with no set paradigm that applies to all. My book, *Animal Talk*, and audiotapes give many examples of how beings may inhabit different species' forms from life to life, according to their purposes. Some choose to stay in one particular species, such as human or feline, because they like it or find it fulfills their purposes. There are as many reasons and patterns as there are individuals.

Most domesticated animals that I have communicated with have had experience in other lives as humans. They are comfortable with human thinking and human problems. They enjoy helping people through their often complex and emotionally turbulent lives. They often easily accept being a cat or horse, even though they haven't inhabited those forms before. In previous lives as humans, they usually loved those animals, understood them, and identified with them, or they are very conscious of their choice of species and quick to learn how to enjoy life as that animal. Some animals who have been human before tend to act like, even demand, the "privileges" of human living.

Animals who have had no human experience, or have never been a domesticated animal, can be fearful of humans and find it hard to tune into often confusing or chaotic human thinking. Some animals may just want to hide out for a while and be "feral," while they maintain a minimal or safe contact with humans. They have made some decision to learn from the path of being close to humans, but it may take them awhile to respond to humans as something besides predators or alien beings. By respecting their choices and understanding their situation, we can greatly assist fearful animals to progress in the direction of amiable coexistence. Experiencing and mastering another way of life is usually the main purpose for changing forms and seeking totally different circumstances.

Some animals are very confused about the form they inhabit. They have never been a cat or dog before and still identify with some other form that they are more familiar with, such as a fox or rabbit. They chose to change their experience at some point in their lives, but they may not be fully conscious or accepting of their choice.

An individual's passion or major concern usually has some past-life thread. For example, people working now to rescue or assist animals may have tried to help animals for lifetimes, or they may be attempting to make up for having hurt them in the past. Horses who easily learn and excel at dressage may have been equine champions previously. Horses who resist an activity may have mastered that activity already and wish to go on to something else.

In counseling animals to resolve unwanted behaviors or emotions, most situations are routinely handled by addressing the current life. However, past-life incidents may surface, and it is helpful and often necessary to review them to release old hurts and injuries that affect the being now.

I talked to Jayla, a Peruvian Paso horse, and her human companion, Karen. Karen wanted to know why Jayla seemed sad. Even under Karen's care, people had mistreated Jayla, almost as if Karen could not prevent it. Jayla was contented in her small herd of horses, but seemed melancholy as a spirit.

As we communed, she quietly began to relay the reason for her gloom. She had died in a concentration camp in her most recent life and had been a Jewish rabbi in a life before that. She was immersed in the concept of atonement for wrong or evil, and she felt that to reach true and eternal happiness, she had to suffer, both for herself and others.

Even as a horse, a form she adopted because she liked horses and needed a change from her human lives, she felt she had to endure agony before she could be happy. As we talked, she was able to release some of her anguish. She then realized that she had already made the necessary atonement to fulfill her life path and could allow herself to feel joy in living.

Johnny was an adopted wild burro. His person called me because he was difficult to work with. I found him very uncommunicative. He pictured himself with his head held down in resistance. After I talked with his person about his history and how she had worked with him, he began to open up and talk about himself.

In his most recent lifetime, he had been a man who lived in Montana, Wyoming, and Idaho, roping and taming wild horses and burros. He did not like people and was generally unsociable, but he identified with the burros, feeling they were a lot like him, steely and stubborn. He felt he could mesmerize the wild equines by the way he talked to them and had a reputation for being able to catch them when others couldn't. He became a wild burro this time around because he liked them and wanted to live a free life on the plains.

He recognized, as we talked, that his job this lifetime was to get closer to accepting humans. His pattern of resistance was getting tiresome for him. He had lived that way for so many consecutive lifetimes, but he wasn't ready to completely change yet.

Now, he just wanted peace and quiet. He didn't like people talking to him and found their voices annoying. His person had noticed that he was more approachable when she talked in a whisper. He said that, if she wanted to get closer to him, she should sit silently on a stump with her back to him. He'd respect her more that way. I recommended that she communicate telepathically with him, without using her voice to get his attention. He loved it when she did therapeutic touch with him, but he didn't like her gazing at him and trying to discern his emotions. She was quite willing to patiently respect his wishes, and they made steady progress in his training after that.

In the mid-1980s, Diana Thompson took on the task of rehabilitating Thoroughbred racehorses. She tried to race them in a manner aligned with their ability and purposes, without the attendant pressure and pain that is usually associated with horse racing. She called me for a number of conversations with Timothy's Hope, who was rejected at the race track for bolting and running amok at the starting gate.

Timothy was an extremely sensitive being and was very affected by all the negative energies around the race track. Diana had great faith in his ability and worked hard to help him have a good time while fulfilling his potential for running fast. Timothy's racing experience was linked with many past-life traumas, and we worked to ease the fear and pain associated with them.

In one session, Timothy hung his head, cradled against my chest, and poured out many images and emotions, especially guilt. He had been a leader, as a human, in a number of lifetimes and tried to save or help or heal others, taking on too much responsibility for the welfare of others and feeling burdened with failure. He sped from one life to the next, not giving himself enough time to contemplate and sort things out. He was driven to help. In our counseling sessions, Timothy worked through a lot of agony and self-blame and realized that he needed to quiet down, take time off to think, relax, and get himself together. I recommended time off in a pasture, away from the competitive atmosphere of racing.

Diana and Timothy went through years of growing together, trying to work in and soften the grueling competition endured by racehorses in a system that wears down even the toughest participants. Although Diana got him through most of his fears about the starting gate and racing, he did not succeed as a racehorse, but went on to be a dressage and companion horse.

Robyn Hood asked me to talk to one of her Icelandic horses. The mare was white with blue eyes, an unusual trait. Robyn felt that she was an odd character and was concerned about her.

The horse approached us in the field and began communicating to me immediately. I first noticed a strange shape to the aura, or energy field, around her head and wondered about it. The horse informed me that she didn't care about the other horses or what people thought. She wasn't a horse, but a caribou, and no one could change her. She would continue to graze and live out her life just as she wanted it. Then I saw clearly why the aura was a different shape than her horse form. It outlined antlers on her head!

Being something other than their current bodies can be disorienting for animals and others connected with them, causing unusual behavior and lack of self-esteem or fulfillment. Listening to and counseling these animals through their past-life stories can help them to clear any traumas that may be locking them in those past images. Then, reorienting them to their present body and the opportunities available within it—as well as asking other animals of the same species who embody confidence and joy in living to help the disoriented one—can further resolve conflicting self-image problems.

In this instance, the "Caribou Horse" seemed quite content and assertive and did not see any point in changing, although she was sometimes a difficult horse for people to deal with.

At a lecture/demonstration at the American Holistic Veterinary Conference, I was asked to communicate with Baby, a two-year-old cockatoo, to find out why she had begun to pick her feathers out and how we could handle it. When I contacted Baby, she was very confused about her identity. She did not see herself as a bird, but as a human baby, and she kept picturing that she was meant to be inside her person's body and be born as her (human) baby.

The woman was definite about not having babies, so the cockatoo had chosen a form that was intimately connected to the woman. Baby was a favorite among her many large parrots. Having been human in previous lives, Baby expected to carry on in that manner. Her confusion and frustration about wanting to be the person's daughter had driven her to pick her feathers out.

Her person was already giving Baby an enormous amount of attention and affection, and even took her to work, where many other people admired her and communicated with her. The name "Baby" may have been adding to her confusion, but the cockatoo was adamant about not wanting to have it changed.

I suggested that the woman gently massage Baby's chest (the feather-picked area), admire her, and imagine her as a totally beautiful, feather-perfect bird. Her veterinarian wanted to know if acupuncture might help, and Baby thought that would be fine, adding that she was very cooperative and a good girl.

Baby had a purpose in life to help others by interacting with them frequently. It looked as if her person could facilitate that. Baby seemed to be clearer about who she was as a result of the brief consultation, and I hoped it would help to handle her destructive habit of feather picking.

Another cockatoo, named Pigalle, had a totally different experience. She was six years old when her person, Donna, called me. Pigalle had been with her four and a half years, after living in a health club. The cockatoo behaved violently with her and other people, having bitten Donna's lip all the way through and broken her nose. Pigalle got ill after she ate plastic and other toys and often woke up screaming from nightmares. She also became sick if Donna had to leave town. Besides trips to the veterinarian, Donna had hired an eminent bird behaviorist to work with Pigalle.

Pigalle related that when she was human, she hated other people. She wanted to fly, free as a bird, and chose to be a wild cockatoo. Unfortunately, she was captured. Then she wished to die, and ended up neglected and abused by several owners. When Donna became Pigalle's companion, Donna had no avian knowledge, although she felt a strong connection with birds. I saw images of Donna as a Mayan shaman, closely aligned with bird gods, taking flight as a spirit moving out of her body. Donna mentioned that she often dreamed of birds.

After these revelations, Pigalle was still confused, and said she felt full of possessiveness, hate, and jealousy. She couldn't decide if she wanted to live or not. This was not something that would be resolved in one consultation, or perhaps even in one life.

Adele Tate had this experience with self-image confusion:

My friend, Sally, called and asked me to talk with her horse, Dee. Sally explained that she and a professional trainer had been trying to sad- dle and ride Dee for several weeks. Dee pictured herself hunching her back with the saddle, then becoming a four-legged pogo stick when a human tried to board her.

It seemed Dee was unable to accept the idea of having a person on her back. She wanted to know "why my person could not walk beside me on a trail ride. That would be more fun, wouldn't it?"

I was curious about Dee's lack of knowledge of her body and decided to ask her more about her background. Specifically, I wanted to know about her most recent life and why she had chosen to be a horse in this life. Before I finished thinking about the question, Dee pictured a beautiful white cat. In her previous life, when she was the gorgeous white cat, her person always left her to "go ride the horse." "The horse is sure lucky to have such a close relationship with my person," she thought, and she decided that she would be a horse someday. What a surprise it was to find out about some of the other aspects of a horse's life, such as work! Dee seemed unaware of her actual size and could not understand why her person wanted to sit on her back. I talked to her about how wonderful her life could be as a horse and wished her well.

The trainer said that, the day after we talked, they had the best training session ever with Dee. Dee seemed to have a better understanding of what it meant to be a horse.

Taco was an Appaloosa horse. At five years old, he was having a difficult time in training. He was nervous and balky. When I talked with him, he relayed anguish about his current condition. He wasn't sure why he was here as a domesticated horse. When last on Earth, about 200 years ago, he lived wild and free lives as an American Indian, and then as an Indian pony. He was shocked to find himself in his condition, living a confined life with people ordering him around.

I asked him why he had incarnated here. As he viewed his decision and the passage into this life, he extricated himself from his grief and confusion. He realized that he could have a sense of humor about the condition he chose and could have fun with people, who were in the same boat as he. He felt he had a new lease on life.

Soon after the arrival of Popiya, my first Afghan, she got to know other people who lived in the house, whom she liked in her reserved way. One woman was eager to take her on a walk, which I felt would be okay in the morning. When the woman came at 7 A.M., Popiya was a bit groggy and didn't really want to go. I coaxed her, thinking that she'd enjoy it once she got going. The woman returned in a short time and felt there was something wrong with Popiya, that she was balky and stiff in her movements. A few minutes after returning, she had her first seizure, as I described earlier.

After getting through that episode, I worked with Popiya to clear the psychosomatic, or mental and spiritual, cause of her seizures. The counseling opened up tremendous past-life suffering. Popiya had died in a concentration camp, as a young German Jewish boy. The woman who took her out for the walk had the look and mannerisms of a concentration camp guard who had tortured Popiya. This appeared to trigger the latest seizure. Popiya had been especially susceptible then because she was tired and resistant to going on a walk. We did a series of sessions to uncover and resolve her traumatic past, along with the reasons she had chosen that path. This went a long way to restoring her physical and mental well-being and ending the seizures.

Popiya's lives since the concentration camp had been equally disturbing. She felt that being human again would be too much to bear. Her unresolved pain, confusion, and resistance swayed her destiny. The result was a life as a German shepherd dog, used for rounding up prisoners going to the camps. This made her a nervous wreck, and she was shot for her erratic behavior. Then she was a very nervous and high-strung Doberman pinscher, and lived a tortured life of seven years.

After these "failures," she stayed out of the earthly game for a while until she chose her Afghan body. Still, she ended up suffering and abused in human hands. She came to me for help to get through her unhappiness and to once again be able to share her beauty and artistic sensitivity with the world.

In the course of counseling Popiya, I discovered that I had known her when she was the young German boy. I was an Austrian Jewish man, and we had crossed paths on a truck taking us to the concentration camps. She had shared some of her poetry with me on the way. In her Afghan form, Popiya dictated a series of haunting poems of her feelings from that life and her struggles to come to terms with herself, which I call "The Popiya Series":

1 JANUARY 23, 1978

I am alone in my vision
And the breeze that haunts me
Is of ages past
Friends gone
Poems lost in the wind.

Brutality claimed my art
My gift to the world
Of rhyme and gentle song.

I caress the day and the sun
In this warm land
Where comfort and love
Ease my mind and coax my tongue

Once again to reach out
To dare to be myself.

Through my friend
My words are written
I ask in quietness
Edging from my sorrow
To have them heard.

I am again here
Peering softly from my hiding
To say hello.
My tears speak
My joy from wells below the pain
Is touched and aches
To touch you, too.

Hello, I want to say
Do not speak loudly
Caress me gently with your smile
And let me put my head
Close to your hand or foot
I am here again
Hello.

2 JANUARY 28, 1978

I am the one from far
Journeys long are not strange to me
I have raced from moon to sun
In pen and song
And in the quiet night when restless.

You will see me again in human form ere long
My safety mission is near complete
The wounds are whole
And I dare to stand up
To fight again.

3   *Discovery*
A sudden change
I have called and I am heard
The darkness of uncertainty
Is struck through with light
My friend has come to me
Now I shall live.

4   JANUARY 31, 1978

The dawn took me away the other day
I awoke, my body still in sleep
To go running through the clouds
Racing faster and further
My body imitating me upon its couch
Feet quivering, spurting energy
To duplicate my waveless, soundless,
Weightless passage.

When I returned, my master friend
Kissing me good morning said
Hello, it's such a beautiful day
I'm glad you're here
I felt such peace
No need to go out for a walk
I'd had my run beneath the stars
And through the sunlit tracings
Hello, indeed, good morning.

5   MARCH 9, 1978

Many roads
Bouncing, crawling, stretching
Moving forward in my backwards way all the same.

Through the harsh necessities of suffering
Consequences of bodies frail and unruly
I reach forward in my backwards way all the same.

Looking out this way and that
Knowing they don't really understand how I feel
I hid it so well in this golden shadow form
Yet this beauty is me.

The gentle one reaching with warm love
Gentle thoughts to soothe and welcome
Can you hear me thinking to you?
Yes, I do love and feel so much
And now, I think of you and others
Reaching forward in my backwards way all the same
Someday to be free.

6 MARCH 14, 1978

Leaves are falling in my life
Dark gusts swirl like whirlpools
Churning out the dust of ages long
I swirl in their wake.

Pausing to look at the hands outstretched
But I have to work this out myself this time
This is myself this time
Moving into a new realm
From confusion to serene existence.

When the tornadoes settle
I will know what I so long have forgotten
From hiding to being once more.

7 JULY 3, 1978

I waver
Huddled at the edge of my indecision
To be or not to be this or that
A fine-cut edge needs to be walked
To take on my role as a listener

Helping others and myself to be strong
Or wait some more in the corner wanting to be heard
But with nothing left to say
No purpose in this form
Worthy of me, my new vision.

I waver to take on this responsibility
The pain of leaving
To begin with all things new frightens me
Yet I know it must be done
Each reminder of the choice
Makes me fight myself and those around me
I am ashamed that I have hidden and they know
I can no longer hide.

Yet breaking free to do as I must
Crushes me sometimes
I do not know
But yet I do
What I must do.

The time draws near
For new beginnings painful and unsure
I waver.

8 JULY 7, 1978

I have decided
Decided yes to stay.

The weariness sheds off
I am interested again
In life, in love, in living
I feel the fun of being myself
In any form, in this form.

The music that sings in my head
Is hollow but sweet

I reach for play and good times
Not to sink to solid sadness in my dreams
To stay and be stronger
I am Popiya still.

When Pasha arrived, Popiya, then about ten years old, didn't want much to do with this energetic puppy. We found other playmates for Pasha, because Popiya growled at him if he tried to play with her. In April 1979, I was planning to take a tour of the country, teaching and having an adventure, with Popiya and Pasha in an old, long Dodge van purchased for the expedition. Popiya was not sure she wanted to go and became ill; the idea of being uprooted for six months of traveling did not appeal to her.

I told her it was up to her what she wanted to do with her life, that if she wanted to go with us, she should get well, and we'd have a good time together. If she really felt that her life purpose was fulfilled, she could leave her body. She didn't eat for a few days. Then we worked out how she could be comfortable traveling in the van, and she decided to get well and go with us.

When we returned to Los Angeles in October, after an adventurous yet relaxing six months, Popiya felt again that it was her time to die. She felt she had completed her cycle in this life and was no longer bound by suffering and denial of her own creativity. She wanted to be human again, but this time to express herself purposefully and happily. She was in good health at the time, better than she ever had been. We wondered how she would make a departure, as she and her body were very attached to each other!

We spent an entire night attempting an exit without trauma, willing her as a spirit from the body. It didn't work. The body wasn't willing to let go of her, and she didn't know how to release herself from it either. She asked me for additional help. Would I take her to the vet to be put down? Gulp. That was a challenging request. I felt her need, and I felt I couldn't let her down, even though it would be a very difficult thing for me to do. We went to a very spiritually aware and understanding veterinarian the next day. Popiya quietly accepted the injection as I held her in my arms, and she was gone in a few seconds. Even now, the tears flow as I write this. It certainly was not an easy thing to do, even though it was what Popiya wanted.

Guilt and doubt are part of human nature as safeguards against rash action, but also haunting reminders of our fallibility, even in apparently definite decisions. My little Popiya Pizzeria! I left her body there and stumbled down the street through my tears. Then I heard her laughing and shouting, "I'm free, I'm free!" How could I cry, when Popiya was so grateful and liberated?

I kept in touch with Popiya as she searched around for a human baby body. She found a married couple in Connecticut with whom she felt a close kinship. They had a baby boy, about two years old at the time, who was not thriving. The doctors could not find what was wrong with him, but he ate very little and was weak and almost silent. The parents grieved for him and their helplessness. Popiya communicated with the spirit who inhabited the baby body, and it turned out that he did not really want to be there and was planning to depart. They made an agreement for Popiya to take over that body and begin her new life.

Upon her entrance into the baby body, he immediately became brighter, more active, and soon was fully healthy, talking, and developing normally. Both Popiya and her new parents were elated. I have since occasionally checked in on her telepathically and found her to be doing well in her new life. I have not felt it appropriate to try and find out the family's name and whereabouts. Who knows? Someday, I may meet Popiya again in her human form.

Most of my own past lifetimes on the Earth have been in human form, but in my earliest conscious past-life memory, I realized that I had been a frog. I recalled that I had spent several wonderful weeks leaping on lily pads in a pond, mating, eating, and exulting in the beauty of the water and plants. I felt that my ease in jumping, when I performed as a dancer, was beneficially influenced by my experience as a frog. To this day, I have a special affinity for frogs.

Another past life on Earth that I thoroughly enjoyed was that of a Bengal tiger. I discovered this in a counseling session in 1971. My first husband, Brian, was very allergic to cats, while I loved cats and identified with them more than any other animal. In my session, images came forth of eating Brian when he was a boy in India and I was a tiger. I recalled how easy it was to catch a frail human and how tasty he was! Now this may sound gruesome from the human viewpoint, but from the tiger perspective, it was a gourmet meal! I didn't take man-eating seriously, because I felt humans were just too easy prey to really enjoy the challenge. I thoroughly enjoyed my tiger life and died of old age, with very few teeth left in my mouth.

You may wonder how this affected Brian, to live with a former tiger that had been his killer! Most of us have lived a variety of lives and played many roles, as humans and nonhumans, in various relationships with each other. Not all of these incidents are necessarily revived in each life, or carry negative consequence or "karmic debt." Brian's encounter with me as a tiger may be just one among his many experiences with cats—having things done by them and doing things to them—that manifested as his allergy.

Many people who are animal lovers have existed as other species in other lifetimes and often have a deep understanding of animals' spiritual natures because of that. Even if you have not lived as animals before, you can learn to exercise the ability to merge with their viewpoints now and feel their experience to enrich your outlook.

Our animal friends can also empathize with us, even to the extent that they choose to return to be with us, to help us find fulfillment as spiritual beings in our difficult task as humans. Goodness knows, we humans need all the support and love we can get. Adele Tate's experience of a horse client illustrates this:

Windstan was one of those big, beautiful quarter horses who possessed the speed and agility to be a great horse, no matter what he or his human companion wanted to do. He could place his feet in the proper position for cutting, reining, trail riding, jumping, dressage, or carefully avoiding the tiny feet of a curious three-year-old human. He was a most gentle individual and cared for everyone and everything. He brought joy to this world through his caring and his humor, making us laugh at the sight of a 1,300-pound horse squeezing every ounce into the 6-by-6-foot feed room with the finesse of a lady pouring her size 8 foot into her size 6 shoe. He also made us cry, admitting that he understood his person's need to physically feel the warmth of his body close to her, or to feel the moisture of his breath as he nuzzled her neck. He told us that we needed to know him spiritually as well as physically.

When I first met Windstan, his person, Sue, suspected that he wanted to be assisted to the spiritual realm. In discussing his desires, he made it clear that he could not be useful in his present condition. His nerves had been removed from his left foot and leg, and he was now feeling the initial pain of navicular disease in the right foot. He told me that he wanted a few weeks to help prepare the family, and assisted me in selecting the Bach Flower remedies for them and his animal companions. He was pleased that Sue understood his desires and assured her that "everyone will know when I go."

On Sunday, before his scheduled departure, he asked me to be with him for a while and write a letter to Sue for him. He was concerned about her, the children, and his horse companion, Demi. He explained that death was the beginning of the resting time before the exhilaration of new life. Death was not a time of sadness for the individual leaving or remaining. He promised to be with his family always and to return to them in the physical realm in a very short time.

The day came to celebrate his earthly life and allow him to gently pass to the spiritual plane. His body was to be placed in the ground "to make beautiful things grow." He walked purposefully to the place that had been prepared to receive his body. He wore a necklace of braided alfalfa and wheat, which his cowboy friends brought to honor him. Even in the last moments of his life, he shared his love with lifelong friends. There, in a circle of friends and loved ones, he passed.

Ralph was a young dog of eighteen months when he was killed by a truck. His person consulted with me just after his death and mentioned that she planned to have his body freeze-dried and to keep it next to her in his former favorite place in the bedroom.

When I contacted Ralph in the spiritual realm, he was a light and free spirit, full of joy. He loved people and life on Earth and felt that while he was here he had lived his life on "fast forward." He wanted to return and planned to do so soon. He felt he had learned to moderate his speed to better suit living in the physical realm.

His person asked if it was okay with Ralph if she had his body freeze-dried and kept it in the house. Ralph communicated that her attachment to that body would keep him from returning to her house. He could not reenter that family under those circumstances and would have to go somewhere else.

As I had not encountered someone asking about this subject before, I wondered how other beings felt about their bodies being freeze-dried. I checked with Freddy, her old dog, who had died the previous summer. He was very happy in the spiritual realm, surrounded by friends and family, and planning to stay there for a long time. He did not feel bothered by the fact of her keeping his old body.

Most animals I have communicated with are not attached to the body after it dies and don't concern themselves about its disposition. Some will ask for their body to be buried in a certain place, or in a certain way. Most view and enjoy the love and cherishing that people give when they do a ceremony in honor of the animal's life and death. It helps to make a completion for all concerned, so that each can move on.

Beings who have gone on generally feel free without their physical forms and are more concerned with how their families are doing emotionally than with what happens to their old bodies. They may hang around, or check in, to ensure their loved ones are okay, sending love and blessings or directing a new animal companion to the family. Some reincarnate if it is the right time for them to do so.

Nature's way is for bodies to decompose and return to the Earth. Mummifying, stuffing, or freeze-drying bodies can keep or attract energies that may not be desirable. Spirits, not necessarily related to the original inhabitant of the body while it was alive, often inhabit or communicate through stuffed animals, such as deer, moose, or elk heads on the wall. Even "fake" stuffed animals, such as teddy bears, can be inhabited, especially if the doll is given loving contact with humans or other living beings. It's a painless way to dwell in the physical, and one certainly can give and receive a lot of love and admiration that way.

Years ago, I visited Disneyland's Pirate Cove, where people travel on a boat through a dark tunnel that lights up at times, with pirate and other figures popping out. I was very aware that spirits had taken up residence in many of these forms and enjoyed scaring people and getting their attention.

It's one way of contacting, communicating, and participating in life on Earth. It may not be your idea of a good life. It may even seem like a form of captivity, but for many, it does not seem any more confining than dwelling in a live physical form. You can come and go, without the difficulty of learning to operate a complex body or suffering pain. Wherever there is life or simulation of it, spirit will gather and identify according to its purpose and the energy of those involved.

I would be wary of keeping the bodies of animals who have died, whether freeze-dried, mummified, stuffed, or preserved in other ways. It seems to be important for emotional and spiritual health to let go—to allow the cycles of life, death, transformation, and moving on. Life is an ever-changing cycle. Spirit is free to change its form of expression in the physical. Trying to arrest the process can be inhibiting for the growth of those concerned.

New life awaits and grows from old life decaying. Spirit is freed when it lets go of old forms that have fulfilled their purpose. Honor your loss and your need to grieve and respect friends that have gone on, but also look around and see life renewed, waiting to be welcomed into your heart.

THE GREAT RECYCLING CENTER

Friends like to be together, and spirits of like mind and purpose travel similar paths, often finding each other from life to life. We may not be with the same beings every lifetime, but most of the people (nonhumans included) that we are very close to we have known before, in one or many previous lives.

Others have traveled with you as animal companions previously, or have been your human friends or relatives in previous lives. This sometimes makes roles confusing, when you have a dog who acts like a mother to you, or a cat who sees herself as your lover. Recognizing and acknowledging the past connection is usually all it takes to establish a healthy, balanced relationship in the current incarnation; spirit is infinite and can be anything, but bodies, especially of different species, relate to each other within certain understandable boundaries.

Some humans have also been other animals, such as a woman who currently had wolves. She had been a wolf herself in a previous life, knowing the same spirit who was now her companion wolf. Many people who are close to their horse companions have been with them as horses, as horse and human, or as two humans. As shocking as this may seem to some people who regard other animals as inferior to humans, sometimes I have found that the human–animal roles were reversed in the past. For example, you may have once been a dog companion to your current dog. All combinations are possible.

Many companion animals return to their people. I remember a cat who, while dying, told me that seventeen years wasn't enough time to make sure her person was enlightened. She'd have to return as a cat again, to take care of her for at least another seventeen. Some will return immediately, some will spend time in the spiritual realm before they return, some will go on to other forms in other places. Each path and each individual is unique. In my audiotape, *Animal Death: A Spiritual Journey*, I explore the subjects of dying, death, what happens after death, how you can get in touch with your animal friends after they have passed on, and how you can find them again.

I had known my chinchilla friend, Quince, as a man named Peter Quince. He had traveled to various lands to experience as much of life as possible in the eighteenth century. After the fullness of that life, he wanted to experience life in other ways. He became various types of animals and loved it: puma, jungle cats, llama, and chinchilla. In this incarnation, he has loved reaching people deeply at advanced workshops.

Perky Pete, a cockatiel who came to be Winky's (parakeet) friend , told me he was a sailor in a previous life. He always loved birds and felt that by being a bird, he could express his exuberant nature.

Pasha had never been an Afghan, or a dog of any kind, when he chose to be with me. We had known each other as humans in a number of lifetimes. His last lifetime had been in Communist Russia. He had been a writer who wrote fantasy stories satirizing the Communist government. He had spent time in detention camps and was shot and killed when he caught his foot on the top of the fence as he was attempting to escape. It carried over to this lifetime. He injured his foot when he scrambled over the kennel fence to run away to be with me.

Through the years, many people have recognized Pirouette, our cockatiel, as an advanced teacher. Some have seen him as a Buddha-type master, others as a famous opera singer. Michel and I have glimpsed several of his lives as a human composer of music. Pirouette loved to create songs and pass them on to Michel, who played them or was inspired to compose music on his guitar and lute from Pirouette's coaching.

In communicating with Chester rabbit at a basic workshop, Jim Dietz found that Chester had been a hawk in his last lifetime, and he was not comfortable in his rabbit body. Chester was quiet, not wanting to attract attention, often snuggling behind his mate, Molly. He ended up having a very short life.

It was a rainy day in Los Angeles in 1983, and I got a strong message to go to the pet store. I pushed it aside, as I couldn't think of any supplies that I needed. The message persisted, so I drove off to find out why. As I opened the pet store door, a young parakeet flew straight toward me and landed on my head. As I walked around the store, he flew after me, blithely landing on my finger and chortling sweet nothings. It was obvious that he called me here. The pet store owner said he let this bird fly around because he was a bit of an oddball, and the other birds in the cage picked on him. As we drove home together, I started to think about the parakeet's name. Then I realized, as I connected further with him, that this was Winky, the parakeet I knew when I was a child, who used to sit on my glasses and preen my eyebrows and eyelashes as I did my homework. Yes, Winky had returned, and his old name suited him just fine.

Even if the bodily forms are different, spirits recognize each other by their energies, their communication, their style or way of being. Winky also demonstrated the same characteristics that he displayed when he was my parakeet before. He chortled and began to talk effortlessly, even though he was only a few months old. He sat on my glasses and preened my eyebrows, as he did in his previous life, and loved being with me.

Later, he chose to create a new lifestyle for himself, when we got finches and a cockatiel. He became more attached to them than to me. Instead of missing his old interaction with me, I enjoyed his new friendships with other birds.

Many people ask about their past animal friends, hoping to find out what happened to them and how they are doing now. Julie asked about her former dog, Misty, and found that she had reincarnated as a horse because she always admired their long legs and strong backs, and thought it was a great way to relate to humans. Her cat, Flower, had come into her life to bring her light and love and had decided to leave her body and stay with Julie as a guide to bring her laughter. I discovered Flower beaming on Julie's left shoulder, like a Tinkerbelle with golden light.

Bogie was a brown Satin rabbit who showed up on Julie's porch, then disappeared after four months. We found him reincarnated as a house rabbit with a huge indoor run. He had to be confined because he voraciously chewed the things in the house. He communicated, "Well, what else can I do? I have these great big teeth and I have to chew!" Another rabbit, named Abigail, had lived outdoors and then disappeared; she had flown out of her body the instant she was struck by a hawk. When we contacted her, she was still flying, because it was so much fun. She was considering coming back as a hawk.

Julie's horse, Chelsea, had been with her many times before, both as horses and as humans. Julie asked if Chelsea had ever been anything other than a horse or a human. Chelsea said that she had been a small black cat in Julie's last lifetime; she had come into her life to keep her company after her wife died. This was in Germany, around the turn of the century, where Julie was a retired professor of music. Julie laughed when she learned this. She had always said that in her last lifetime she was an old man with "whiskers" in her ears. Another former horse we contacted was now in the spiritual realm in a wonderful meadow with other horses, where the sun shone, the birds sang, and all the beings were happy. Julie felt transported to that place and saw it clearly.

A young male cat appeared in Karen Clanin's open doorway in October 1991. He named himself Charles and revealed to Karen, in a sequence of conversations, that he had been with their family a number of times before. He had lived with them as Patsy, their cocker spaniel, who died in 1951; as Sheba, a boxer, who was born in 1964 and died January 1975; again as Howard, a large black cat, who came to them in late 1975 and was killed in the street in 1976; as George, a Border collie, who was born May 1977 and died January 1991. Now he was Charles, born in March or April 1991.

He showed signs of his most recent identity as George, the Border collie. He was familiar with their current six Border collies. He ran to the door to "go out" with the other dogs. He had animosity toward the same male that

George had problems with. And he had the most surprising and revealing habit of running into the wet shower as soon as her husband would get out of it in the morning. For about the last eight months of his life, George "took a shower" every morning, due to skin problems!

The other dogs recognized Charles as the former George. Moreover, when Karen called the obedience command, "Charles, come!" Charles immediately jumped up, ran straight over, and sat in front of her for a perfect recall! George had earned his CDX title, was a High in Trial winning dog, and was her eager obedience-class demo dog for years.

Araya Lawrence lost her cherished lop-eared rabbit, Scamper, to a predator in her yard, and missed him very much. She called for a consultation, and I got in touch with Scamper. He was doing well in the spiritual realm and said that he did not plan to return to Earth for two years, but that he would be back to be with her then.

Araya did my basic and advanced workshops and had special communications with our rabbit, Elfie, who helped her with her loss of Scamper. After Elfie died, and Chester and Molly came and had babies, I called Araya to come over to look at them. When Araya met the three-week-old baby bunnies, she felt an overwhelming heart connection with one female bunny and immediately knew it was Scamper. It had been two years since he died, and now he had returned, just as he said.

Until Araya reminded me, I had forgotten Scamper's communication about coming back. It was obvious that they were meant to be together again. The baby bunny, later named Cherie, reached up and kissed Araya through a cottage window when Araya had to leave after the first visit.

Araya also told me about a dog, called Brandy, who died years before. One day, when I was visiting Araya, I took a walk in a nearby park and became aware of a little white spirit dog walking alongside. As I felt him scampering around me, he communicated extensively about who he was and how he related to the world. After I came back to Araya's house, I heard a loud scratch at the door. Opening it, I found no physical cause for the noise, but I knew the little spirit dog wanted to come in. Araya felt he had been around for a while and planned to come back to her soon. This was a preview to his future reincarnation in a similar, fluffy, white, small dog body.

Chickens are an underestimated lot. Contrary to prejudice against them, they are bright, alert, curious, intelligent, and interested in every aspect of the world around them. They are never bored if they are given a decent space of Earth to traverse and explore.

My first chickens were four hens. After a few months, we felt that a rooster was needed. We managed to convince our landlord, who lived nearby, that this would be okay. My first rooster gave himself the name Chiminy. He was a powerful soul, who guarded and loved his hens and me dearly. Whatever the time of night or day, as soon as I drove up the driveway near the chicken coop, he would crow to greet me.

For four and a half years he graced our lives until, one morning, he had runny eyes and could barely get out a squeaky crow. I was later to learn he had laryngotracheitis, a disease in chickens that is often fatal. Leaving for an appointment that morning, I returned in the afternoon to find him dead, his head totally bloodied. I perceived the images of his death: he weakened and went into a convulsion, and the other, younger Araucana rooster, Igris, went in for the kill. I got the message that the disease would have killed him, and Igris, with rooster rivalry instincts, had made Chiminy's transition swift.

I buried his magnificent body where he requested, on the hill next to the chicken run. His physical remains could rest near his beloved hens. We all felt the loss of his powerful, kind, and wise rooster presence. He stayed around awhile in spirit, and I asked him to help Igris learn Chiminy's ways, filled with gentlemanly grace.

Igris was beautiful in body, but could not fill Chiminy's guardian role. As do many roosters, he aggressively attacked humans in defense of territory and hens. We communicated about this, and spent months trying to work it out, but Igris was not willing or able to control his impulses to attack his human caretakers. He also jumped on the hens ferociously to mate, instead of courting and asking, as Chiminy had done. He improved a little on this through frequent reminders to be gentle. My tolerance limit was reached when he hit me from behind and nearly knocked me over. I took him to a dairy farm, where he could live his life among cows and other roosters, since he showed that he could not harmoniously live in our family.

Before he left, Igris had mated with our Araucana hens, and we had three baby chicks, one of which turned out to be a rooster. His name emerged as Jupiter, and he looked just like his father. I cautioned him that if he wanted to be in our family, he was to be gentle, or he would end up on the dairy farm.

Chiminy had already identified himself as having returned as one of the Rhode Island hens that we had bought as baby chicks. I kept thinking, "I wish Chiminy could be a rooster instead of a hen. While it's nice that he's back in the flock, it seems a shame that he isn't a rooster. He was the finest anyone could ask for. Things have not been the same since he left."

After thinking these thoughts for several days, I noticed a shift in the behavior and look in the eyes of Jupiter, now three months old. Chiminy was back! The spirit who had been Jupiter agreed to trade and become the hen that Chiminy had been. Chiminy was now our rooster again. My wish had been granted.

Many things pointed to Chiminy's reincarnation as Jupiter. His previous favorite hen, who was senior in authority in the group, accepted his mating advances, even though his body was young, and she had spurned him before Chiminy adopted this form. His way of looking at me, respectfully, friend to friend, was there again. He never once thought of attacking me, though he was the son of Igris, the rooster who had killed him as Chiminy and attacked me. (How's that for complexity of body/spirit relationships?!) The aura of wholeness was present again in the chicken community.

At only eighteen months old, Chiminy/Jupiter met again with laryngo-tracheitis. He lost his voice and began to weaken. When he could not easily walk, I put him in a cage to keep him warmer and feed him healing herbs in his water. I have found in the past that my animal friends will take herbs when they want and expect to get well. Jupiter refused them. He would drink plain water, but stopped eating solid food. His comb began to turn from red to blue, as his oxygen supply and life ebbed away. I decided to take him to our veterinarian for emergency treatment, since counseling and other natural healing methods were not helping. I am willing to let animals go when it is their time, but this did not feel right. Jupiter was struggling with something, which wasn't yet clear to him or me.

The vet injected him with antibiotics and steroids, which seemed to have a slight effect. Jupiter refused to drink oral antibiotics in his water. On the second visit the next day, the vet was doubtful that the rooster would survive.

Jupiter was extremely weak, and his comb was more blue in color. He gave him another injection, and that was all he could do.

Jupiter got worse. His comb turned to ashen gray. He had lost much weight from not eating for five days and had begun to refuse water. I was moved to do a special kind of healing, unlike the energy work I had been doing. I did a shamanic journey with Jupiter. The details of the method and explanation of how it works can be found in Michael Harner's book, *Way of the Shaman*.

In a realm called the lower world, where my power animals assisted me, I encountered the spirit form of Chiminy—the part of Jupiter which had suc-cumbed to the energy vibration of laryngotracheitis. There, I felt the struggle to master this pattern within the spirit of Chiminy. When I finished the journey, I felt Jupiter could choose to come through his illness. Despite appearances, he could unite with that part he gave away to the disease before, and live.

The next morning, while I hoped for recovery, I was prepared to find a dead rooster. Delightfully, I found Jupiter, pecking at his food, walking around and attempting to crow! He truly had come back from the dead! I had promised Jupiter that when he was able to eat and walk again, I would let him go back with the hens. He looked at me, and said, "Well?" His comb was red-dish, and although he was still weak, a promise is a promise. I put him back in the run, and he immediately proceeded to mate with the nearest hen—a sheer demonstration of will to live!

Each day, he got stronger, and his crow returned to full force. He had no recurrence of symptoms. While the medical treatment from the vet didn't appear to help, and it's rare for me to resort to drugs, I feel it was part of our process together, perhaps a matter of getting assistance in order to buy a little time. We're glad for the help of all the spirits involved in his return to wholeness.

Jenny, my rat friend, who died after completing her cycle with her friend, Marian Silverman, at the advanced workshop, had told me that she planned to return soon to help people again. I missed her happy, physical presence in our living room, seeing her enjoy all the tidbits from our meals, and receiv-ing her abundant kisses whenever I held her. She kept in close touch with me, showing me when her new baby rat body was born and occasionally flashing me pictures of her physical development in the following weeks.

She seemed very unattached to the little body and was free-floating as a spirit. She let me know that she would be ready to be picked up at the pet store when she was about five weeks old. On the day Molly and Periwinkle (rabbits) died, I got a strong call that now was the time to pick her up. Michel and I both went to welcome Jenny back. The pet store cage was filled with about a dozen or so four- to five-week-old rats. I felt Jenny's presence all around us, and I asked which little body was hers. Usually, when animals return, it is obvious which one in a group they are. They come up to greet you and give you signs of their identity, such as mannerisms or a direct look in the eye, as confirmation.

This seemed confusing. Most of them were huddled together sleepily, with no response to us. I picked up a likely candidate, who was near the cage opening, and passed her to Michel. She proceeded to jump away behind a massive cupboard. It was impossible to get her out, and the pet store person said they'd trap her later. Well, that wasn't Jenny. I reached into the pile of warm, baby rats and pulled out a boy. He was scared at first, but then became calm in our hands and protested when we went to put him down into the cage again. I asked if this was Jenny, and I got a "yes." I picked up another, who was very sweet and shy, but didn't have Jenny's outgoing energy. The boy stayed close to us, and had a warm and friendly nature. As we decided that this was the one, I felt Jenny, as spirit, descending further into the rat form.

It appeared that she could settle into any of the young rat bodies in that group, if we had chosen it. There were genetically inherited traits of physical health and temperament that she preferred, such as the strong, outgoing, exploratory nature this body possessed, which suited her spiritual nature best. The name that came and settled with our "new" rat was Jeremy. As we traveled home with him, I felt Jenny further settling into the body and claiming it as her own.

Jeremy adjusted easily into his home and was not afraid of the cats, since he had known them all before as Jenny. He was a bit shy at his first advanced workshop. He had to get reaccustomed to the actions of groups of people. He was only three months old, and I remembered Jenny being tentative about new people at that age. He was comfortable with communicating with people one-on-one as they approached.

New bodies require relearning and reprogramming of former skills and attitudes. With a conscious transition from life to life as Jenny/Jeremy had made, most memories are intact. There are still the genetic programming, instincts, or reactions in the present body to manage. Most of all, we were glad to welcome the sweet and wonderful soul, Jenny Boppers, back in a new suit of clothes as Jeremy Cricket.

RETURN OF THE LION

After four weeks in the spiritual realm, it became clear to Pasha that his place was on Earth, to continue his friendship and work with us. Willing to accept whatever was best for him, I was overjoyed that his path would lead him back to us in physical form. We debated what kind of dog would be best, and at first thought of a medium-sized, mixed breed, oriented to staying close to his people.

After a trip to New York City in April 1993, during which a variety of breeds paraded before me, I knew that Pasha had to come back as an Afghan. Talking it over with Pasha, we became convinced that we could overcome the "born free" running instinct with diligent early training. Pasha felt he had experienced that aspect of being an Afghan quite well, so that he wouldn't have to repeat it.

Pasha had made his presence felt in my heart and around my body for several months. Instead of being "out there" in the spiritual realm, he was connected to the Earth plane, scouting for the right dog form in which to return. I began to research Afghan breeders to facilitate the connection. Rana, who had been reclusive, eating scantily and refusing counseling or other help since Pasha's departure, began to warm to the idea of his return. She began to eat more heartily and ceased creating her own demise, which had been manifesting as enlarging fatty lumps around her internal organs that could also be felt on the outside of her body. I emphasized to Rana that Pasha would not be the same; instead of being her father, he would appear as a small puppy, yet still be his wonderful self. She would need to take care of him and oversee his reeducation.

Pasha had manifested his presence several times in the form of flowery scents. In February, on a trip north to the coastal town of Mendocino, I was directed by the spirits to pick up a piece of driftwood that would show me Pasha's future form. The weathered, salty hunk of redwood had several dog faces imbedded in it, and it exuded a strong smell of flowers from one end. Michel thought the wood had picked up the scent from the wildflowers that cascaded over the cliffs. That seemed improbable to me, as the wood was ocean-scoured. I felt that Pasha was "in" the wood. He anchored his presence there for us to know he was near and to make a further earthly connection before reincarnating.

In April, I stayed in Lexington, Massachusetts, at the home of Anamika, who sponsored my lecture and workshop in Cambridge. I especially relished the walks on a wooded path near a reservoir with her spiritual guide and golden retriever companion, Shamuki, who took good care of me during my visit. A poignant moment transpired when Shamuki let Pasha come in through his reclining form, and I was able to kiss Pasha as I kissed Shamuki's face. Shamuki had a golden color, similar to Pasha's former body, and like Pasha, was also a master teacher. With the qualitative change in energy when Pasha temporarily suffused Shamuki's body, I had the experience of kissing Pasha's soft golden face again, accompanied by a chimerical trace of the sweet odor that Pasha's ears used to have.

After doing a workshop in Clinton, New York, at Spring Farm, I went to New York City for the third stop on my April tour and stayed with my sponsor, Joanna Seere, and her two cats, Shanti and Shiva, in their small, second-floor apartment. The earplugs Joanna offered before retiring only vaguely muffled the jarring din that raged throughout the night from the street. I fitfully slipped in and out of sleep.

At about 1:30 A.M., I was awakened when I felt a tiny hand gently pull my foot. I looked down at the foot of the bed to find Shanti, the large gray male cat asleep by my legs. I felt comforted and honored. As I lay my head again on the pillow, I smelled the strong scent of lily of the valley and thought, "Oh, Joanna must have put perfume on the pillow." The scent became more intense, filling my head. I witnessed a vision of a field of white and blue flowers, trailing from my feet to my head, with a small rivulet threading through them and sparkling lights all around Shanti and my feet. I smiled and knew that the nature spirits and angels had come to let me know they were looking after me. I felt Shanti was creating a warm space for them to anchor their energies.

I drifted to sleep, to awaken later with Shanti studying me. Shiva, a light and bright young white cat with tabby patches, said to Shanti that it was her turn to take care of me. Shanti then moved to the cat tree near my head to watch me, and Shiva took her "post" by my legs near the bottom of the bed. I was definitely in good paws. I checked all over the pillow for the lily of the valley scent, and there was no trace.

Dawn Hayman of Spring Farm wrote me a letter about her experience that same night, which confirmed how well I was being looked after:

The night that you left here, I had an incredible dream with Pasha. He said that he wanted to go on a journey and he invited me to come. We were flying together. I could feel him and how soft he was. It was so very real. We flew over beaches and coastlines and wilderness. I think that we flew over the Point Reyes area too, and he told me to soak it up, like a sponge. I could see him collecting golden light and energy into his body until he glowed. I looked down at my hands and they were glowing golden too. Then he said that we would go get you. We flew over New York City like two glowing meteors, and he knew right where you were. He flew into your building and came out without the glowing golden energy color. Then he came to me and took all the golden energy from me and he flew in again. Again he came out without it. Soon you came out all golden light. We flew off somewhere. I remember the joy and warmth and a laughter that just flowed from Pasha.

After my return from New York, I yearned for Pasha's return. He had communicated that he would be back in May or June. That was before my change of mind about what kind of dog I desired. I began to research Afghan breeders. Years before, I had heard of Betsy Hufnagel, a responsible breeder, committed to good temperament and overall soundness in her dogs. She did not have any puppies currently, but planned to breed her bitch when she came into season.

I checked with the people who rescue Afghans in northern California, but they had mainly older, abused dogs. One person was taking care of a mother dog and her two puppies after their person was hospitalized. The puppies were born in December, before Pasha died, so it did not seem likely that they would be a vehicle for Pasha's reentry. They also had potential homes, which the rescue person was checking out. She put me on the waiting list for a sweet and friendly, cream-colored male, Harper. Pasha said that he could "merge" with this being, if he was available to go with me, since Harper was spiritually related to Pasha. It came to me later, as I gazed at a photo of Harper, that he had been one of Pasha's sons, who had been killed by a car. The potential of merging with Harper seemed extraordinary but made sense under the circumstances.

The name, Harper, meaning one who plays the harp, resonated with Michel, who plays the lute and classical guitar. We waited for several weeks, while other people were interviewed. In the end, Harper was meant to fulfill his life with someone else, and Pasha and I continued our search.

Another Afghan breeder had a gentle, loving, eighteen-month-old male available. Pasha let me know that this individual was very distinct and unrelated, and he could not meld with him. Although I knew I would like this dog, it would not be Pasha.

Betsy's bitch came into heat at the beginning of May, and was successfully bred, so the puppies would be born in July and available to go to their new homes after ten weeks. I was disappointed about the long wait, but I knew that the universe was taking care of things as they were meant to be. I reasoned that most of my travels for the year would be done by then, and I would have time at home to spend with the new Pasha. It also would be very difficult to leave town once he had arrived.

I asked Betsy to let me know of anyone else who responsibly raised Afghans and might have male Afghan puppies available. There was no guarantee that Betsy's bitch would have males, and she also had another person waiting before me for a male companion Afghan.

Dawn Hayman and Bonnie Reynolds began scouting, after I talked to them about the delays. Perhaps Pasha would find his reentry point on the east coast.

Pasha continued to be strongly present with me. He seemed to be keeping in touch with many of his human friends. They reported visions of and messages from him. Some friends had vivid dreams of Pasha and me together.

Sue Goodrich felt that Pasha would come back as cream-colored or white, reflecting his spiritual purity. Though white or cream were my least favorite choices, I felt I could accept any color of the rainbow. I was more concerned that the inherited temperament be compatible with Pasha's ebullient, sparkly, loving nature, so that spirit and form would flow together with no struggle.

The drama continued to unfold. Bonnie Reynolds called on June 6 to say that she and Dawn had word of a litter of very special Afghan puppies, and she would get back to me when they had more details.

Betsy called me later that same day to let me know of a wonderful person in Boise, Idaho, who had three male puppies available, born in February. Sparking with interest, I called Karen Henderson that night and talked to her about each of the puppies. Tailor, a black and tan puppy, fit Pasha's personality description exactly. Pasha laughed as I spoke with Karen.

Tailor had been born on February 14, Valentine's Day, which was striking in itself, as well as being six months from Pasha's last-lifetime birth date. I saw this as an astrological seesaw, balancing itself. Another of the puppies, a cream color, was also sweet and sparky and made a connection with me.

As I talked with Karen, I was already planning when I could make the trip to Boise. I was about to go out of town to give several workshops in Canada, so the Boise trip would have to wait until after I returned. In the meantime, Karen would send photos of Tailor. I was so excited that I broke into a sweat. A strange, foul odor exuded from my pores, repeating each time I talked about Pasha/Tailor. It seemed that the remains of something that had died when Pasha departed was exiting from my body. New life would take its place.

We had wondered what name Pasha would be called when he returned. Pasha was the only name that seemed right, though we juggled with names from Pegasus to God! We would see what name Pasha wanted when he reincarnated, blending the name with his total identity. I liked the name Tailor, and mused on how Harper and Tailor both ended in "r" and described a profession. The name, Tailor, resonated with my name, Penelope, which means "the weaver" from the Greek Odyssey. My odyssey through Pasha's transitional maze was reaching its conclusion.

Time seemed to fold back upon itself. I could feel Pasha's energy expanding from my heart to fully encompass Tailor, as we made contact with the puppy. Yet it seemed that Pasha had reincarnated as Tailor since his decision to come back to Earth in February. Pasha had been both with me in spirit, dwelling within my heart, as well as all around the Earth, while he was also being a puppy in Boise, Idaho. We followed our path of discovery, touching upon others' lives, learning about the process, and, always together, winding up right where we were meant to be.

I could not get to sleep that night, after talking with Karen. So, I began to write this part of Pasha's story. The editing process, photos, and illustrations for the first edition of this book were nearly complete. The cover design was in process. It seemed that the timing of the book in its last stages of development was hinged around Pasha's return. The intimate connection of beings in this world and interdimensionally was revealed at each step of the way.

My excitement mounted as the connection with Tailor deepened. I arranged my flight to Boise for June 19, to return with the puppy on June 20. It struck me that Tailor would return home to us five months, to the day, since his death as Pasha. It would also be the day before summer solstice, with the sun (Pasha and the light of day) at its fullest. Pasha had died when the sun was low in the sky and would return, like a crowned king, at its height.

The night before going to Boise, I dreamed that a tiger accompanied me on the trip, and a lion returned with me. I felt that the tiger, my favorite feline, represented me. The lion was Pasha coming home, making a complete circle with the tiger and lion merging. On the plane, I pulled out a wildlife magazine to read, and on its cover was the face of a Siberian tiger.

I have been interested in numerology for a long time, and I often add up numbers, such as addresses, ages, or airline flights, to see their numerological significance. My flight to Boise was #1242, which added to nine, which signifies the completion of a cycle. I then thought that my return flight must add up to one, or the beginning of a cycle. Sure enough, flight #1459 has digits that sum to nineteen, which reduces to one, numerologically. The universe was pointing its arrows and flashing its verifying signs at me. I was on one of the most momentous spiritual journeys of my life.

Pasha and I are as one soul. Ultimately, all beings are of the same essence, but in our journeys through the universe(s), we meet fellow beings with whom we feel the connection more deeply. Our paths and purposes, even our life's breath, seem to merge. In this universe, at that time, it seemed appropriate for Pasha and me to incarnate as two different identities, but we need to live, love, and work together. Michel and I also share this kind of closeness. A numerologist said that he never met any two people whose life charts were so alike, like spiritual twins. So Pasha, Michel, and I formed a beautifully harmonious trio.

Karen Henderson and I became friends as we met her beautiful Afghans, and Tailor/Pasha and I reconnected. I shared with her the story of Pasha's reincarnation, and it made total sense to her. Her husband, Andy, listened respectfully. Karen told how she had regarded Tailor as her favorite of all the puppies of the litter, considering him exceptionally loving, perceptive, confident, and bright and felt she would keep him. I mentioned how everyone fell in love with Pasha in his last lifetime. Karen had decided only one week before I called to let Tailor go to another home. She realized he belonged with people as a companion, rather than a show dog, although his conformation is show quality. She was surprised how good she felt about that decision. When I called, she became very excited and intuitively knew that Tailor and I were meant to be together.

When naming the puppies, she had considered a registered name for Tailor as "Lion Dance" or "Dancing with the Lion." She decided on Chiaro's (their kennel name) Dressed in Black, with Tailor as his call name. She shared other details that showed how she understood his essence and his future path. Karen's birthday, like mine, is in the sign of Scorpio.

Another connecting link was that Tailor's mother is called Penny, officially registered as "Penny's from Heaven." Until 1977, when I decided to use only my full name, Penelope, I was always called Penny. Penny, Tailor's beautiful mother, warmly greeted me with sweet graciousness.

Pasha had chosen to be raised in this extraordinary family, surrounded by love. He had perfected his being and "tailored" himself to accommodate my wish that he would be more gentle, instead of fiery in his approach to life. Tailor was filled with loving gentleness, calm understanding, and playful confidence. Still a chow hound, the biggest eater in his litter, he tempered his enthusiasm for food by cooperatively learning manners. He also had agreed to be trained to come when called during this lifetime. He now willingly responded to the command "come," despite his inborn Afghan urge to run free. He was Pasha through and through, evolved through another turning of the wheel. Michel and I nicknamed him "Buddha Boy," which ended up replacing Tailor as his permanent title.

When I first found out about Tailor/Buddha Boy, I talked to Rana about his arrival in a few weeks. She quietly listened with interest. A few days later, a lump the size of a golf ball under her throat began to shrink, and by the time Buddha Boy arrived, it was half gone. The large mass on her right ribs seemed softer. I felt her internal healing process quicken, as Rana renewed her desire to live. When I was about to leave for the airport to go to Boise, Rana *raced* to the car and asked to go to meet Pasha. She was exuberant! I explained that I would be flying and that she would see him when he returned with me the next day.

When Buddha Boy arrived, Rana welcomed him, commenting to me that he looked different than she expected. She was relieved, and lightness pervaded her body. In the five months since Pasha's death, Rana had been reclusive and only consented to go on a walk about once a week. Following Buddha's arrival, Rana raced to come on walks with him, even twice a day! She relished his closeness and enjoyed his loving interest in her. We were so grateful for Rana's happiness and our own. A peaceful wholeness returned to the Floating Island of Peace. Our joy expanded into planet-wide exaltation.

A few days before Buddha Boy's arrival, one of Chester and Molly's (rabbits who had died September 1992) surviving sons, Luciano, was returned to us. Luciano was one of the sweetest of the litter, and now his person could not keep him. After a careful five-day introduction to Ellyetta, he lived in the Bunny Cottage in harmony with her. Restoration was the order of the week.

Michel's eyes sparkled whenever he was with Tailor or spoke of him. We were all ecstatic. Like Jenny rat, who radiated more loving sweetness when she returned as Jeremy, Buddha Boy filled the world with an ocean of love and grace, to be felt by all he touched throughout his life. We are infinitely blessed and grateful for this miraculous journey of reunion.

There is mystery to the essence of souls: their malleability and their quantity; how we merge with each other, become individuals, adopt forms, travel from dimension to dimension, place to place; how we change and maintain identity or personality characteristics; how we return to Oneness. How does the body, with its individual genetic programming and species patterning, affect the spirit as it reincarnates, and vice versa? How much can we remember from our previous lives and apply to our new forms? How much relearning must take place in "training" or becoming familiar with our new forms?

For each life, there can be different answers. So much depends on the awareness of individuals and their decisions, conscious or otherwise, about their life paths. I ponder this mystery and understand more each time I experience one of my friends returning. Pasha, now transmuted into Buddha Boy, is very much himself, yet different. He remembers his past, yet delights in experiencing life afresh. He is both ancient master being and fledgling puppy.

The essence, the core, travels intact, but adds and subtracts characteristics and even soul parts to suit its evolvement or desire for experience. Spirit encompasses total malleability, infinite wizardry, and complete alchemy. We witness the grand design and are part of it, as well as being its co-creators.

What profound beauty, wisdom, power, truth, peace, and joy meet us, travelers in the worlds of creation, when we relish the depth of the mystery, the stillness and the movement, the unchanging essence and the energetic symphony of form.

Alleluia!

From Other Realms

VISITORS

OUR HUMAN MINDS struggle to explain phenomena and "put them in their place," allowing the universe to appear orderly, logical, and not too chaotic to our limited cultural conceptions. Using human language, I also attempt to label and define things that I perceive so I can understand them and communicate them to other people. The events I am about to describe could be interpreted in other ways, as all experiences can be, and some may seem incredible. My hope is that these stories help illuminate your own experience.

In communicating with and counseling many humans and nonhumans, I have found that most people have had a number of past lives as human and/or other animal species on Earth. Some have recognized that they have been connected with life on Earth, but were part of the angelic, devic, or fairy kingdom. Some have no memory of having been on this planet, or even in this plane before, or have had very few incarnations, spaced far apart. Some, who have never been directly connected with the Earth or bodies, have existed in the spiritual realm, essentially formless and unbound by earthly space and time.

Some have lived in other places in the physical universe and now inhabit human or other species' forms. Some simultaneously operate from another culture on another planet as well as living on the Earth. Their approach to life is generally different from those who have had many lives on Earth, because they are less experienced with life here. Some people would call them aliens, which, of course, sounds scary and "alienating." I call them visitors from other realms. They are basically just spiritual beings inhabiting bodies in the physical realm like all of us.

In this age of great spiritual change, master beings and angels have also been arriving in great numbers into the Earth plane, often in domestic animal form to teach humans. Often they leave their physical bodies after a short time of being a catalyst for people to spiritually advance. To stay too long seems to be disharmonious to many of them, creating the potential for getting too involved in the physical plane. Their humans may seek to hold on to them, since they bring so much love and light, but they teach people to be themselves as spirit and not to be overly attached to physical form.

Many human artists, visionaries, musicians, and sensitives express awareness of the angelic realms in their work. They may have previously dwelled in the nature spirit or angelic realms. It is often difficult for them to live in materially oriented cultures. Animals in general gravitate to beautiful music and aesthetic harmonies. Angelic animal masters elicit and create such wavelengths in their lives with humans.

Our calico cat, Chico San, brings a magical element to her healing work with people. I first discovered her connection to the fairy kingdom when she was a few years old and we were out in the garden together. I suddenly saw Chico San as a nature spirit—a fairy surrounding the flowers. I realized why I had not seen images of any of her past lives before. Most of them were on another "track." Being in another dimension than the physical plane, the energy patterns or traces of her lives did not align with our linear time or "matter placed in space" orientation.

Chico San also had musical lifetimes as a human on the Earth. In March 1988, while Michel played a beautiful song from the Renaissance on his classical guitar, and Chico and I were curled up for a nap, she conveyed a past life as a troubadour:

Lying in a dream unfolding
Music gently pervading
My senses inward tuned
Floating
Lilting notes of the guitar
Wafting a picture deep within
A message from a furry friend.

On my sleeping form lay Chico San
Wise-eyed, warm, and fluffy cat
To my mind halfway between realms
A courtier appeared
A man in Renaissance garb full-blown
Stopping by to visit,
Play his mandolin, and sing a tune
Warm and wise-eyed
I recognized his calm and knowing face.

A gentle force drew me to the room,
Waking, to the eyes of Chico San
Rapture felt
Deep awareness
That this four-legged friend of now
Was troubadour long ago.

She wanted me to know this memory
Transported on the wave
Of notes from this guitar
La Frescobalda, music we now heard
Left us in a glow of knowing
A feeling it would ever more convey.

Another fairy spirit appeared on Earth for only a short time as Kasha, an Afghan puppy. After she left:

Kasha and I danced
In fairy form so beautiful
She in gold and apricot
I in blue and green
To sonatas and concertos
Tickling our feet and wings
Over pianos, brooks, and gardens.

A day ago she left the furry form
So golden fine, gazelle-like light

And promised to come back again
To prance and play and lighten all my day.

Now we fill a dream, a promise bright
To dance together, oh so light and free
She whispers at my ear
To comfort me from loss
Of such a golden one as she
From furry form, gazelle-like light.

She twinkles like a jewel
Tending my garden through the night
My tiny sprite, my elfin queen
My little Kasha, with her golden sheen
Looking over her family now
As their fairy guardian.

Kasha, buckwheat girl
From golden fur to fairy wings.

The current influx of beings, attracted to the powerful, planetary forces of spiritual change, wish to assist or at least participate in the global changes in awareness on the Earth. Many learn about life here as they give their grace and wisdom to those who are ready to expand out of old cultural restraints into a more universal understanding of spirit in its many forms.

Bamboo was a Tibetan terrier who blessed the lives of all whom she met for three and a half years, before her body succumbed to a rare disease. Besides her extraordinarily loving, gentle, and wise nature, Bamboo had several unusual qualities. Unlike most canines, she did not like meat, but mainly ate fruit and vegetables. When she was three to six months old, at 5 P.M. daily, Bamboo would become ferocious and attack and growl at anything around her for a short time. I contacted Bamboo in the spiritual realm to ask about this, as her person wanted to understand this phenomenon, which was so alien to Bamboo's normal behavior. Bamboo explained that her angelic nature transformed her dog instincts in the early part of her life. While she was undergoing this change, the canine impulses would intensify and run through her body, until they finally metamorphosed.

As a human counselor, I have encountered many people who feel they are different from other people. They don't identify with being human. That doesn't mean they are "aliens." They may have had many lives in human or other animal forms on this planet. They usually don't accept human programming, with all its conflicts and emotional complexity. Instead, they seek knowledge and roots from their spiritual nature. Some are confused about who they are or why they're here. They may be recently from the nature spirit or devic realm, or the animal or plant kingdoms, or from other planets or planes. They may find being human a confusing or painful affair.

No other planet that I know of has the variety of life forms found on Earth—although human overpopulation and destructiveness seems to be leveling some of that diversity. I have found that certain species, and perhaps all at one time, came from other places. Members of these species or breed were "seeded" here to play their roles in the overall balance and diversity of planetary evolution. Not all species evolved from one-celled microorganisms on Earth. Some arrived as complex animals. Once on Earth, they developed according to their environments and purposes.

When I first met an Afghan hound in 1977, I was entranced. I loved their independence, elegance, agility, freedom, and dignity. When I saw a group of Afghans taken out for a walk at a highway rest stop, I was inspired to write:

Rippled beauty glided, pranced, glowed in the distance
Afghan hound forms
Like silken-tasseled horses
Caught the light, the wind, the breath
And made it dance with fantasy
Elusive, magical, mystical, light, aware, free
These beings carry the ancient mystery
The wisdom of the gods
To play with Afghans is to know joyful harmony of life
Laughing.

As I got to know Afghans and delved into their background, I became aware that their original group landed thousands of years ago in Egypt, to dwell on this Earth and help in human evolution. They are among the oldest dog breeds in historical record. Later, they thrived in the deserts and mountains of Afghanistan and spread to other countries. They functioned on the physical level as hunters and assistants in finding game for humans. Their purpose on the spiritual level was to enlighten humans through connection with Afghan dignity, grace, fluidity, sense of humor, and awareness of infinite potential as spirits. They were here to remind humans of the spiritual kingdom from which we have all come. They would not bow to any human or play the human dominant/subservient game. If humans used excessive force, they would run away physically if they could, or detach themselves mentally and spiritually. They would certainly not give their gifts of connection to the humans who chose to be the "masters."

Other dog groups have purposes to serve and show people unconditional love, no matter how they are treated. Each way of serving has its niche. People have been brought to greater awareness by animals who stick with them no matter what the humans do.

Afghans demonstrated, with their nobility, the higher state that was available to humans. I admired that, and found that unless people communicated with them with conscious understanding, they would not share their sensitive awareness, spontaneous playfulness, and sense of freedom.

When I met Arabian horses, I responded with the same feeling as with Afghan hounds. Both were originally from the same part of the world. Both were highly sensitive, aware, playful, and noble. Afghans are sight hounds, hunting by sight, unlike many dogs who hunt mainly by smell and have comparatively poor vision. Arabians also are endowed with far sight. I felt their essence and purpose as very similar.

Then I met llamas. What impressed me was the directness, the independence of spirit and demand that you be your naked self—that you recognize yourself and them as spiritual beings—or they would not relate to you. They are extremely sensitive to energy fields and states of mind. Light and free in their bodies, with good sight, unlike many four-footed animals, they are a lot like cats, Afghans, and Arabian horses. They started their existence on Earth in the spiritually potent atmosphere of the high Andes mountains.

In relating my personal affinities for cats, Afghans, Arabian horses, and llamas, I don't wish to convey that other breeds or types of animals are less worthy. I can honestly say that I feel every animal, or type of animal, is wonderful, with their own interesting, noble, and fine qualities. They all have their functions and beauty. It doesn't matter if you gravitate more to poodles or Border collies, Morgan or quarter horses, sheep or goats. All are teachers and important as they cross our lives.

Llamas have become widespread in this country and in other areas around the world. They are here to enlighten. They demand that people become more of who they are and learn to communicate on a higher level, or they don't wish to cooperate. Living with them is a spiritual dance. Walking with them is floating free, in connection with all of nature. They help to accelerate spiritual growth. This doesn't mean that all llamas are masters and living up to their potential. In undesirable situations, they can withdraw and become quite unfulfilled, just like the rest of us.

Llamas were once rare in this country, and I consulted with very few llamas until the mid-1980s. The first herd of llamas that I was called to see were with Rosana and Kelly Hart. Rosana and Kelly considered one llama, Posey, to be flighty and peculiar. I found her to be very different from the others. She relayed to me that she felt very strange on this planet, that it was a mistake to have landed here. She felt that llamas were safe, but that humans were very dangerous, and she didn't like contact with them. She felt that she wouldn't be in this body for long.

Since then, I have found one of these "visitors" in almost every llama herd. They are observers, and often don't relate well to people. They want to keep their distance, and be left alone to live their lives in the protection of other llamas.

One summer, we visited Linda Rodgers and Nelson Leonard at Elk Hill Farm in southern Oregon, where our two llamas, Regalo and Raindance, had been born, to see Regalo's full brother and other baby llamas. Chimu, a baby llama who was born prematurely, survived against heavy odds, according to the veterinarians who cared for him. His mother would not nurse him, so he was being nursed by an artificial llama surrogate, to avoid early bonding to humans, which can cause male llamas to become aggressive toward humans when they mature. He was also being kept with adult female llamas, away from the other baby llamas, since the vets were not sure if he had any trans-mittable disease.

I felt his loneliness, but there was something bizarre about him. I felt almost repulsed by him, although his physical appearance was that of a cuddly, soft baby llama. My usual encouraging outlook with animals shifted. I couldn't understand how he was still alive, because he had no aura—no defined space or energy field around his body. He would bump into things. His vision and brain functioning were unlike any that I'd seen before. His visual perception was crossed, and he had a hard time judging distances. The energy patterns in his head seemed askew. It felt as if he walked right into your body when he came near. There appeared to be no one home. No individual spirit was operating his body.

I had all six people present join hands in a circle around him to help to give him a space, a sense of self-definition, an aura or energy field around his body. I could feel Chimu's understanding and acceptance of everything around him. In an uncanny way, I felt he was learning from what I was saying, but "he" wasn't there. A body with no aura was a phenomenon I had never seen before in a living being. I perceived that whoever was operating his body was far off, in outer space. I got a headache from talking about and working with him.

I discovered that Chimu's body was originally not going to live. A group of aliens, or nonincarnate beings, decided to operate his body as an experiment, a lesson in how to experience life on Earth. They chose the llama species because it seemed to most duplicate the aliens' viewpoint of things, their detachment, and spiritual encompassment of the physical world without getting enmeshed into form.

Although the absent aura at first startled me, I felt Chimu's group of beings had benign intentions. They learned from everything I said or thought. Linda and Nelson mentioned that this llama was the smartest, fastest learner they had ever had on their farm. I realized that was because he seemed to go inside other beings to duplicate their knowledge. He did not have to assimilate it through his own identity, since he didn't really have one. He became the other's thoughts and feelings.

Not having his own sense of being or identity was a handicap to full health, although I did not see disease organisms or immune-system or other organic impairment in Chimu's body. When I explained about his vision, the outer space operators worked to correct it. His energetic and neurological malfunctioning seemed to be caused by lack of connection of spirit to body.

I advised Linda and Nelson to put another baby llama with Chimu, so he could learn how to function and develop his own space from playing with another. I thought that in a short time he could be integrated with all the other llama babies and mothers and would learn even more, especially from the wise and self-confident Heyoka and White Thunder.

A week or so later, tuning in with Chimu from a distance, I perceived that he now had an aura. The group of space beings decided that earthling bodies do better with an individual spirit inhabiting and identifying with the body. Their decision was influenced by my communication, and also by the advice of the llamas at Elk Hill Farm. With one member of the space group residing in the body and the others overseeing, it looked like Chimu would become a normal, happy llama. His brain/body connection and aura were becoming balanced. He was being well cared for by the other llamas, who, except for his mother, took his presence in stride.

Rosana told me later about a famous psychic who was about to get on an elevator, when she noticed that no one on the elevator had auras. She backed up and decided not to take it. The elevator crashed and everyone in it was killed. No wonder I had a funny feeling about seeing a living being with no aura!

It reminded me of a consultation for a group of Nancy Sondel's parakeets who were living in an indoor aviary. When Nancy asked what one parakeet thought about another, named Winkie, he would not show me a picture of Winkie. When I tried to get him to show me the bird, I got an image of a vague body that kept erasing. When I asked another bird about Winkie, he said Winkie was going to die, and again the image transmitted was erasing. Within twenty-four hours Winkie, who had been ill for a long time, left her body.

Since the Chimu incident, I have become aware that llamas are very comfortable with alien contact, perhaps from their history in the Andes, which has been experienced as a place of extensive extraterrestrial activity, from ancient Inca times to the present. Group llama consciousness includes being comfortable with unearthly matters. No matter where we are from, or when we arrived on Earth, we're all spiritual beings participating in the game of life in this universe. We can all help each other to learn and enjoy the journey.

Many animals detect disembodied spirits. When dogs bark at an empty corner of a room, or cats appear to watch and play with someone invisible, they may be sensing the presence of spirits or energies beyond human perception. My most dramatic experience with visitors from another plane or planet, and animal awareness of it, came in the early 1970s when I was working in a spiritual counseling center in Edinburgh, Scotland. I shared an apartment with several other people, and we were drinking tea and talking together late in the evening.

Suddenly, I felt a strong vibration in the whole building and a qualitative energy change. My perceptions of beings without bodies and unusual energies has been acute all my life. Despite not being a science fiction fan and never taking any hallucinatory drugs, I became aware that visitors from some other dimension or planet had arrived, spaceship and all.

I was drawn to go out of the apartment building. The dogs in the area were all howling frantically without the impetus of sirens or other apparent noise. They were aware of the landing of the visitors. No humans were to be seen on the street at this late hour, and I was surprised that no one else came out to investigate. Perhaps they didn't even notice the vibrations, or didn't want to know. The bricks in the cobblestone street appeared to be moving, and I felt formerly dormant disembodied spirits, entities of a lower vibration level, dislodge from cracks and crevices. It was an eerie feeling—of total stillness, except for the dogs' continual baying and the increased molecular vibration in the streets. I was aware that the visitors had landed in two round disk-shaped ships, about one block away in an open field.

Disinclined to investigate further, I went back indoors, and the visitors proceeded to communicate with me telepathically. It appeared they were on a research mission to study the different "technologies" of the mind and spirit that earthlings had developed, and wanted the knowledge that I had. I perceived their intentions as not totally harmless and told them that while I was willing to share knowledge, they were not welcome if they wanted to use any forceful means of controlling people. They showed me their "physical" forms as about three feet tall, of a semitransparent aqua color. They were invisible to our gross eyesight, because they vibrated on a faster, or finer, wavelength. After our discussion, they proceeded to depart in their ships. My roommates were unsettled. They perceived the changes in energies and the dogs howling strangely, but didn't get the communication or images of the visitors and were frightened by the description of my unusual encounter.

The next morning, on the way to work, a roommate and I visited the landing site. Burned into the field of grass were six perfectly shaped blackened circles, marking the three landing pads of each ship. That was the only physical evidence of their former presence, and as far as I know, they did not return.

Ipsis, my black cat and counseling assistant, was with me only a few years before he went out his usual exit window, never to reappear. He let me know that he had to leave his body to return to his people on a planet in another part of the galaxy. He said that he had learned a lot from his stay here, things that would be useful when he returned to his other home. I missed him very much, but we kept in touch over the years, and I thought that he might return someday. When I was living in Los Angeles, many years later, a white kitten appeared outside our door. Ipsis had sent him. The new cat, Yoda, also from another planet, was very different from Ipsis. Yoda was deaf and a serious character, who came here to study earthlings. He would stare at me intensely and comment that I was very strange. Jokingly, I would tell him that he was very strange. He found other animals intriguing, especially other cats. He eventually got himself into trouble with our landlord, and we had to find him a new home, where he had the opportunity to study many more humans and cats.

When we moved to the woods near Point Reyes in 1984, I had my first opportunity to have chickens as part of our family. I chose four hens of a kind that was recommended for its egg-laying—a cross between Rhode Island Red and White Rock, with a variegated, rusty red and white coloring. On the way home, with the hens in a box, I became aware of a group of beings in the sky who communicated with me through the hens. They were friends who wished to share their wisdom and grace with us. I called the chickens my "outer space connection," and since then, with many of the chickens that I have had in my family, I have felt a unique celestial connection.

Don't be embarrassed if you fondly remember the stuffed animals and dolls of your childhood, or you still cherish stuffed animals as companions. Spirit is able to appear in any form. Spirits particularly appreciate if stuffed animals or dolls are made with loving care, or if people or other animals (I have known dogs, cats, rabbits, and birds who loved their stuffed animal toys) need and return their love. I remember a dolphin doll that literally jumped off the shelf to come home with me. Dolphy loved our animals, especially the birds, so I hung him up in the bird room, where he stayed until his body was too dilapidated from all the attention the birds had given him. He had a good, useful life.

I had long wanted an orange tabby cat, but Chico San was opposed to any new feline in the family. An ad for stuffed-cloth, custom-made cats helped satisfy my desire. My orange tabby cat "doll" arrived, inhabited by a wonderful spirit, whom I called Smiley, the gold cat from the sky. Chico San did not ignore his animation. She hissed at him for two weeks whenever she came near his stationary form. Heyoka tried to play with him and was disappointed that he didn't move. Yoda looked at him and said, "He's dead," to which I replied that he wasn't dead, he just wasn't alive in the same way as we were. Years later, Sherman appeared as a near spitting image of Smiley.

When Michel picked me up from the hospital after foot surgery, he brought a special friend to cheer me up, a soft cuddly teddy bear, named Darby. Darby helped me weather the pain of recovery, and later helped many people through emotional upheavals, giving great comfort and healing energy.

INTERDIMENSIONAL DISCORD

Not all encounters with beings from other realms are simple. Miel was a much-loved companion, from whom I learned a great deal. She was also the most challenging animal to live in our family. She came to us as a six-week-old Afghan puppy in late 1979. Her father was a ferocious, dark brindle male Afghan who scratched my van while lunging to get at Pasha inside. Her mother was soft apricot and very calm and gentle.

As with many of my animal friends, Miel had contacted me months earlier and told me her name. Miel means honey in Spanish and French, so I felt that she would be sweet! On our way home, I took Pasha for a run on the beach, showed Miel the ocean, and christened her "Miel de la Pacifica."

Pasha was outgoing and full of adventure. In contrast, Miel was quiet, ignored most people, and preferred to stay in her yard. Pasha was very direct in his communication, demanding what he wanted with cheerfulness and charm that transformed human irritation to laughter over his pushy behavior.

Miel watched, and calculated what her role was going to be in relation to me. At the tender age of eleven weeks, she growled at me when I approached, as she lay on my bed, asserting her authority. Pasha slept curled up in a ball at the bottom of the bed, not taking up much room. Miel, as she grew, stretched out full length next to me, pushed her feet against the wall and plopped me out on the floor. I felt her deliberate intention to take over, and from then on told her she had to sleep on the floor rug. She was insulted, and after that slept on a rug outside our cabin.

Miel belonged to a group of beings from another dimension who found humans and life on Earth to be inferior and disdainful. Miel felt I was spiritually advanced and her best friend, but her companions cautioned her to maintain a distance from all humans. I told them that they were not to interfere with our happiness and goodwill, and it was totally honorable for a spirit to be human, Afghan, or any form. Miel had made her choice to be here. If they didn't like it, they could leave.

They left, along with their negative influence, but Miel never really felt comfortable being in her body and associating with life on Earth. Although she had lived on Earth as a whale and a dolphin long ago, she felt that these forms were vastly different from human and other species. Cetaceans were spiritual guardians and advanced souls with total harmony in their natures. Miel loved the spiritual connection and love that we shared, but as time went on, her distaste for being incarnate became apparent.

I did not have Pasha and Miel neutered. Despite the dog overpopulation problem, I fell into the same thinking I have since cautioned others against: Because Pasha was so wonderful, it would be wonderful to have his puppies, and my friends wanted them. Had I foreseen how Miel would change after having puppies, I would have had her spayed at puberty. Perhaps it would have made no difference.

Until Miel had puppies at two years old, Pasha and she had played happily with each other. After that, Miel became more defensive and aggressive toward other dogs, including Pasha. She started to growl at some people when they came into the yard and occasionally barked and postured aggressively at strangers during walks. I worked with her on each occasion, and at first, she was willing to change. The only time her protectiveness was valuable was when two men threatened to attack me early one morning in Griffith Park in Los Angeles. Her fearsome growling and lunging scared them off.

Miel killed squirrels, opossums, rats, and pigeons, and when she was pregnant and nursing, ate them. She was also aggressive toward cats, including our own, and once killed a kitten. I worked with her on this, and as long as I was there to supervise she would be calm with cats, but would revert later. I warned our cats to stay away from her, and they did. Afghans are natural hunters, so this behavior aligned with her genetic background. Pasha loved to chase animals, but he listened to me when he was young and I asked him not to kill. He would catch up with small animals, jump back, and tell them to run—even when they were frozen in fear, certain that they were finished. He was shocked when Miel killed other animals. He'd ask her why she did that when, now, they wouldn't be able to run.

When Michel came into our lives in July 1980, Pasha and he quickly became best buddies. Pasha had always been amiable with anyone who visited, but not overly friendly if he did not feel a strong connection. When he met Michel, he curled up next to him and melted into his body. He looked at me and said, "Now, here's a man that's worthy of you." We got married in December 1980, with Pasha and Miel as attendants.

Miel was aloof to Michel at first. She warmed up to him later, and especially appreciated his classical guitar music. Miel was very attuned to aesthetics and spiritual awareness and became best friends with people who were gentle and sensitive in the same way. She judged harshly and sometimes acted aggressively with people who did not meet her high standards. Despite my efforts to increase her tolerance and encourage or enforce gentle behavior, as the years went by, she would turn her head away and say that she knew best.

A dominating, willful individual to be sure, Miel, at her best, was still one of the most spiritually beautiful beings ever encountered. Her awareness was other-dimensional, filled with depth and peace. On the physical level, she was very unhappy with being incarnate and gradually refused to control her instinctual impulses. Several times she bit children who startled her when she was in her doghouse or asleep. She had no conscious awareness afterwards that she did that. It made it hazardous to have children or people she did not approve of around. As she got older, she acted more aggressively, like her father.

I tried various ways of working with Miel. Communication, counseling, and being firm with her were not yielding consistent results. A prominent dog psychologist said that I was not dominant enough with her, but dominance in attitude or behavior did not seem to be the answer with Miel. At times when Michel had reacted to her in a dominant way, she had responded even more aggressively. She was very different with strangers who handled her, such as veterinary technicians. She would detach herself and just go with them passively. She didn't care about them and acted uninvolved while being maneuvered by them. When we moved from Los Angeles to the woods of Point Reyes, she became even more protective of me and her territory. We were much more remote from people, and she viewed people who suddenly appeared on the trail as intruders. I ended up keeping her leashed except in remote places where no other people visited.

Dog trainers and behaviorists may have their own solutions for a dominant individual like Miel. I researched and used several training methods and holistic approaches, from counseling to herbs to homeopathy. None helped consistently or permanently, because Miel was not willing to change. As time went on, she wanted to be with me and me alone, isolated from the rest of the world. She enjoyed life on Earth less and less.

It made life very difficult for me, because encounters with Miel and people were unpredictable. Sometimes she would be pleasant with people or ignore them. She would be friendly with some guests, and then suddenly attack them when their backs were turned. I began to chain her away from people. The turning point came one day in March 1986.

Rana was Miel and Pasha's daughter, born December 1981. She was a sweet and gentle soul, and loved to play with her dad. Pasha loved his puppies, playing with them and massaging them with his teeth to calm them. After the other puppies found homes and we kept Rana, Miel became more and more dominant with her, growling and chasing her if she was too exuberant. Rana was spayed at eight months, and Miel was spayed after her second litter of puppies were weaned, but this did not ameliorate Miel's heavy dominance with Rana. If Rana came running to greet Pasha or me, Miel would attack her. Rana never fought back, but would hold still and then quietly move away. My attempts to handle the situation did not change Miel's behavior appreciably. Rana learned to be very cautious around her mother.

Pasha, Miel, Rana, and I were taking a walk together. Michel was away, doing some errands, so he did not go with us as usual. We went to a remote trail in the woods, about a mile from our home, so I let Miel off the leash for exercise. Pasha and Rana had already run well ahead of us, and Miel was sniffing around near me. Rana raced back towards us, exuberantly telling me what fun Pasha and she had had. Miel lunged at her, snarling, but this time Rana decided she wasn't going to submit anymore. She attacked Miel with a vengeance.

Those of you who have ever been present at a dogfight know how difficult it can be to get two dogs apart. A mother–daughter fight certainly ranks among the most ferocious. In the melee, I tried to grab Rana's collar and felt her fangs go deep into my hand. She wasn't deliberately trying to bite me, but my hand got in the path of her snapping jaw. Now bleeding and desperate, I cried for help, with no one around to come to the rescue. When Pasha appeared I clipped on his leash before he joined in the roiling mass of dog fur. We watched as they fought and rolled down a stream bank.

Rana was younger and stronger and got her mother by the neck and was holding her head underwater. I tied Pasha to a tree, slid into the stream, and found an opening when Rana backed off because she figured Miel was finished. I got Rana on the leash, pulled Miel sputtering out of the water, and all three of us stood there wet, breathing heavily, full of mud and debris. Neither dog tried to fight again as we made our way home, with Miel choking, me crying, and Rana very quiet.

I let Pasha loose to run ahead of us, and he told me he would have joined in to finish off Miel. I was not repelled by what he said. At that point, I wondered why I had saved her. I didn't blame Rana. Her mother had suppressed her enjoyment of life far too often, and I saw exactly what happened. Miel started the fight.

I had groomed the dogs before the walk, but now they were full of brambles, mud, and blood. Miel had a number of puncture wounds on her neck.

Rana had barely a scratch. I cleaned the wounds, dried their fur, and gave us all Rescue Remedy (an essence made from flowers that helps in extreme emotional states and shock). Rana told me she would not apologize, that she meant to do what she did and was not sorry. They agreed not to fight again. I tried to call several friends for comfort. No one was home. I felt I was being pushed to make a decision regarding Miel. I could no longer tolerate her aggression and the discord it created.

I went to check on Rana and Miel and found Miel breathing with difficulty, her gums very pale. I took her to an emergency vet about thirty minutes away for treatment, concerned she might get pneumonia. Rana came along for a checkup, as well. When we got back, with the physical emergency under control, I tried to think of solutions to the Miel situation. One option was to put her down. That, of course, made me feel miserable, though at the time I didn't consider it out of the question.

I remembered that a client named Kathy, whom I had known for years through working with her cats, had just moved into her own home in Santa Rosa, about an hour's drive from us, and was building a fence in order to have some dogs. Kathy had a strong, dominant personality, and although Miel nipped her when they first met, they had come to know and respect each other. After explaining the situation, I asked Kathy if she would consider taking Miel. She agreed to do so when she finished the fence within two weeks.

Miel and I communicated about the decision, and she did not want to leave me. I was firm. I had been pushed to the wall, and there was no turning back. While Miel liked Kathy, and she didn't mind being the only dog, she came to this world to be with me, and she didn't want to be here otherwise. When I visited her at her new home, she would howl for days afterward, so I stopped visiting, except at long intervals. She communicated to me from a distance that she wanted to come back, that I could keep her chained or in a kennel, and she wouldn't mind. I couldn't live with that and held my ground.

Right after Miel left, everyone at home breathed a sigh of relief. The cats came onto the deck and in the yard, where they couldn't go freely before because of Miel. People coming to visit weren't terrorized anymore. At first, Rana thought she had to assume Miel's role and started to be aggressive toward people. Rana had always been so gentle. The nice thing about Rana, as opposed to Miel, is that she listened. I explained that she didn't have to do what Miel did. We didn't need that here, and she returned to her natural, peaceful ways. Later, some of Miel's protectiveness came out again in Rana, but we were able to handle it quickly. Miel had refused to conciliate.

Seeing Miel over the next year was difficult. When she developed mammary tumors, we tried herbal and nutritional methods to heal her, but she told us that she didn't want to heal. She wanted to leave her body, and this was her way out. The veterinarian wanted to do surgery to remove the tumors, which continued to grow, but Miel was adamant. She wanted to go, and if surgery were performed, she would just grow them back or develop some other disease to exit this world. I was faced again, as with Popiya, with a request to participate in ending a dog's life. This time, although the circumstances were different, the communication was clear but heartrending all the same. Miel's will prevailed at the end.

When Miel left her body on December 22, 1987, she was filled with joy. She had been so sad and tortured in her body, especially after she had to leave me. Now she was free and glad, and from her exalted, expanded dimension, sent us all many blessings and her spiritual guardianship for a time. She said she would never come back on Earth again, but we would be friends forever.

This was a very difficult story for me to write—accompanied by tears as the memories were refreshed, but a cathartic exercise. After Miel departed, I asked the powers that be to have only those animals in our family who come to serve and help people to expand in a peaceful, harmonious way. While we all grew through our struggles, and sharing Miel's beauty was beyond words to express, I didn't want to deal with this kind of aggressive nature again.

The experience has helped me to understand others' struggles with similar characters. Diana Thompson, who has worked with many difficult horses, encouraged me to tell about Miel, for many people have to deal with unyielding individuals, and it isn't easy. Other people marvel when I mention difficulties with Miel—that I, with my skills, would have any problems with animals. As I have said, telepathic communication does not equal obedience or control of others' life paths and choices. With awareness of our limits comes the grace of humility.

Sherman, the orange wonder-cat, has had to learn how to balance and use the power given to him from the angelic realm. While he has been a great helper to people at workshops, he has also created some serious mischief as a cat. From his arrival, Sherman has been a very active, dynamic, adventurous individual. As a kitten, he boldly went right up to dogs and other cats to greet and meet them. He thought everyone of any species was interesting and wonderful. When he was about five-months-old, I jumped up when he screamed loudly outside my office window. I saw him racing toward the house as a big feral tomcat headed out through the fence. Sherman had tried to make friends with the wild cat, who attacked him, scaring Sherman so much he stained his fluffy back legs with diarrhea.

Wherever he went, he greeted cats warmly and expected reciprocation. He tried this with the five cats of a neighboring couple, Tory and Janine, who lived about half a mile away through the forest. The people welcomed Sherman's visits, but their cats did not. When his fellow felines rebuffed him a number of times, a frustrated Sherman began to attack them. Tory reported this terrorization of his cats to me and asked me to keep Sherman inside during the day, since they generally kept their cats inside at night.

Keeping Sherman confined in the house is like trying to leash a tornado. He is so full of dynamic energy that he simply has to find adventures outdoors or he bounces off the walls. I advised Sherman to ignore the cats if they were not friendly. It was their home and their choice, and we all wanted peaceful coexistence.

Sherman was good about staying away for a while. Then back he went, causing trouble again. I tried to explain Sherman's viewpoint to the neighbors and asked them to discourage his visits by spraying him with the garden hose if he returned. They didn't think they could be out there at the right time to do that. Tory felt that Sherman was becoming a real bully, trying to take over the territory, since the feral tomcat had disappeared. One of their cats had an abscessed wound because of Sherman, and they were getting angry.

I recoiled at the accusation that Sherman was an aggressive bully. I knew his side of the story, although it certainly didn't justify causing such distress. Sherman got along with all the other cats in the neighborhood. Tory and Janine had a reputation for conflicts with people. Roaming dogs had twice attacked their previous cats. I did not want to add to their difficulties.

With the cat door locked this time, Sherman became very restless. His normal playfulness with our other cats turned to harassment. They also did not have free access to go in and out as usual. Taking this approach devalued our respectful regard for each other, and I felt it was not a permanent solution.

Sherman and I sat together for a talk, and he began to clearly see my viewpoint. I wanted to ensure that he would not go back and bother the neighbors again. I sought guidance, since it seemed Sherman's angelic mission was going awry. The angels and I worked together to surround our neighbor's home and land with a circle of harmonious white light, filled with love and well-being. We did the same with our home, making a circle of light that was to be Sherman's roaming ground, which did not cross over into our neighbor's circle. I clearly visualized that Sherman would not enter their circle, and harmony would reign within and without. Weeks later, Janine and Tory thanked me for keeping Sherman indoors. I didn't mention what we actually did to resolve the conflict. I was so grateful for the end of hostilities.

It was over a year later when the neighbors again reported a Sherman attack. This was the time I related earlier, when Sherman almost left his body. Besides working with Sherman, we renewed the circles of light, with the same results.

Michel and I were walking Rana and Pasha down the dirt road past Tory and Janine's home and noticed how they had cut down some huge, old pine and fir trees, as well as native shrubs and smaller trees. I was shocked, as Tory loudly complained about others cutting down trees or changing the natural environment. He had once said to me, "I don't care about people; I just care about the environment." We figured it was a preventive measure, because years ago trees had crashed down in a storm and destroyed part of their roof. Since they were very private people, it seemed especially amazing that they would open a clear view of their home from the road, where before it had been hidden.

A few days after that, Tory called to report that Sherman had attacked his orange cat, Kalo, who had to be taken to the vet to handle the wounds. Appalled, I asked, "Sherman, how could you do this?" Sherman did not want to listen when I told him how much agony this was causing all of us and how this was bringing negative forces into our home. I had to have his promise that he would never, never do that again, and not go to the neighbors' home at all. Sherman struggled with this. I wondered how Sherman could be so far from his purpose of creating harmony. Sherman pondered this and conveyed that he would kill himself first before he followed an impulse to attack those cats again!

Later Sherman told us this story: Kalo, the orange cat he singled out for attack, was not living up to his connection with the Orange Cat Contingent. Kalo was withdrawn in fear, instead of expansive and friendly, as he was meant to be. Sherman wanted to wake him up, like a Zen master who hits students in the head with a club when they do not comprehend as expected. He did not feel that he could reach Kalo with gentle communication. I countered that the Zen student asks for guidance from the master and agrees to the use of traditional methods. Kalo and his people were not directly inviting Sherman's teaching. His methods were not working. Sherman understood.

Days later, while the neighbors reported that Sherman had not been seen, and Kalo was healing well, I still was concerned about a recurrence. For my own reassurance and to avoid temptation, I had advised Sherman to sleep at home most of the day if possible, or if he went out, to stay close to home and mainly go out at night. He kept to that arrangement.

I wondered why this had happened three times, each time apparently resolved. I searched more deeply for answers, which came gradually in this multifaceted learning experience. I discovered that when the neighbors had cut the trees and drastically altered their landscape, they had made themselves vulnerable to negative energies. The protective angel circle surrounding their area was broken. Sherman had also been feeling tremendous upsurges in power, which he did not know how to handle—hence the "Zen master" approach. I suggested to Sherman that he use his power to help solve big conflicts on the Earth, in the Middle East, for example.

For my part, I had been uncomfortable with these neighbors for years, because they were sometimes quite critical and hostile and seemed to stir up conflict over neighborhood issues. They also could be very friendly and kind, and Tory said he followed the Hindu path of ahimsa, or nonviolence to all living things. I could see that they were afraid of being hurt by people, and so they sometimes adopted a defensive, angry position. I was grateful when they both communicated very peacefully about the last Sherman event.

To fully resolve the problem, I had to handle my negative feelings about my neighbors. I have always avoided conflict with people. My parents had been alcoholics, and I had enough of interpersonal physical and mental abuse when I was growing up. I realized that I was critical of Tory and Janine and did not focus on their wholeness as spirits. I certainly didn't love them unconditionally. When I let go of my fear and judgment and sent them non-judgmental love and peace, I felt much relief. My intolerance and fear of them had added to Sherman's harsh actions. After all, he came and stayed on Earth to help me. Acknowledging my responsibility in the whole situation, I focused on sending unconditional love to my neighbors and others toward whom I had felt critical.

As I looked this situation over, I realized that in the past my dogs Miel and Rana had each nipped Janine once as she was jogging by. Rana had also bit another man who had acted antagonistically toward us. The dogs had their own reasons for doing so. They didn't bite everyone I ever had a critical thought about, but I could see the connection between their actions and the attitudes of the people involved, including my own. While animal companions make their own choices, obviously we influence each other's actions. We all need to do our part to create harmony. The growth and evolution of all beings on this Earth are interconnected. I felt that Tory, Janine, their cats, and all of us were uplifted by all the positive actions we took and the positive energies we sent.

I checked with Sherman a few days after giving him the Middle East assignment. He definitely was channeling positive energy to heal the area, but said it was very tiring! I had noticed that he was sleeping more than usual. Weeks later, he felt he had finished what he could do. He said that the people who were fighting did not want to stop. They enjoyed the conflict and the intense feelings it created. He could not help change people and situations where there was no willingness to change. He managed to put a spiritual safety net over the area to help contain the conflict so that it didn't spill over to other areas. I pointed out other areas of the globe where he might help, and he promised to channel energy in those directions as he was able.

THE DARK SIDE

We know that life on Earth isn't all joy and delight. There are dark sides to life. Some phenomena may seem evil or frightening, particularly if we don't know how to handle them, or our belief systems don't allow for examining, understanding, and shedding light on them.

One of these potentially forbidding phenomena is spirit possession, which can result in multiple personalities. Instead of the usual single spirit in charge of a body, there may be other entities, thought forms, or individualized spirits who may vie for control to manifest or express themselves through the body. This appears to happen more commonly in humans than in animals, but I have run across it occasionally during consultations with animals.

Happy was a young Samoyed-mix dog, adopted as a stray. He had some difficult behavior patterns that his people were trying to help him overcome. He seemed scattered and confused. Sometimes he bit people. Other times he was friendly with them. For many days in a row he would refuse to eat, and so would have to be fed by hand or even force-fed. After his receiving treatments of therapeutic touch known as TTEAM, he would settle down for a while and eat, but then have a relapse.

When I met Happy, I found it very difficult to connect with him mentally and spiritually. He radiated dissonance and jagged energy. I found that his body was being operated by three beings, all with different intentions. A shattering blow to his head when he was a puppy drove out the main individual spirit and allowed these three lesser ones to enter. No one confidently inhabited the body, causing confusion and negative impulses. Two of the beings weren't even sure they wanted to keep the body alive—hence the eating difficulty.

One of the beings was more communicative, benign, and gentle, and I recommended that he be focused on creating a life as Happy. Teaching the dog how to behave and encouraging him to benefit from the therapy could promote positive dog behavior. The other beings were not willing to leave the body at the time. However, I felt that if the more benevolent being were given encouragement, he might be able to integrate the others into one personality and live a balanced life as a dog.

Spirit transfer usually occurs with young animals. One being enters the body after another departs, as in an accident or severe shock or with the agreement of the resident being. It can be confusing for those involved.

Our chinchilla's four-story condominium habitat was under the deck that surrounded the south- and east-facing sides of our house. Pasha lay on his cot on the deck, just above Quince's dwelling, when the vet helped him to leave his body. Quince acted very strangely after that and became terrified when anyone approached, hiding and grunting. I could get no information from him or help him through his trauma. He acted like he was possessed or insane. I realized that the energy of Pasha's departure had severely affected him. I thought he would get through it and calm down, but several weeks went by with no change.

Then I realized what had happened. Quince, the wonderful, intense, powerful being who had inhabited the chinchilla body, was gone. He had left when Pasha sailed out of his body and the veil opened to the other side. He no longer belonged in the chinchilla, and he had no intention to return.

A spirit who had no experience with humans or domesticated life had entered when Quince vacated. We wondered what we would do with the wild-being chinchilla we now had in our family. I got the name Gaylor for him. I asked the universe to help this spirit accommodate our mission here or be able to vacate in place of someone who would want to help people to telepathically communicate with animals. After my recognition of the situation, Gaylor calmed down. A spirit sent by Quince and aligned with our purpose here combined with Gaylor's presence, to strengthen him and help him to grow. He was very different from Quince in mannerisms and energy, but he was very interested in learning.

Most domesticated animals I have met try to give love and helpfulness to people. Sometimes people misinterpret animal behavior as negatively intentioned when it is not. Animals who do not have proper outlets for natural behavior and energy may express themselves in ways that people cannot accept. People may erroneously consider them malevolent. Most animals mean well, but there are exceptions.

In 1977, while I was working at a spiritual counseling center, a black kitten came up to me. No one knew where she had come from or how she had gotten there. My cat had recently died, so I took the new kitten home. She called herself Dania. She was with me only a short time when she began to do some very odd things.

Cats have a special place in my heart, and I delight in the playfulness of kittens. Dania was different. She studied me quietly, trying to decide what made me tick. As I exercised and practiced my dance, she would wait until I looked at her. Then she calculatedly hit the arm of the record player to make it skid across the record. It was eerie how her behavior lacked kitten curiosity and playfulness. She coldly stared at me to see my response. I felt her motive was to stop the spiritual form of dance that I practiced. I could see in her eyes and feel in her heart what I could only call evil. I felt she was sent from somewhere or someone to bring negative energy. She had access to outdoors whenever she wanted. I told her that I knew what her intentions were, and that if she couldn't bring harmony to me and to the area, she could leave. I never saw her again.

A milder and more mundane form of opposition came from an Arabian mare named Ariel. When I approached her eight-month-old filly, Emerald, who had previously been sweet and cooperative when I talked with her, Ariel zapped her daughter with messages of danger. Ariel wanted to manipulate Emerald to be tougher with people, and she vehemently opposed her daughter's communicating with me. Poor Emerald was frenzied when I tried to ask her about the matters her person wanted to know. Ariel, by her overpowering nature, caused conflict, wildness, and extreme dependency in Emerald.

Ariel's attitude was arrogant toward most humans, while Emerald was basically soft and trusting. I recommended that Ariel be taken away temporarily to another ranch so that Emerald could be socialized properly and not end up with neurotic behaviors. After separating the two horses, Emerald's gentle, cooperative nature came to the fore.

Donna called me to see her Western performance horse, Gaucho, because of his unruly and sometimes dangerous behavior toward people. She haltered the horse and stood next to him. When I approached the corral, Gaucho told me that if I came in, he would kill me. He started to paw and rear to prove it. Donna laughed and seemed almost proud of his dominating behavior. I stood outside his corral, but he refused to answer questions posed to him and was not willing to cooperate or change.

It became clear to me that this was a game perpetrated and enjoyed by both human and horse. My inability to elicit two-way communication and cooperation brought a smug confirmation to Donna that she was the only person who could control him. My help was not wanted here by either species. I made a few suggestions for his training, but she wasn't really interested, since she already had the result she wanted. Fortunately, these kinds of situations are extremely rare. Most people and animals who call for help really want to change and grow together.

This is what I have always considered my mission on Earth: to help others realize their wholeness as spiritual beings with the capacity to be full of joy in living, and to facilitate more communion and harmony among beings. At various stages and places in my life on Earth, I have met with opposition or forces that seek to dampen or challenge this purpose. In this universe of polarities, of forces opposing and balancing each other, it appears that if one creates positive energy or seeks higher levels of harmony, the dark side of the force is drawn out of the woodwork to be exposed to the light.

The ending millennium seems to be full of this contest. The game of polarities—good versus evil, light versus dark—that appears to make the world function as it does, seems to be coming to an end. The polar opposites are striving for integration as never before, not only within individuals, but also on a planetary basis. The negative forces seem to be asking for us to help them join the creation of unity and harmony. In doing so, they are releasing their chaos of energies into the world and challenging the "good" or light side to accept them.

My first trip to New Mexico to offer a lecture, workshop, and consultations, in May 1990, brought me face to face with the dark side. That part of the world, with its intense transformational energy, demands that you face your shadow—the repressed or denied aspects of your being that do not fit your preferred self-image, that which you do not like about yourself. Many people find that when they first move to New Mexico, their lives undergo great trials by fire, including severe illness or divorce. Around Santa Fe, I found the dichotomy strong. It is a fire center, a crucible. The contrasts of positive and negative are put into a sharp light, and everything is laid bare. The thin air and the stark landscape, generally not softened by large trees and water, as well as the hot sun and red mineral mountains demand that you face that which you fear. The very positive and very negative energies there can be used for planetary balance and change.

I was asked to see an Arabian stallion on a ranch outside of Santa Fe. I was told that he could be difficult and dangerous. Standing near him outside his corral, I could get very little communication from him except for images of a shattered mirror. My mind felt fragmented as I attempted to understand him. My head began to ache, and surges of emotion coursed through me. If I had gone into his corral, I knew he would have attacked me. I moved away, seeing that he was not going to cooperate by answering the questions his person posed.

When I turned to see his young son, the stallion then spoke to me and told me his name was Ashtar (not his given horse-name), that he was from another place and group of beings, and that he was a spirit of great power and darkness. Then he struck me with waves of force, and I felt weak and began to cry. As I sat with the ranch owner—a very spiritually powerful artist and animal lover—and a few other people, it became clearer to me what was going on here.

The artist revealed that the stallion had been very wild and had even tried to kill people. They had used various approaches with little effect, and considered him dangerous. I felt that the energy of this area had attracted Ashtar, to facilitate the dark side being pushed into the world in a new wave, in order for all of us, on a planetary basis, to face and integrate it.

They had considered destroying the stallion, or at least gelding him, since there had also been some doubt about the mental stability of his sire. After I left, the spirit force, Ashtar, left the horse body to do his work in the world. Since that time, we certainly have experienced major planetary upheavals and are rebalancing from such events as the downfalls of the Berlin Wall and Communism.

This New Mexico journey was also a personal test for me to face the powers of darkness. We all have to confront the dark side to attain positive integration as spirits in this universe. It was startling for me to experience this being through a horse. Animals mainly express such positive energies. But why not? Animals also experience the polarities and conflicts in this plane, and help us in our human challenges.

I felt New Mexico had unleashed its power on me on my first trip, to help me grow and to strengthen my resolve to continue doing my task on Earth. I did not relish returning, but when I did, that same year, I had a very different experience. The spirit of New Mexico and I were now respectful friends, and I felt her beauty.

My first trip to Hawaii, in March 1991, featured another meeting with the dark side through an animal. When Michel and I got off the plane at Oahu and were driven to the hostess's home, we took a walk around the neighborhood. It was lined with houses, fences, and lawns. I was eager to see more natural surroundings, so we began a descent down a lane with more vegetation and a stream. My psychic antenna started to vibrate, and I got the message that this area was dangerous and we should turn around.

Had I been by myself, I would have heeded the warning and reversed direction. Michel was with me, and I felt safe with him to explore the area. I got that eerie feeling several more times as we walked on, and then the danger materialized. A large black German shepherd came charging out at us, snarling, and intent on attack. Reacting to the sight of his huge white teeth, I turned to Michel on my left. The dog lunged and bit my right side below the ribs. Before the dog could attack again, Michel bellowed at him and chased him off to his home. When a very unsavory looking man came out and the dog stood by him, I urged Michel not to talk to the man, as he had intended to do. Bleeding and hysterical, I just wanted to get out of there.

Welcome to Hawaii! The dark side of the force, in the form of a large black dog, faced me squarely. We discovered later, when the police interviewed me, that we were walking in an area of drug dealers and cockfighters. While my lecture and workshop went well, and the people attending were wonderful, I wondered where the spirit of Hawaii had gone. Traveling to Maui to a ranch to do consultation with horses, I witnessed endless pineapple and sugar cane fields. Where were the holy places of this sacred land? I left with a feeling of desolation, a pain in my side, and a fear of aggressive dogs.

On my second trip to Maui in early 1992, besides enjoying the people at the lecture and workshops, I was determined to find the holy places and the sense of spirit alive in the land. I was enchanted when I visited Mount Haleakala and the sacred pools and forests along Hana Road.

The number three must bring the magic of integration. In the first trip I met the dark side, and on the second trip I was graced by the holy places. On the third trip to Maui, in September 1992, for the American Holistic Veterinary Medical Conference, Michel and I found the beauty in nature, the welcoming generosity of the people, and the spirit of Hawaii throughout.

Late summer, fall, and early winter are the dying time of year. All of nature gives its fruit, prepares to shed its old forms, and shelters the dormant seed through the winter, to prepare for new birth after darkness turns toward the light again in the winter solstice. At this most transformational time of year, we are asked to review, turn over, and examine anything stored in cracks and crevices. New layers of being are exposed from the depths.

Always a passionate person, I have espoused living life with full and deep feeling. Opposing my joy in living was my shadow side of sometimes becoming impatient or hypersensitive and irritable with those I am close to. In late 1992, my tendency to be at times impatient and short-tempered with my husband was brought to the fore. I didn't like it when I flared up at him, but my attempts to control this anger had only been temporarily successful. Obviously, Michel didn't like being the brunt of this bad humor and urged me to get through it. His nature was less fiery and more balanced emotionally, so he had difficulty understanding my outbursts.

Many people—especially native shamans, who work closely with natural forces—find supportive interaction from the wild animal kingdom in dealing with spiritual issues. In the throes of trying to handle this force rooted deep in my psyche, I was awakened about 3 A.M. by a fierce, high-pitched squeaking. I went to the living room and found an injured bat, flailing on the carpet. Surprisingly, none of our cats were visible to fend off or remonstrate. I scooped the bat up in a container to take him out to the woods. I felt the pain from his severely mangled wing. I knew he could not live like this, so I hoped a predator would quickly end his misery.

A deeper connection surfaced. The bat had come to help me through the struggle with my shadow, to help transform darkness into light. The bat became my dark side, caught and broken by being unearthed and exposed and threatened with dissolution. As this wounded friend expired and was liberated from pain, a part of my dark side also died and was freed from a seething, tortured existence. Darkness merged with the light and became beauty. I thanked my bat ally for coming to help me and freeing us both from darkness.

That night, an angel appeared in a dream in the form of a sprite-faced boy. He told me that I needed to be aware and control my impatience for five days, to say nothing about it, and I would start a new phase. It took many stages to get to the root of this pattern and expunge it from my inherited and learned temperament. I felt my bat partner helping me through each step.

communicating with the spirits of nature

THE UNIVERSE *is God extended*
God available in myriad forms
God stretched out and stretched in
Merging and rearranging
Beyond the visible into the invisible
The unknown, unknowable
Encompassing and extending beyond all universes
Playing within them from many perspectives
Playing without them in stillness divine
I am God—a spark of divinity
As you are and every cell and drop of sand
We are all God
Looking at each other through different lenses
Different windows
Wondering about the whole
Each of us needing the other
To be expanded, complete, whole-some
What a game
A blending of realities
God is laughing at her/himself.

July 2, 1992, on the plane from New York to San Francisco

TREES AND OTHER PLANTS

Living beings are a composite of forms, an amalgam of spirit. There is the individual spirit in charge of a body, known as the identity or I, usually given a name by humans. There is spirit infusing every cell, every particle, and every minute life form. There are the nature spirits who assist all living beings and natural environments to keep form and function growing and changing in orderly progression.

The spirits of Nature have various ethereal forms and functions. They are given different names or identities by different cultures. They are called plant spirits, flower fairies, sprites, elves, gnomes, leprechauns, landscape or mountain devas, angels. They dwell in the woods, seashores, deserts, waterways, gardens, earth, and air that have not been dispirited by human pollution or other desecration. You can communicate with the individual spirit inhabiting a tree, a flower, a rock, a mountain, and also with the attendant spirits who assist the functioning of the physical forms or areas. I will not indulge in categorization, hierarchies, and naming schemes for all the different spirits, but simply share some of my experiences communicating with the spirits of Nature.

One of my favorite places to be is in my garden. Gardening is a soulful process of renewal for me. I love digging in the soil, hauling earth, compost, and manure (which our chickens, rabbits, and llamas amply provide), designing and tending the garden in communion with all the nature spirits around. The more I feel creative joy in the garden as chief laborer/caretaker, the more the bees, birds, plants, soil organisms, other wildlife, and nature spirits hum with approval and contribute their vitality to help everything grow. I get many messages from spirits in the garden about the garden itself and the world of which it is a part, and my role in it all.

Sometimes while working at my desk the energy rises in my body to the extent that I will vibrate "nervously" unless I heed the call to go outside and create and renew. I spend meditative time with the plants and animals of our land, which we call "The Floating Island of Peace."

I have not always been a gardener. My father loved his lawn and nurtured it carefully, along with border irises and roses. My mother had some houseplants. I always loved trees and considered them my confidants and protectors.

I've planted flowers and herbs at some of the places I've rented over the years, and I've created ponds out of plastic swimming pools, so I could take them with me when I left. I seldom had houseplants unless someone gave them to me as a gift. My attitude about plants was that they belonged out-doors in the ground where they could live naturally among all the elements. When we bought our own home in 1988, I went into gardening with great abandon, removing the ubiquitous ivy and planting native and compatible-climate plants, herbs, fruit trees, and vegetables.

I read dozens of gardening books, but mainly took the advice of the plant spirits regarding where they should be planted and what they needed. Experienced gardener friends would come over and tell me that I couldn't transplant such a plant in this or that way or in that season (for some important reason), or the plants will die. I would reply that I had asked the plants, and after I had explained what I wanted to do, they told me how they would flourish in some new location and how I should take care of them. To other people's amazement, the apparent violation of gar-dening rules did not deter the plants from growing abundantly. Often, after I got messages from the plants about where they wanted to be planted, and next to what other plants, I would read gardening books and find that the plants had directed me to the microclimate and conditions that they indeed were found to have needed.

I take an eclectic approach in gardening, as I do with many things in life. I listen to the plants and all the accompanying delightful spirits in the gar-den, and I listen to my own creative impulses as human caretaker, artist, and sister spirit. Our garden is lush with growth, and it's hard to get me to leave, once I'm knee deep in digging, weeding, planting, trimming, and enjoying. As I pull weeds, I let them know they will be heartily enjoyed as food for the llamas, chickens, rabbits, or birds, or even find their way into our salads. They are all appreciative of the love and the communion we share.

I listen to the garden spirits, but I don't feel a slave to them. I let myself play freely among all the elements, and am constantly sparked by things to do to make the garden better. We have a happy, nurturing coexistence. I find a deep communion with Spirit in the garden that gives me courage, inspiration, thoughts, and love to share with people (of all species) in my work and travels.

Tending to the needs of animals and plants can soften the edges of human nature, increasing compassion and understanding. The more we are aware of the feelings, ideas, sensations, and desires of all forms of life, the more responsible we are for acknowledging their purposes and our intimate interrelationships. When we wantonly grab, manipulate, or conquer other life forms, we violate other parts of ourselves in the vast unity of life. This doesn't mean we must tiptoe around the universe and fear squashing a bacterium or breaking a twig. That would actually serve to put us out of communion. Conversely, it seems we can practically do anything with other life forms, as long as we do it with respect and lovingly, knowing that in doing unto others, we are doing to ourselves.

I wondered how plants felt about being pruned, cut, and uprooted. I have experienced how plants will give of themselves for food, as will animals, if we give loving respect, communication, and a request or prayer for their bodies as nourishment. I have had fruit almost leap out at me to be eaten, exchanging energy with me by changing form and becoming one with my body.

One day I was sitting in my car watching a tree trimmer prune the trees in front of a restaurant. I felt the trees experiencing both pain and exhilaration. The initial feeling was "ouch" upon having a branch sawed or cut, which quickly changed to a rush, somewhat like adrenaline, as the sap—or "blood" of the tree—ran to the rescue to heal the wound and quickly rebuild. The trees felt that they would grow better after the pruning. It stimulated their growth, and they enjoyed the feeling of being an aesthetic part of the environment and being admired for it. So, for the trees the momentary "pain" seemed to be worth the end result. The woman doing the pruning seemed both competent and happy in her work, all adding to the trees' sense of pride and feeling of being cared for.

When we need to prune for a tree's health and beauty, if we let the tree know in advance and approach with respect and love, we can receive a lot of help. The tree will let us know which branches and how much to take off to fulfill the purpose. Just as in communicating with animals, in answer to our questions on what to prune or how, we can receive impressions, thoughts, feelings, or images, or just know what to do. It's a nice feeling of harmony, doing a job together.

As you approach plants and other beings in this sensitive way, you increase your ability to feel what is going on with them and learn a tremendous amount from them. Trees can respond to the way they are pruned—not just what is done to them, but how it is done to them. A negative emotional state in a person pruning or tending plants can make them feel punished and inhibit their growth. Positive human energies and a feeling of being part of their creative spirit nurtures their growth and beauty, just as it does with all the rest of us.

Trees have always been special friends to me. When I was a child, my mother told me the telephone linemen were coming to cut down a big, old cottonwood tree in our backyard in Chicago. I cried as I felt my tree friend about to be taken from me. It turned out the men only trimmed the limbs that were interfering with the phone lines, but I went through an afternoon of grief, since I expected the tree to be felled.

I learned many lessons about communion with plants when we moved from Los Angeles to the woods of Inverness Ridge at the edge of Point Reyes National Seashore. I had to do some clearing of bushes and branches to make a yard space for our dogs and make the driveway more navigable. I felt the trees and bushes did not mind a bit of trimming back. However, I got into a frenzy of clearing shrubs to make space.

I heard from the plants numerous times that I was overdoing it, and they were getting upset. Despite my awareness of this, I proceeded in my manic action, ignoring emotions and thoughts from the plants, denying their sensitivity and my own. After many hours, over several days of hacking and clearing, my arms were sore, especially my left arm, which I used for throwing the branches away after cutting them with the right arm. I figured the muscle soreness was to be expected, and it would heal up in a few days.

Weeks went by, with my arm ache partially clearing up and then the soreness returning and shifting. At times my arm was so weak I couldn't lift anything. Weakness changed to partial paralysis, coming and going for months. Pain and stiffness traveled into my left shoulder, lodging in my neck and upper back. Four months after the pruning spree, I could barely move and thought I had developed arthritis.

This chronic pain astounded me, since I had been basically very healthy all my life and did yoga, dance, and stretching, ate a whole food diet, and was generally in tune with my body and its needs. I was accustomed to helping myself and others with their bodies as a health practitioner doing bodywork and nutritional counseling. After applying myriad natural arthritis remedies and being mindful of food and exercise, my condition only worsened. I had also searched for every spiritual cause behind this condition, meditated, studied, and prayed to find answers. The wonderful awareness about all the intense spiritual changes I'd been going through since moving to the Point Reyes area did very little to alleviate my physical condition. When I could barely move from the pain, my husband pushed me to go to a doctor.

The doctor I chose was holistic, a very wonderful person who also discussed the possible emotional and spiritual causes behind my condition. Through his spine-aligning bodywork and electro-acupuncture, I gratefully experienced some relief. I spotted some influences in the environment causing stress and handled them. That helped a bit, too.

My husband tried to help with every healing mode he knew and used his psychic awareness to find clues. We had discussed several times in the past four months that maybe my condition had something to do with cutting down all those branches, but nothing came of that. Then, after three more weeks of pain and difficult nights of little sleep, Michel relayed some insights from the plants after he came back from an early morning walk. He had noticed the piles of cut branches here and there along the driveway, talked to the trees about what I had done, and asked them to help in my healing. When he said that, I felt a lightening of pressure and slept more peacefully.

Then, it became very clear to me that the violation of all those bushes and trees, boldly cutting away their arms, without paying attention to their feelings, was not okay. I felt a rush of reprimands from the forest spirits. The trees told me that I had no right to come here to a very sacred wood and treat the wild trees and bushes as if they were domesticated and could be pruned and treated according to human desire alone. Chastised and embarrassed by my insensitivity, I asked forgiveness.

If I had clearly listened and communicated well with the plants, we would have come to an agreement about how much could be cleared without offense, recognizing all of our needs. Since I am generally aware of the thoughts and feelings of my sisters and brothers in the animal and plant realms, ignoring their communication had been a grave error. After receiving forgiveness, my shoulders, neck, and back felt greatly relieved, and I could feel healing taking place and balanced energy returning.

There were other factors involved in the painful condition of my left upper body. A tick had bitten me under my left collarbone a short time before the symptoms appeared, and a red swelling appeared in a large circle all around the tick bite. I later learned that the swelling and the arthritic pain and stiffness were all symptoms of tick-spread Lyme disease.

In working with the holistic doctor, I also realized I had a backlog of valuable experience to communicate to people about telepathy with animals. When I started working on audiotapes, which became the Interspecies Telepathic Connection Tape Series, my pain decreased and the mobility in my arm and neck increased. After six months of chiropractic and other body and nutritional work, communing with the plants, and getting my tapes completed, I was through the agony, with many lessons learned.

Laurel Airica wrote about her experience with plant helpers:

On many occasions, when meditating in nature, I've seen how a moment of revelation within me was greeted by a synchronous nod of assent by the flora around me or by the sudden dispersion of a cloud that had placed itself before the sun. This sense of shared vision, and the impact of insight, was reinforced for me by reading *The Education of Little Tree* by Forrest Carter, and Michael Road's *Talking with Nature*.

I was motivated to test and extend this conversation with the natural world while working as a psychic on a nationally advertised "hotline." Under pressure to respond to a rapid succession of distressed and curious callers from across the country, I felt compelled to turn to the trees outside my window for assistance. I had never studied any formal system of divination (as the tarot, astrology, or numerology), and my natural intuitive abilities were being severely taxed by the constant demand placed upon them. It was clear I could not continue to ask my body to be the instrument by which to "divine" other people's experiences.

Using the trees and the wind as an ally, I began focusing on the movement of leaves and boughs in the breeze as I spoke with each caller. The first time I employed this technique, a young woman from New York challenged me. She simply demanded, "Tell me about myself." At $3.00/minute, she had the right to expect some genuine insight and assistance.

Without a specific question from her to initiate the direction of my intuitive inquiry, I simply shrugged my shoulders and looked out the window to see what a nearby jacaranda could tell me. Its graceful wind dance said, "She loves to dance and sing and is an excellent performer."

When I repeated this to her, my caller confirmed that she was a rap singer and dancer and was performing all that month. A more distant tree then described her boyfriend and the close relationship she enjoyed with her mother. It further suggested she encourage the development of her mother's latent artistic talents, untapped since childhood, with the gift of some watercolors and paper. The trees, to the delight of my caller and to my own surprise, provided this information and more.

The synchronicity was always amazing. On one occasion, a gust of wind went racing through the trees just as my phone rang. Struck by this sudden dramatic display, I told my caller her energy reminded me a good deal of *Wuthering Heights*. She was quite startled! "That's my favorite book," she told me. "I've read it seven times!"

After gaining confidence in, and some sense of dependence on, this process of reading "tree leaves," I accepted a job giving approximately twenty readings in two and a half hours at a Christmas party atop a high rise in downtown Los Angeles. I was concerned not to have any trees to consult, but felt a bit heartened to find I'd be sharing an office with a small potted plant. Though there would be no wind to whisper secrets through its leaves, I felt better just having it there, and sensed it could help me.

But I nearly forgot all about it as I flowed through the majority of readings. Finally, a young woman entered the office and sat down before me. This time, I thought to myself, I am going to see if I am receptive enough to let this plant assist me. As it turned out, this was her office and her plant, so it had plenty to say about her!

I've recently turned to my own houseplants for insights and clarity. Who knows me better than they do and who better than I can witness and appreciate their wisdom?! This exchange between us has heightened the flow of beauty and love energy in my home.

Each plant, of course, has a different character, tone, and type of information to convey. For instance, the plant that lives beside my place of meditation is always ready with a deep and helpful reflection on my momentary state of consciousness. And the huge multi-stalk corn plant in my living room has brought into focus powerful truths about my way of relating to the world. The messages they've shared have helped me understand myself better, view situations from an improved perspective, and thus adopt a more positive attitude.

I decided to extend this conversation to edible plants, and began joining in silent communion with fruits and vegetables before eating them. One by one I hold them in my hands, close to my heart, to allow them to communicate not only their assent to becoming part of me, but also any other type of information they might wish to share while they're still intact.

They are grateful for the acknowledgement and opportunity, and open themselves to reveal a precious treasure of love-intelligence. Not only do they let me know whether they are ripe and ready for eating, but they also remind me to check in with my body if I am proposing to consume beyond her needs.

Some rapidly relate the wisdom and affection of their kind and of their own unique individuality. It puts me in mind of the "fruit of knowledge," for it feels rather like speed-reading through nature's invaluable library, though I don't believe I could consciously interpret all the information I am given. Ultimately, I like to feel these beings melt into me, in essence, before I take the first bite. It's a wonderful exchange that I know improves digestion.

Because these life forms exemplify Givingness, they are capable of bestowing a high level of nourishment, balance, and wisdom, even prior to consumption, if we slow down enough to partake of them first in spirit. It takes only a few moments to witness and honor their exquisite beauty and divine purpose, and to absorb that into ourselves.

Trees have often given me valuable personal and planetary insights. I wrote this arboreal communication when it occurred in 1989:

Our home and roof over our heads is the wind and the sky. The wind nurtures and shapes us, even when it breaks us. We love human houses. Out of our bodies, they have been made. Humans live inside our bodies, as other creatures do. We are pleased that your house is made from many trees that you appreciate so much as your shelter. The love and unitive energy of the house increases with your appreciation of it and of us, the trees, as shelterers.

Killing plants and animals for food is part of sharing forms, keeping the unity alive with transformation of energies, one form into another. Sometimes killing of other life forms, for eating or to get rid of parasites or pests, is necessary to sustain and transform other life forms. Pay attention to your manner, proceeding with thankfulness, letting live as you can, and only taking life—plant, animal, or mineral—as needed for survival.

If I had to pick a favorite type of tree, of the many that I love, I would choose the redwoods. These ancient, tall trees have given me physical, emotional, and spiritual comfort. I have seen visions of a time when they moved slowly on the Earth, hence the legends of the walking trees. This is why their roots are so shallow, although they are so gigantic. This poem crystallized as I leaned up against a giant redwood:

When I grow up, I'm going to be a tree
I'll stand straight and tall
And nothing will bother me
The world will be mine—all.

The stars will shine on me
The rain will fall on me

The moon will beam on me
The wind will whistle through my branches
And I will love it all.

I will love the ants crawling on my bark
The birds alighting on my limbs
The children climbing on my gnarled trunk
And when it comes time for me to die
I will love my death
A dance, a slow parade of releasing
And transforming my power through all the Earth.

My life will be full of experiences with other beings
Nurturing and sharing my life with them
I will thrill to all the usefulness they find in me
I will laugh and love and sing
And remember it for all time.

My legacy will live and die
And live again for everyone on Earth
What greater joy could one being have
Than to share the multitude of forms, functions, energies
In every pore to every soul in every form.

When I grow up, I swear I'll be a tree.
I'll understand the ways of all life and accept them all
Even when humans chop my limbs or cut me down whole
And my death is apparently hastened
I'll not grieve or feel any pain
For I know that I'll live
As my fellow beings' houses, fences, sheds, or shelters
And nourish them all—humans, animals, plants alike
And parts of me left in the forest will grow and change
As home to many creatures small and large.

My spirit great will spread throughout the world
My roots will reach the power that holds the Earth alive

I'll know the joys and woes of all the world
And feel the pulsing of the universe.

I know, I know, I deeply know
When I grow up I'll be a tree.

With an eighty-year-old Bishop pine, I felt the timelessness of trees. As I melded with and became the tree, I had a sense of permeation with all of life. All living beings appeared as energy forms interacting—wave shadows going by and coalescing with all other life forms. I felt infinite tolerance, even for death, and the sense of my tree energy form as continuing, indestructible, and connected with all trees that ever are, were, and will be. My awareness was high and wide, experiencing all life as one and continuing, no matter the change of the solid, outward form. Infinite wisdom, eternal singing, fusion with all rhythms.

I assumed my own viewpoint again and conversed with the tree. The Bishop pine mentioned that most young trees are more concerned with survival, more emotional, close to instincts of self and others, and more threatened by death. The older, wiser trees consoled the young trees who were hurt or dying and encouraged them to carry on. Among species of plants there was a whole support system, a spiritual and energetic connection.

I became a group of *Tagetes limonii* (Mexican marigold) and experienced life forms around as energetic wave forms, with feelings and purpose, touching me in friendly or neutral ways. Giving to bees and butterflies and receiving their gift of pollination was a tender love affair.

The plants do not get bored with their seeming inaction, compared to human or other animal movement. They exude an endless *ah-h-h-h-h* in rhythmic participation with all the elements. The plants are conscious of their essential nature, their interconnection and continuance, smoothly shedding old forms and giving rise to new ones. Humans need the wisdom, continuity, and sense of timelessness that are experienced by plants.

Humans often focus on visual features. Plant perception is less concentrated on seeing images and more subtly attentive to the nuances of experiencing energies. The awareness and intelligence of plants is so broad, it can escape a narrower human focus and understanding. Human states of altered, expanded perception found in quiet meditation or attuning rituals are the natural, nearly constant state of awareness of plants and other species.

ROCKS AND COSMIC CONSCIOUSNESS

Humans may be the most mobile species, capable of rearranging forms and energies in the physical universe. Of the animal, plant, and mineral kingdoms, the minerals or rocks are the most grounded in magnetic, earthly energy and, at the same time, expanded in cosmic consciousness. In most instances, I have found that the more solid or still the form is, the greater the sense of timelessness and union with all life throughout the universe. For example, elephants exhibit that quality more than humans, and mountains embody that quality more than trees. This is why we can feel so rooted yet expanded in their presence.

Rocks have relayed to me a constant connection not only with the Earth, but with all the planets in the galaxy and beyond. Humans have used the mineral kingdom to help connect with space, energies, and the stars, through use in radios, telescopes, and radar. In direct communication with rocks, I have felt myself whirling among the stars and in touch with far galaxies. The link is powerful and immediate.

It appears that mineral forms have the broadest awareness of the cosmos. The view gets narrower going from plants to animals and, finally, humans. For physical survival, humans are also the most dependent on all the others. Without the contribution of the mineral kingdom, all the rest could not exist. There are symbiotic relationships among all life forms, and the elements of earth, air, fire, and water enrich all the kingdoms.

THE ELEMENTS

Storms, floods, earthquakes, winds, and all the elemental forces of the Earth energize me to write poetry or run outside screaming and laughing, or digging in the earth and planting. They are healing forces, releasing, washing, cleansing, and bringing new life.

The wind is a lover, gently caressing, and a gleaner—sweeping clean of debris, breaking those who will not bend. The wind has often talked to me. I feel its guidance, care, and discipline. Wherever I have gone to do workshops, I have asked the spirits in charge of wind and weather to help us by moderating weather patterns where needed. In Santa Fe, New Mexico, the clouds covered the sky during the outdoor workshop to soften the searing heat and brightness of the upper altitude, and disappeared when the workshop was done. In Clinton, New York, we experienced the only weekend of sunny weather the area had that summer, permitting an outdoor workshop under a nurturing tree. The following year, Clinton experienced a blizzard a few weeks before the April workshop, but we had sunny spring weather during our time there. Immediately afterwards, the area experienced cold rains and flooding. For most advanced workshops during our foggy coastal summers, the spirits have brought us warm, sunny weather in the hours needed, to make it comfortable for people to communicate with the animals in their outdoor habitats.

Often at workshops, the wind will rise and swirl to emphasize a point to those gathered, or make a statement or prayer of its own. Conversing with the wind is easy; it speaks in voices. It is our voice and all voices.

Water, water web of life
Magic threads enfold
Tapestry gold and silver
Youth and age enmingle perfectly
Ancient rhymes and melodies
Pour out from the deep
And flood the Earth with joy.

Wherever there is a confluence of water and rocks, such as a waterfall or rapids, the nature spirits will be very active. You can feel joy and excitement in their motion. The spirits echo and enhance the water's liveliness. Once, at the top of a waterfall, I saw a ring of fairies playing, their evanescent forms weaving in and out of view. They were relishing the upwelling water energy and blessing the plants all around.

One night when we pitched our tent in the Sierras next to a mountain stream, there was so much laughter and conversation in the nearby rapids that our two dogs barked profusely. I explained to Pasha and Rana that the water spirits were having a festival, but the dogs remained alert. They hadn't heard anything quite like that before. The voices of these nature spirits were louder than I'd ever heard. You could pick out individual voices in conversation. We had to put the dogs in the car so they could rest calmly. Then we let the spirit bubbling and babbling lull us to sleep.

The transforming and strengthening power of the elements supports us in our spiritual growth. During a winter's shedding of old patterns and spiritual rejuvenation, I had asked for increased power to understand and do my work well here on Earth.

On the evening of January 12, 1991, when I acted on an impulse to turn on the television, I came across a movie called *The Highlander*, with Sean Connery, one of my favorite actors. The action began in Scotland several hundred years ago and chronicled the century-spanning struggle of a man with other members of his group of nearly immortal beings. The driving force and motto of each challenger was "There can be only one." After each fight and killing of an opponent, the "quickening" occurred, wherein lightning struck the winner, conferring increased power and understanding. In the end, a spectacular display of lightning fiercely buffeted the Highlander after he vanquished the last evil challenger. In this final "quickening," the Highlander knew everything and became everything. He knew what people were thinking and dreaming all over the world, and could help them understand each other.

I was impressed with the synchronicity of my request and the answer in this movie. That was just the start! That night I had a dream in which a wise being in a cave gave me increased power to know all beings' thoughts and to understand and help them. I was told to use the ability wisely. Thunderstorms on the coast are rare, but as I dreamed, thunder and lightning rumbled all around us. I began to wake as I noted the time between the thunder and lightning flashes narrowing.

Boom! A huge jolt hit our house, accompanied by a flash, causing Michel and me and our cat, Yohinta, to leap from the bed. This strike had more impact than the earthquake we experienced a few months previously. The television flashed with a crack, and a ball of light danced around the living room.

The electrical transformer outdoors, 50 feet from our bedroom, was burned out by millions of volts of lightning energy, and the water main burst underground. Michel went around the neighborhood to help turn off water main valves, since many houses met the same fate. The lightning struck simultaneously in a number of places on the ridge where we live. About 150 feet down the road, a huge Douglas fir was stripped of bark in a spiral from top to bottom.

The thunder and lightning had come to confer my spiritual gift, as it had in *The Highlander*. Significant, too, is the fact that we live in the highlands of our area. I felt transformed, exalted, and sealed. The lightning and I were one. The next morning, I spent hours meditating indoors, watching the downpour of rain. Many computers and other electrical equipment in the area were blown out by the blast. Our computer screen was magically transformed to rainbow designs of orange, pink, and blue. A neighbor told us that we could get that fixed through demagnetizing it, but I knew it was a sign of the gift of light, and I didn't want to change it. The bright colors gradually faded until they were hardly noticeable months later.

In September 1992, we rented *The Highlander* as a video. It was again a spiritually transforming experience. These were my thoughts after watching it:

The power of unity, oneness, being the other, knowing all things, being the master of understanding and compassion, uniting good and evil, integrated power-to-do from a base of total understanding. Handling that power requires grounding with the Earth, all truth, and all beings. There is only One. There can be only One—no separation.

Power to understand inseparably can be very hard on the physical body. It is too much for one vessel, or even a few vessels, to hold. When there are enough to hold the understanding in physical form— the wise ones of all species—we shall not blow each other away or burn out. We will burn together in an everlasting flame. Unity, consciously shared, will elevate us all.

There is Beauty here—peace and beauty. Quiet, Silence, Power, and Sharing bring it all together as a recognized creation and help us see the swirling energies that are our paintbrush and paints.

I feel my Timelessness—an ageless understanding that the animals, rocks, trees, plants, air, and all Spirit know.

I am a flame, an everlasting fire. Passion runs deep for truth and union, communion. Those in spirit and those in form who have not lost the connection can understand. I am moved to do the things I do by a Force within that is greater than the universe and permeates every pore of every being. I am/we are God, beauty, truth divine.

There is so much ignorance when spirit is divorced from self. Feeling is limited by form, time, custom, habit, and thought patterns. There is so much wisdom in every cell, every atom infused and conscious with itself as Spirit. We are One. There is no choice. Separateness is a lie that dies when faced with itself in any form. Form dies but Life goes on infinitely as Itself, uniting with form in energy patterns ever changing. We are tormented and unhappy until we go home to meet and love and unite with ourselves as Spirit, the All. That is completeness. That is knowledge. That is truth. That is power—the Unlimited, the Infinite, and the Force eternal.

SEASONAL CYCLES

People throughout the ages have celebrated the seasons with a profound consciousness of their lives being deeply connected with the rhythms of the Earth. Most modern urbanized humans have lost that intimate sense of pulsing with the sun, moon, and stars. This is both a sign and a cause of their alienation and spiritual malaise.

The seasons are alive with their own spiritual qualities. They blend and change into one another—dramatically in some areas of the world, subtly in others. Getting in touch with the seasons and being aware of what they give to self and all of life has a profound effect on the integration of body, mind, and spirit. It gives a sense of grounding and purpose to being here on the Earth plane, in unity with all other forms of spirit.

Who cannot love spring, with its renewal of life, sprouting and bringing rich smells and abundance to us all? Summer is a time of growth and plenty. As the summer ends, the harvest of fall is upon us. We are reminded of our mortality as fires rage and trees lose their leaves.

In our coastal clime, winter is a time of extreme changes. Wild storms bring pelting rain and winds that bend the tallest trees. Stormy days shift to sunny, mild days that invite hiking over the hills and through the forests in the cool, fresh, scent-filled air. As winter brings its cold winds and rains, I often relish the depth of solitude it imposes. The necessary inwardness brings a time of contemplation, of facing the darkness. Winter tears us from complacence and forces a reappraisal, a stripping away of accumulated trappings, ideas, and worldviews that bind or smother, a seeking of the light in deeper places.

A quality difference
The winter solstice set
The light reversing.

Magically
I feel my heart lifted
From focusing on the deep and still
The dark side
Velvet and foreboding
Fascination with a violence
Seeking integration
To the brighter side,
The thought of crocuses
Pushing through the snow,
Life reaffirming itself.

Still death has its sparkle
Its quiet depth
Restful and alive in its own way
New energies waiting in the seed
Pulsing
Quickening.

Thank you for the light
I could not live forever in the quiet night.

THE EARTH

Many people have experienced the Earth as an entity or spirit, with its own consciousness, life plan, and relationship with all its inhabitants. Some who have experienced being in planetary rapport, or within the consciousness of the planet, report that they sense neither alarm nor concern on the part of the Earth for our current ecological crises.

Members of the plant, mineral, and animal kingdoms have feelings, but none seem to get wrapped up in emotional reactions and to project emotion onto others as humans do. Like the Earth itself, many species have a sense of oneness and expansiveness as spirit that permits a more dispassionate, detached way of being.

The Earth has been known to look upon humanity with the sort of compassionate indulgence of a fond mother for her errant children. Earth changes and cleansing are intended. Humans, by their actions in disharmony with the rest of nature, may be unwitting instruments.

This message about the Earth's nature came through me one February day:

Everything is so beautiful, so true upon the Earth if we but see the abundant harmony and enchantment there. We make it so or make it different. The woods, the fields, the oceans, lakes, rivers, and streams, all cry out for joy in their growing and flowing.

I see the magic. I see the grace. I see the harmony even in the death and the dying and the disease. All make way for life renewed, grace restored.

Cling not to forms unchanging. See the glory in the dance of form, dissolving and resolving. Don't fight the shifting molecules with orders, chains, tears, and cries of "No, it cannot be." Flow with the spirit, ever changing in its guises.

See the wildflowers bloom and die and give their seeds to the Earth. Nothing really dies or fades. It dissolves into unity and flows into another sea, or shower, or puff of air.

Flow your own tears with the tide. See your changes. Watch as spirit laughs, and like a blind magician, magically transforms death, decay, and destruction, to rebirth, new growth, and creation abundantly harmonious.

Cease to fight. Grind not against the wind, but weave your patterns in the unity of rainbows and melting snow, nourishing the senses and the pulsing, breathing, living Earth.

Be the creator, weaver, magician, spellbinder that you are, always were, and will be endlessly, even when you, too, dissolve in the light of endless artistry.

MESSENGERS BETWEEN REALMS

Some forms of life have the role of being interkingdom or interdimensional messengers, adjusting their vibrations to interact with the life rhythms of several dimensions. Among these envoys are butterflies, hummingbirds, dragonflies, dragons, and Yeti.

Marcia Ramsland observed a young white pine tree with a yellow-green cast. She was considering chopping it down when a butterfly materialized and said to her, "I wouldn't be so fast in chopping down that tree." Marcia realized that the butterfly acted as a representative on the tree's behalf, with advice she would heed. In time, the tree's color changed to a more normal appearance, showing that it was not deteriorating as Marcia had thought, but only going through a growth phase.

Butterflies exemplify transformation in their own life cycle. They often arrive to encourage humans at crucial moments of spiritual expansion. Many people have had the experience of butterflies appearing and vanishing in the blink of an eye. Try to watch their erratic movement for long, and you may be transported to their other abode in the fairy kingdom.

Hummingbirds and dragonflies, often depicted in fairy story illustrations, can shuttle between dimensions and relate to fairies as easily as they do to animals and plants in this realm. Other animals are aware of nature spirits, and even act as messengers in times of need. As I was writing this section, I was informed that insects, particularly flying ones, are also emissaries. "We appear and then we disappear."

Another group of beings that consciously dwells in several dimensions is the Yeti, also known as Big Foot or Abominable Snowmen. They have been sighted and even photographed and videotaped, but their tracks end mysteriously, or they seem to vanish when followed.

Hundreds of years ago, I was a Yeti in a secluded region of the Himalayas. It was a very solitary, monkish existence. Some Buddhist monks knew of me and regarded me as a brother. I adopted the Yeti form to make a subtle connection to the physical plane without being immersed in it. Occasionally, I would save human travelers caught in avalanches, trying not to let them see me and be frightened by my large golden-white-furred appearance. Because some of them were in altered states from their traumas, or were otherwise spiritually aware, they did perceive my form.

The Yeti form did not die when I departed, but served as a vehicle for another soul. Some beings chose to experience life as a Yeti as a break from human existence, or to integrate their earthly experience from a quieter point of connection with the Earth.

In my experience, dragons do exist on the Earth—although now there are only a few, in very remote mountains, who spend time in the Earth plane. Hundreds of years ago, and more often thousands of years past, dragons were common in mountain caves and physically appeared to help increase or align Earth energies and interact with humans. Some tribes of dragons were very benign, and others were fierce. Over two thousand years ago, when I dwelled as a lama in a Tibetan mountain cave, a dragon regularly visited me, and we exchanged knowledge telepathically.

Unicorns and winged horses, such as Pegasus, appear to reside wholly in ethereal realms. Humans have been able to tune into them and experience their reality, just as we can experience the reality of fairies, devas, elves, and leprechauns, by shifting or expanding our perception.

All of us can be linked to other dimensions, especially if we allow the ones who vibrate at these different rates to show us the way. As the veil of dimensions appears to be thinning and opening in this age, more and more people will experience the interconnection of dimensions, forms, and experiences. Who knows what beings will be visible to human eyes and awareness in the near future?

COMMUNION WITH NATURE

Every step I take
The Earth speaks to me
Every breath I make
The Earth wakes to me
Joyful ringing
Singing with each breath
I see the creatures all around me
Happy, waking, shaking
Taking notice of all the Earth
Every breath, every step
Life is in me, out me
Pulsing, waking
Me to it, it to me
Us together.

Ever since I was a young child, I communicated with animals, plants, rocks, and unseen spirits. I knew that there were angels, saints, demons, fairies, and leprechauns dwelling invisibly around us. I communicated with them, prayed to some, had pleasant and scary experiences with them, and made deals with them. No amount of discouragement from adults, acculturation, or acceptance of scientific rationalism managed to remove the awareness of the unseen world from me.

I met Peter Caddy, co-founder of the Findhorn Community in Scotland, when he lived in the San Francisco Bay area in 1985 and I attended a nature spirit workshop he was co-leading. The day was filled with bubbling enthusiasm, as the nature spirits, elves, gnomes, fairies, and devas all came out to play. I continually transmitted their communications and joy. Peter felt the nature spirits were really having fun with me. It was wonderful to freely share my awareness of these unseen spirits with people who were receptive.

At the end of the workshop, I got the image that Peter and I would be leading these workshops together, adding my focus on communicating with animals. We did co-lead workshops for a few years, until Peter moved to Germany. I continued to lead them myself. These "communion with nature" workshops have been a relaxing, powerful time to get people in touch with the nature spirits, bringing out the playful child within us.

People have asked, when they get profound and personal messages from animals, plants, rocks, or the wind, "Are we just receiving our own projections, or thoughts rebounding?" Most of the time, when people are being open, receptive, and attentive and have put aside their own expectations of what will happen, they get genuine communication from the other beings they are addressing, whether human, animal, plant, rock, or nature spirit. The other may communicate just what the listener needs to hear, or in ways that are similar to the person's own thought patterns, translated through the person's framework of experience.

Don't be surprised at the depth of wisdom or personal understanding that we receive from other forms of spirit. We are all conscious and capable of knowing. In our spiritual essence, we are all the same and reflect the truth of existence. We are communicating with the other and ourselves at the same time.

Are things alive and communicating, or are we just projecting those qualities? The answer lies in the direct experience. Which rings true, and brings more fulfillment and joy? Acknowledging aliveness and spirit in all things brings a sparkle throughout your life. Dissecting and denying life and communication brings alienation and misery. Take your choice! As soon as two beings of any kind respectfully communicate, more energy, more life is born. Good relationships bring out abilities and intelligence for all involved.

In preparation for the communion with nature workshop at Point Reyes National Seashore, I would follow where the nature spirits lead me to get inspiration and instructions for guiding the upcoming workshop. Once I was told to sit under an old Douglas fir tree, near the Woodpecker Trail, and instructed that we would all meet there to start the workshop. The theme I received was "The Meeting of Earth and Sky." I was directed to various places where I would guide people in exercises to connect them with the spirits of nature. There were several vistas overlooking the surrounding hills and valleys or ocean, with the sky magnificent in its expanse. I could feel the spirits of the heavens above swirling, connecting, and interchanging with the spirits of the Earth and water below.

On the evening before the workshop, Michel and I attended a concert of world-famous lutanist, Hopkinson Smith. The beauty of "Hoppy's" musicianship and his gentle, harmonious spirit brought visions of the nature spirits and angelic beings weaving their harmonies through and around him and all of us. While he played, the theme for the communion with nature workshop came across with clarity and expanded itself into a fuller understanding. During the concert intermission, I wrote this poem, which opened the workshop the following morning:

Come with me and let us sail
To the meeting of Earth and sky
Where angels meet with spirits of Earth
To play and dance and sing
Where energies mate and meld between realms
To enrich all beings involved
Where mortal/immortal become as one
Sharing webs of common ground.

Let us watch and listen
See the air waver before our eyes
Hear the tinkling sound so light and clear
The fairies call us there
See the rainbow bubbles of light
Enshrine the plants as they reach to the sun
Feel the energies streaming from heaven so high
Yet so near that they permeate ground.

Watch, feel, listen
So deep that barriers melt away
Feel your kinship so warm with all spirits
Air, water, earth, and fire
Play inside the magic dimension
Where memory knows no bound
Feel the mystery wind inside yourself
And meander all around.

Surround yourself with communion
Of all the spirits so bright
Who aid the Earth in spinning
Turning the elements into light
Light and sound reflected upon themselves
Become the music of form
The plants, the rocks, the humans,
The trees, the animals all are made
In the energies swirling in spiritual realms
That find their home in our hearts
That permeate everything everywhere
A symphony constantly played.

We are invited to come and share
To see and hear and know
The spirits that help us
Reach us and teach us
And make life on Earth a joy
To recognize our kinship with them
To see all of life in form
As energies changing
Blending, rearranging
A harmony sublime
Not a trap or a bore or a pain or a chore
But a joyful co-creation.

Join with me
Come let's fly
Come let's sail in joy
To the meeting of Earth and sky.

Edward Rockett had this cherished experience after taking a communion with nature workshop:

My wife, Lorin, and I planned to take your workshop prior to leaving for Sequoia Park for a five-day backpack. The day we spent with you and the participants of the workshop truly opened us up once again to the beauty and magic of nature. Both Lorin and I felt a deep and satisfying connection with the Point Reyes environment, and we left for the Sierras in a very joyful and calm spirit.

After a week filled with all the excitement and challenge of being in the High Sierra wilderness, we decided that before we left we would venture into one of the tourist attractions of King's Canyon Park, the grove of giant sequoias at Grant's Grove. We planned to arrive at the grove at sunset, hoping that the crowds would be thinned out. We were pleased to find we nearly had the sacred place to ourselves. The soft lighting of the setting sun reflected up underneath the massive bodies of the trees. The air was absolutely still, with the first hint of coolness falling from the sky. My heart opened up to the deep spirituality of the setting. I wanted to embrace each tree and fall to my knees in awe and humility. Yet, here I was on an asphalt trail restrained by wooden fences. I understood and accepted this separation created by the Forest Service to protect the trees, yet it was frustrating to me.

As we walked the loop around the General Grant Tree, there was a pathway leading away from the asphalt trail and up a hillside to an enormous sequoia without any fencing around it. Immediately I raced up the hill to be with that tree. Slowly I circled around, filling my being with its beauty and majesty, making intimate conversation, crying with the joy of discovery, learning its wisdom. It was a Master of inner strength through perseverance and longevity. It said to me that I shared the same inner power and that I stood next to it as an equal.

Just below the Master Tree was a large outcropping of granite rocks which I hardly noticed as I ran up the hill. On the side I was facing there appeared to be a set of stairs notched into the rocks that led up to the top. As I walked up the stairs, I had the sense that the ancient Earth people had used this rock face for sacred rituals. At the top of the rocks there was a large flat area, and as I walked to that area I found myself directly facing the majestic Grant Tree.

A flat, diamond-shaped stone, big enough to stand on, lay in the middle of the open area. I seemed to know what to do. I climbed onto the rock just as the last blush of light filled the top branches of the

Grant Tree. I spread my arms out and took in a deep breath of air, in total awe of what I was viewing. It was then that my whole body began to vibrate perceptively, and after a short time a large Spider Monkey-Man appeared at the top of the tree. I existed in an ecstasy of loving communion with the Monkey-Man for what I take to be a few minutes. Then I stopped vibrating, and the Monkey-Man was gone. I stayed up there for a while in a state of bliss, and then I came down the hill, feeling exalted.

This experience has been an opening to go deeper into my spiritual life. The connection I made with nature remains a high moment of my life. A friend recommended that I read a translation of the *Ramayana* [Hindu sacred text] to acquaint myself with the power of the monkey god, Hanuman. Ah, Hanuman! He is the unyielding force of love and undying service.

I am sometimes called to go to special places to meditate and rejuvenate. One of them is the rocky shore of Mendocino, a town about four hours' drive north of our home, following Highway 1 along the California coastline. When spiritual energies were swirling and entering the Earth atmosphere in increasing intensity, around mid-August 1987, during the Harmonic Convergence, I felt myself spiraling in a surge of expansion that was exhilarating, but also dispersing and ungrounding. I was directed by the spirits to go up the coast to Mendocino.

While walking its cliff-lined shore, I first discovered the Fairy Grotto, carved by a stream winding down the steep bluff to the driftwood-lined beach. The fairies beckoned me to restore myself among the flowers there. I slept on the beach, communed with all the spirits, and found my center again. I returned to that grotto afterwards like a pilgrim to a holy shrine.

When I was called again to go to the Fairy Grotto, and these are the messages I received:

THE SPIRIT OF THE GROTTO: You are welcome here, sister, our friend and representative on the Earth. You who sing our voices, who tell our tale upon the Earth, who let the humans know in their dominion, they are not alone. We all share the Earth and love it so.

You have a big heart, and your love will grow as you share with all your wisdom, our wisdom. Humans are a part of us all and contain us, if only they reach and see and enjoy the Earth in a balanced harmony.

I am a bird, a SONG SPARROW, and welcome you. See how I flit from spot to spot, busy, having fun, looking for my food—the insects and seeds that love to feed me and share my body form. I enjoy each moment. See how much there is to be interested in, how much fun it is to be alive. And when it is fun no more, we die. We leave the form, sail the skies of spirit and prepare to enter the Earth atmosphere again, perhaps as a bird, perhaps as another form, always to enjoy each moment.

Humans could learn this from us. Enjoy the interest and joy of each moment. When it is time to go and the energy of the current form is used up, we gladly go, to return to spirit, to return to life anew. It is our path of growth and change and living fully each experience that a spirit has to live. When beings stray from this and struggle against the flow of change, then life becomes a chore, a meaningless event.

Each moment filled with life and joy in living is meaningful—full, so full. How wonderful it is to breathe the air, to feel the wind, to sing our songs, and to find insects and seeds and plants to sustain our bodies. Life is good. Death is necessary. Renewal is constant. Spirit is ever present. Take this message to humankind, so that they can be happy, too.

We do not think as you do. We do not ponder and strain and suffer the pain of wondering why. We feel each moment as it is. Each second has its feeling, its meaning, and its fullness. It has no reason. It is the reason. We are the same in essence. When we are free, being our true selves, spirit incarnate, there is no need to suffer under ponderous thoughts and circles of analysis. Humans find this out, often after long labor. We know it from the start. We never lose our essential knowing, our essential feeling, and our facing life and all that lives square on, with true feeling and expression of our purpose.

We are spirits who fly in feathered bodies, and we express ourselves with full range of feeling. We don't hate ourselves for being who we are. We enjoy our endowment, our way of being and doing. We don't stop ourselves from fulfilling our lives to the fullest.

I watch how humans rush around oblivious of all around them sometimes and wonder at their busyness and lack of consciousness. But, I accept them as they are. That is their being, what they have to be, what they are. I love them and know that they are part of life. Life and beauty will go on, just as I will go on being a bird till I am not, till I am called to other forms or ways of spirit.

Learn to laugh and sing like us. We can teach you that. And take life and death as it comes. That is the secret of never losing yourself as spirit, even when you fully enter the physical. Take it as it is. Float through it all. Fly and be free. Hail, oh sister, sing our song.

The SLUG speaks: We are gentle creatures, making our way slowly, savoring every delight that the Creator of All gives to us. We feel, exquisitely, every lump, every cranny. We wholly know every texture. To protect our sensuous, soft, and sensitive bodies, we have been given a coating, an elegant slime, that softens our way over textures, and helps us to our goal.

Our senses are so different from yours. It is hard for us to relate to your vision, the sense you so emphasize. We touch and feel and "see" waves of energy, heat, vibration, as a picture of what is around us—undulating waves of motion having their own smell, shape, size, texture, feel, coarseness or softness of energy configuration and motion. In some ways this is not so different from your seeing.

We love the world. We are made to crave the smells and textures that nourish us and that long to become one with our bodies. We pass these things through and leave behind our nourishing dung and slime, our signature that we have done our jobs. We are the cleanup crew. We love the effluence of other creatures, the strong-smelling food from their bodies. We love the tender morsels of plants of all kinds—lighter energies and tastes to nurture us.

We are gentle creatures, wending our way through the tiniest spaces to do our job and provide nurture to all. Sharp movements, harsh sounds, and heavy vibrations offend us. We savor the world around us and love each moment as a jewel. The greatest gourmand of your humankind, the greatest eroticist, does not know our long and slow, sensuous savoring of life around us. Not only eating and sexual connections are a continuous delight, but every morsel of life, every moment of movement or stillness is cherished as infinite.

We move and breathe in the rhythms of life, the growing of the plants, the falling of the rain. The speedy creatures pass us by. We support them all in our daily rounds, our sensuous wanderings, our profound and delightful contemplation, touch, consumption-union with all that we pass. We are the nurturers of all, the patient, loving, timeless ones. Feel our rhythms. They are love's harmony and peace, undulating warmth and beauty. We give you our feeling and enjoyment. Hear us.

The SONG SPARROW returns: Speak for us, Penelope. Take down our essences, our voices, our signatures, for all to know who we are.

Humans are a race of compilation—a sum of many creatures' parts. That's why they seek to understand us all and study us in parts. Let them know that to be human, they must feel us all, feel our warmth and our essence, our part and connection to the whole, of which they are a part. Humans are the only creature divorced, apart, destroying. It's a hard task to have the ability to analyze and separate and not destroy the union, communion, and essential link to all that makes life complete and worthwhile. If humans emphasize analytical, linear patterns and separation, they will end up dead, blighted. While they will apparently take many down with them, we are all a part of the ever-changing unity and will survive to play our part another day, as it is willed/allowed by the Spirit of All.

Humans are the caretakers in their own way. They have to be, with their powers of manipulation, creation, and destruction. They are more free-ranging. Will they, in their shortsighted disconnection, render themselves poisoned and extinct? It would be sad, but all life has its ways, its patterns, and its necessity. We enjoy each moment of the game, as it changes, and never worry about it all.

There are other dimensions, other places, other games for us to experience. Only those capable of destruction mourn the loss. We keep moving, and let go when the time dictates. The Spirit in all moves us in different ways to experience infinite creation. Figuring out *why* is not our way. We know deep in our cores. *Life is its own reason*. There is no more to understand.

Message from the SPIRIT OF ALL: Each wave, each rock, each particle of sand, each gust of air, and every molecule moves through me—is me. I am the Spirit of All. I am the motivator, the reason, the way, the enjoyer, the achiever, the mover, and the floater. I am you. I am everyone. I am Spirit everlasting, all-knowing, ever-laughing, that moves through all things. I am all of us, as individuals and as unity. Never forget that you are not the form. You infuse the form through every pore. You are the Essence.

The next day the SONG SPARROW appeared, different from the night before—in a hurry. I asked, "Are you my teacher?"

"Well, I am a teacher. I teach you to look and be quick [darting about]. Take advantage of each moment." And he flew away.

I watched the water trickling, providing lush plant growth, and patiently carving paths into sand and stone.

The SPIRIT OF THE GROTTO: This is a time of rest, Penelope, a time to take it all in. Enrich and dissolve into unity. Go now and take it all with you.

SPECIES LINK

Many humans think that other species can be driven to extinction, never to return. I have become aware that energy forms always exist in the ethereal as potential physical creations. They can return, according to their purpose in the whole, when the energy and conditions are right for them to survive and flourish. Humans, of course, must fulfill their part in restoring and maintaining the natural balance and harmony through conscious thought and action. We all have our interconnected roles in the web of life on Earth.

It takes a leap away from current social conditioning and intellectual, categorical thinking to encompass the truth of Spirit in All Things. It takes a return to simplicity, to wholeness, and to basic knowing for it all to make sense. We understand it fully, not with the limitations of human intellect. We need to go through and beyond human reasoning, to total experiencing, knowing, and feeling the inherent unity in the changing patterns. We can then see the beauty of it all and our part in it, as participants and co-creators.

The animals, plants, rocks, and all know. Go to them to know, too. Your highest joy, ecstasy, unity, pleasure, and peace will be in that knowledge. We are all *anima*.

Telepathy
A grace, a skill
A mixed blessing
To feel the joy
And the pain of millions
To hear the screams of the tortured
Saving grace
To be able to selectively tune in and out.

To request and get the gift so deep
Can be a searing agony
A turning inside out
Requires a ritual cleansing
A dying to self
And being born again
And again consciously
Deeply.

Each time a skin is shed
And new life emerges
More tender, more sensitive
The soul renews
Yet sets the pace
For those behind
Still searching.

A skill returned from babes innocent
Requiring honesty of purest caste
The time is not yet ripe for all to know
Each other's deepest yearnings—
Transformation is required
A deeper innocence than is now present.

The containers are too full
Of secret ways and private thoughts
Held by many
There is nothing to fear
Nothing to hide
When all souls know each other
As themselves
No shame, no guilt, no cutting pride.

All sharing harmony
Oneness
What does this mean?
Unity of purpose and intention
Leaner fare of mind
Discipline and quiet
Bonding, joining hand to hand
Mind to mind
The freeing of the chains of time.

You are like me
You are like mine
We are each other
Outside time
Freed in space
Flying.

So when you say it is my gift
I say it is yours
Mine is faced
Cherished

Developed
There is nothing to hide.

So when the world is ready
To love, to cherish, to be kind
All shall hear and know each other
Heart to heart
Mind to mind
No pain to mar the reaching
No ugliness so blind
That it ignores the beauty inside
Each a treasure
A mine of gold, deep and pure
Crystal waters will reflect the shining
Of the souls united
So sublime.

Telepathy
The reuniting
Of heart to heart
Soul to soul
Mind to mind
Outside the chains of time
And self-seeking
Oh, the harmony sublime.

Over the years of working with interspecies telepathic communication, my title has evolved to try to clearly communicate what I do. I started out with the inoffensive and broad "Animal Consultant." It was a title that could mean all things to all people and required that I explain my abilities and services. It encompassed the consultations, lectures, and healing work, but some people thought I might also be a trainer or behaviorist.

The title "Animal Communicator" is very obvious and straightforward, but never struck me as inclusive enough.

Later, while seeking a title that was more precisely evocative, I had a dream in which a book opened and across it was the title "Animal Communication Specialist." An alternative, which was not as emphasized, was "Animal Communication Therapist." I took the former.

Later, I felt a new title evolving. As the thought of it stirred in my mind, it traveled by telepathic transmission. Without prompting, journals and announcements of my books and public appearances referred to me as "Animal Telepath." I had long avoided using the words "psychic" or "telepath" in my title, as many people find the popular connotations of these words scary or confusing, not understanding the true definitions. Now, it seems, people are more ready to hear the word "telepath" without feeling it is something strange, or far from their experience.

Our local baker conferred my favorite title. When we first moved to Point Reyes, he heard about my work with a friend's parrot, and one day, as I came in for bread, he said, "Oh, there's the Animal Psychiatrist." I laughed and quickly corrected him on that appellation.

A few months later, after he had talked to other people whose dogs and horses I had seen, he called me the title that sounds a deep spiritual chord in my heart, "Animal Mystic." Seeing the mystery of life—the spirit eternal, in our animal friends and all of life—is what my work is all about. I hope that this book has brought out the "animal mystic" in all of you.

Anima, anima, anima, anima
Sisters and brothers of light.
Anima, anima, anima, anima
Sisters and brothers of light.

Sharing with us your myriad forms
Beauty in sight and sound and soul
Anima, anima, anima, anima
Brothers and sisters of light.

Reaching to us in myriad form
Taking us back to ourselves
Away from the noise, away from the night
Brothers and sisters of light.

Anima, anima, anima, anima
Sing to us—souls who fight

To find our way to the glorious day
Sisters and brothers of light.

Grace us, bless us, lead us home
Distance from you is our plight
Anima, anima, anima, anima
Brothers and sisters of light.

Swimming through waters
Soaring through skies
Walking through forest
Tunneling through earth.

Please hear us, please reach us
Please touch us, please save us
Our brothers and sisters of light.

Knowing you from places of old
Cherishing you in the wind and the cold
Of our dark days clouded by humankind's woe
Seed us with wisdom
Lead us back home
To spirit and truth
Never alone
Anima, anima, anima, anima
Our brothers and sisters of light.

Humans will know
The truth you do show
Oh brothers and sisters of light.

Whales in the ocean
Birds in the skies
Lead us to be you
Spirit never dies.

You wait and you watch
You listen, you live

You send us your message
You silently give
In myriad form.

We must see the way
That simple reunion
Will bring back the day
When gaily you roamed
In forest so free
You swam purest oceans
You flew over tree
With no interference
From human machine
You shared with us gladly
The spaces so clean.

Anima, anima, anima, anima
Sisters and brothers of light.

Teach us to serve and to understand
To bring back the beauty of ocean and land
To share in the sweetness and greatness of Earth
To recognize rightly our friendship from birth.

Reach us and teach us
Take us back home
Let us join forces
Never alone.

Learn all the lessons
Find life anew
Bonded in beauty
The good and the true.

We know you are with us
Your song's in our ears
Gratefully calling
Through hardship and fears

Calling us out to our nature, our way
With you in glory
The world's rainbow day.

Anima, anima, anima, anima
Brothers and sisters of light.

Sisters and brothers
Brothers and sisters
Heal us
Touch us
Heal each other
Heal the Earth
Make each other whole.
Anima, anima, anima, anima
Sisters and brothers
Brothers and sisters
Sisters and brothers of light.

ANIMA.

appendix

IN 1990, as more of the people who had studied with me and other teachers began to venture out as animal communicators, I saw some novices mixing their communication abilities with their own agendas or emotional shortcomings and invalidating people through their interpretations of what the animals said. I could not and did not want to police or control the actions of others, yet I felt responsible for helping them on the path they had chosen, and wanted to offer some beacon to guide the way. I meditated and prayed for guidance, and what came about was the following Code of Ethics.

CODE OF ETHICS FOR INTERSPECIES TELEPATHIC COMMUNICATORS

Our motivation is compassion for all beings and a desire to help all species understand each other better, particularly to help restore the lost human ability to freely and directly communicate with other species.

We honor those that come to us for help, not judging, condemning, or invalidating them for their mistakes or misunderstanding, but honoring their desire for change and harmony.

We know that to keep this work as pure and harmonious as possible requires that we continually grow spiritually. We realize that telepathic communication can be clouded or overlaid by our own unfulfilled emotions, critical judgments, or lack of love for self and others. We walk in humility, willing to recognize and clear up our own errors in understanding others' communication—human and nonhuman alike.

We cultivate knowledge and understanding of the dynamics of human, nonhuman, and interspecies behavior and relationships, to increase the good results of our work. We get whatever education and/or personal help we need to do our work effectively, with compassion, respect, joy, and harmony.

We seek to draw out the best in everyone and increase understanding toward mutual resolution of problems. We go only where we are asked to help, so that others are receptive and we truly can help. We respect the feelings and ideas of others and work for interspecies understanding, not pitting one side against another, but walking with compassion for all. We acknowledge the things that we cannot change and continue where our work can be most effective.

We respect the privacy of people and animal companions we work with, and honor their desire for confidentiality.

While doing our best to help, we allow others their own dignity, and help them to help their animal companions. We cultivate understanding and ability in others, rather than dependence on our ability. We offer people ways to be involved in understanding and growth with their fellow beings of other species.

We acknowledge our limitations, seeking help from other professionals as needed. It is not our job to name and treat diseases, and we refer people to veterinarians for diagnosis of physical illness. We may relay animals' ideas, feelings, pains, and symptoms as they describe them or as we feel or perceive them, and this may be helpful to veterinary health professionals. We may also assist through handling of stresses, counseling, and other gentle healing methods. We let clients decide for themselves how to work with healing their animal companions' distress, disease, or injury, given all the information available.

The goal of any consultation, lecture, workshop, or interspecies experience is more communication, balance, compassion, understanding, and communion among all beings. We follow our heart, honoring the spirit and life of all beings as One.

about the author

PENELOPE SMITH is a pioneer in the practice of interspecies telepathic communication and has become the world's foremost teacher of basic
and advanced courses in this field. In this capacity, she has helped launch the
careers of numerous professional animal communicators.

Having communicated with animals telepathically throughout her life,
Penelope discovered in 1971 that animals could be relieved of emotional
traumas and other problems through the same counseling techniques that
benefit humans.

Contributing to her success are her degrees in the social sciences; years
of training and experience in human counseling, nutrition, and holistic
energy balancing methods; research into animal nutrition, anatomy, behavior, and care; and the firsthand education gathered from the thousands of
animals she has contacted. She has composed books, audio- and videotapes,
and magazine articles. She also publishes a quarterly journal, *Species Link*,
and is internationally known as a lecturer and workshop leader.

Penelope feels that the sacred connection we make with other species
through telepathic communication is essential for human wholeness. She
believes that everyone is born with the power to communicate with other
species; although most people have put aside and forgotten this gift, it can be
reclaimed for the benefit of all beings on Earth. She lives with her animal
family in the woods of Inverness Ridge, adjacent to Point Reyes National
Seashore, northwest of San Francisco.

OTHer PUBLICATIONS
From Penelope Smith

AUDIOTAPES

ANIMAL DEATH—*A SPIRITUAL JOURNEY*

The death of an animal companion is often a painful and confusing experience for those left behind. The subject of animal death from a spiritual perspective is explored by this audiotape. Both informative and comforting, it fathoms the process of dying (from animals' and people's viewpoints), working through guilt and grieving, recognizing when to consider euthanasia, understanding what happens after animals depart from the physical body, and coming to terms with reincarnation—meeting your friends from life to life. The recording includes a guided visualization to help you communicate with a departed animal friend.

ISBN 0-936552-09-3; 90 minutes; $14.95

THE INTERSPECIES TELEPATHIC
CONNECTION TAPE SERIES

This series of six digitally recorded audio-cassettes on four major topics covers the theory and practice of direct communication, mind-to-mind and heart-to-heart, with other species. The cassettes offer guidance in breaking through the layers of cultural conditioning that inhibit clear reception of communication from animals, solving problems and understanding an animal companion's behavior, and realizing deeper levels of mutual understanding and cooperation. Filled with timeless wisdom, these cassettes can be played again and again to further personal growth.

Tapes 1-4 below conveniently packaged in an aesthetically delightful album. ISBN 0-936552-12-3; 6 hours; $59.95

1 **HOW TO COMMUNICATE WITH ANIMALS: THE STEPS**

A do-it-yourself mini-workshop for those eager to become more attuned to animals.

ISBN 0-936552-13-1; 1 hour

2 **ANIMAL INTELLIGENCE AND AWARENESS**

How intelligent are animals? Is *Homo sapiens* the only species that is self-aware? Learn how other animals' comprehension, reasoning, and awareness compare to human ability, based on actual telepathic communication and observable responses from animals. This cassette is guaranteed to jog your preconceptions and stimulate your intelligence and awareness.

ISBN 0-936552-14-x; 1 hour

3 UNDERSTANDING ANIMALS' VIEWPOINTS

Get the "inside story" on how animals view humans and the world around them. Numerous experiences reveal animals' purposes, sense of humor, deep feelings, and spiritual insights. This cassette helps to release preconceived notions that can block your communication and connection with other species, and opens you to seeing through your animal companion's eyes.

ISBN 0-936552-15-8; 2 hours

4 HEALING AND COUNSELING WITH ANIMALS

Learn straightforward methods to help animals work through emotional trauma, fear, injury, illness, and death. While not a substitute for veterinary assistance, this cassette promotes the understanding of physical and spiritual healing: bodywork and counseling, both in person and at a distance; contacting animals who have died; spirit transfer; entities. The listener gains insights into Penelope's seasoned approach to communicating with and counseling animals.

ISBN 0-936552-16-8; 2 hours

VIDEOTAPE

TELEPATHIC COMMUNICATION WITH ANIMALS

This videotape is an introduction and overview of the subject—an eye-opener for skeptics! Penelope Smith demonstrates ways of increasing our understanding of and harmony with other species. She also clarifies the fundamental importance of heightening our awareness of other animals' spiritual nature and expanding our abilities to fully communicate with them.

We witness consultations and interviews with people who, together with their animal companions, have benefited from Penelope's communication, counseling, and healing work. In scenes of workshops, we view a sampling of techniques that help people regain their power to telepathically communicate with other species.

ISBN 0-916289-11-7; VHS, 46 minutes; $29.95
Produced by Kelly Hart/Hartworks (non-VHS formats available)